Agnès Varda: Interviews

Conversations with Filmmakers Series

Gerald Peary, General Editor

Agnès Varda

INTERVIEWS

Edited by T. Jefferson Kline

University Press of Mississippi / Jackson

www.upress.state.ms.us

The University Press of Mississippi is a member
of the Association of American University Presses.

Copyright © 2014 by University Press of Mississippi
All rights reserved
Manufactured in the United States of America

First printing 2014
∞
Library of Congress Cataloging-in-Publication Data

Varda, Agnès, 1928–
  Agnès Varda : interviews / edited by T. Jefferson Kline.
     pages cm. — (Conversations with filmmakers series)
  Includes bibliographical references and index.
  Includes filmography.
  ISBN 978-1-61703-920-1 (cloth : alk. paper) — ISBN 978-1-61703-921-8 (ebook) 1.
Varda, Agnès, 1928– —Interviews. 2. Women motion picture producers and direc-
tors—France—Interviews. I. Kline, T. Jefferson (Thomas Jefferson), 1942– editor of
compilation. II. Title.
  PN1998.3.V368A5 2013
  791.4302'33092—dc23
  [B]   2013028808

British Library Cataloging-in-Publication Data available

Contents

Introduction

"I am a woman," Agnès Varda tells Andrea Meyer, "working with her intuition and trying to be intelligent. It's like a stream of feelings, intuition, and joy of discovering things. Finding beauty where it's maybe not. Seeing." She has pursued this search for "beauty where it's maybe not" over a remarkable lifetime in art, beginning her search first in the medium of photography and then, from 1954 to the present, moving to the medium of cinema. Few who know the full range of her work could doubt that Varda has succeeded in her quest.

Agnès Varda has been called "the Mother of the New Wave" and subsequently "the Grandmother of the New Wave" for very good reason. Years before Truffaut burst onto the scene with *Les 400 Coups* (*The Four Hundred Blows*) and Godard broke every rule of film grammar in *A Bout de Souffle* (*Breathless*) Varda had already made the first "New Wave" feature.

Having spent much time on the Mediterranean coast of France, in a neighborhood of Sête called "La Pointe Courte," Varda decided in 1954 to make a film of the same name about the area's fishermen and their families. With an extremely limited budget and no prior cinematic experience (either as a filmgoer or as a film student), Varda had the tenacity and intelligence to produce a remarkable piece of cinema: a story that alternated between scenes of a couple in crisis (Philippe Noiret and Sylvia Montfort) and a community of fishermen struggling to survive economically. Although the film was hardly a box-office success, it would set the stage for the New Wave because of its low-budget, minimalist story-line (based in part on Faulkner's narrative techniques in *The Wild Palms*), neorealism and expressive cinematography.

Born in Brussels in 1928 of a Greek father and Belgian mother, Varda spent much of her youth in Sête. When her family moved to Paris during the Occupation, she began to study photography; and her first jobs included working for the Galleries Lafayette taking four hundred pictures a day of kids sitting on Santa's lap and taking archival photos for the SNCF. Varda was invited in 1951 to join Jean Vilar's *Théâtre National Populaire* as the company's official photographer. For the next ten years she made stunning portraits of the most famous actors in France: Vilar, of course, in his various roles, Gérard Philipe, the heartthrob of France, and many others.

Varda had had the great good fortune of attracting Alain Resnais to edit *La Pointe Courte*, and Resnais would introduce Varda to the future "surfers" of the New Wave: Jean-Luc Godard, Claude Chabrol, François Truffaut, Jacques Doniol-Valcroze and Eric Rohmer. All got their start in the cinema by working for André Bazin's *Cahiers du cinéma*. The *Cahiers* crowd grew to be known as the "Right Bank" group, to distinguish them from the more openly political "Left Bank" group which included Resnais and Chris Marker—and, eventually, Varda herself. It was also Resnais who would introduce Varda to the Cinémathèque Francaise, where she began her education in the history of world cinema.

Varda's cinematic career was given a boost in 1957 when the French Office of Tourism commissioned her to do a short film about the Loire valley, *Ô Saisons, Ô Chateaux* (*O Seasons, O Castles*) which was selected for the Cannes Film Festival and by the Film Festival of Tours in 1958. It was at this latter event that Varda met the love of her life, Jacques Demy, whose career as a director paralleled hers for the next forty years. Demy introduced her to Georges Beauregard, who, excited by the success of the New Wave (and particularly Godard), agreed to produce Varda's next feature film, *Cléo de 5 à 7*, in 1961. Varda had prepared for this film by making another short film, *Du Côté de la Côte* (*Along the Coast*) for the Office of Tourism as well as a documentary called *L'Opéra-Mouffe* (*The Mouffetard Opera*) Pregnant with her first child, Varda described this second documentary as a film "which tells how one can be at the same time pregnant, blessedly happy, and yet also aware that life is also about misery and aging, which are more than anywhere else omnipresent in the Rue Mouffetard. The contradiction fascinated me all the more because it was so unavoidably evident" (Amiel).

Cléo de 5 à 7 (*Cléo from Five to Seven*), shot in mid-May 1961, presents a two-hour segment in the life of a popular singer (Corinne Marchand), on a day when she becomes convinced she is dying of cancer. But then she meets a soldier going off to fight in Algeria and seems, in his presence, to achieve a new kind of peace and sense of self. The film was well-received and was selected as France's official entry for the Festival in Cannes. In the thick of the New Wave, but not yet recognized as having had a significant role in anticipating it, Varda was now "launched" and invitations started pouring in. Also, she and Demy were married in 1962, after *Cléo*'s success. Finally, she traveled to Cuba that year, and, upon her return made *Salut les Cubains* (*Hey Cubans!*) (1963) using a montage of the four thousand photographs she'd taken there as well as material from a personal conversation with Fidel Castro. This film won the Silver Dove award at the Leipzig Festival and a bronze medal at the Venice Festival of Documentary films.

It was during this period of work that Varda began to conceive a more theoretical approach to her art. She says, "[My work] deals with this question, 'What is cinema?' through how I found specific cinematic ways of telling what I was telling. I could have told you the same things that are in the film by just talking to you for six hours. But instead I found shapes" (Warwick). To give a name to her very particular and personal search for a cinematic language, Varda coined the term *cinécriture*. As she explains to Jean Decock: "When you write a musical score, someone else can play it, it's a sign. When an architect draws up a detailed floor plan, anyone can build his house. But for me, there's no way I could write a scenario that someone else could shoot, since the scenario doesn't represent the writing of the film." Later she would clarify, "The cutting, the movement, the points-of-view, the rhythm of filming and editing have been felt and considered in the way a writer chooses the depth of meaning of sentences, the type of words, number of adverbs, paragraphs, asides, chapters which advance the story or break its flow, etc. In writing its called style. In the cinema, style is *cinécriture*." (*Varda par Agnès* [1994], 14).

We see multiple examples of this idea in Varda's interviews, particularly when she speaks of her design for *Le Bonheur* (*Happiness*) (1964). In this film, the main character, François, is happily married with a child. But he seeks even more happiness with a new lover, leading to his distraught wife's apparent suicide. Although *Le Bonheur* delves into the dark side of "happiness," Varda was determined to focus, visually, on the "color of happiness." She tells Yvonne Baby (*Le Monde*, February 25, 1965), "I was thinking of the Impressionists. In their paintings light vibrates and the color corresponds for me to a certain sense of happiness."

When the film premiered, it was called "extremely shocking" by the press. Clearly, it troubled far more spectators than it delighted. They were horrified by François's amorality and, even more, by the film-maker's refusal in the film to condemn his actions. Her interests were far more subtle and philosophical. She tells Jacques Fiecschi and Claude Ollier: "What I try to understand in this film is: What is the meaning of happiness, this need for happiness, this aptitude for happiness? What is this unnamable and slightly monstrous thing? Where did it come from? What form does it take? Why is it there? Why does it leave? Why can't the people chasing it catch it? And why can some other people catch it? Why doesn't it have anything to do with merit? This sense of well-being and of happiness seems to have little to do with anything physical, spiritual, ethical, or anything else: there are just some people who feel happy." In other words, her film is intended to provoke a series of moral and psychological questions rather than tell a satisfying "moral" story. It is perhaps this tendency that has best characterized Varda's cinema and may be the reason that she has never reached a larger "popular" audience.

Two years after filming *Le Bonheur*, Varda followed Jacques Demy to Los Angeles and, while he shot *Model Shop*, she threw herself into a series of short documentaries: *Oncle Yanco* (*Uncle Yanco*) (1967), a short study of her Greek uncle, and *Black Panthers* (1968), which included favorable interviews with Eldridge Cleaver and an incarcerated Huey Newton. Although French Television (ORTF) commissioned this film, it was considered too radical and was never broadcast. In 1980, she returned to Los Angeles to make another politically oriented documentary, *Murs Murs* (*Murmuring Walls*), about the murals in the Mexican neighborhoods of the city.

While in New York the previous year, she had met Andy Warhol, who, in turn, introduced her to the actress Viva. Now Varda gathered Viva, two actors from *Hair* (Jim Rado and Jerry Rangni) and the filmmaker Shirley Clarke in a rented villa and let them loose in a game of nudity and free love, with injected images of Michael McClure's play, *The Beard*, and TV footage from the assassination of Robert Kennedy. The result was *Lions Love*. When asked about the subject of this very loosely structured and diverse film, Varda replied, "I could give you twenty different answers that would all be more or less true and more or less limited. I wanted my film to express two great currents in America: sex and politics. The film, which I'd prefer to call a collage, is about: nostalgia for the stars of yesteryear and, as I've already said, the political stars; my attempt to make a film in Hollywood; a certain mysticism, the mysticism of the hippies; Hollywood, the magical city with its typical streets, enormous boulevards and enormous studios; the end of youth since the characters are too old to be hippies, too young to be adults; and contradictions—between political events and private life."

As we shall see, *contradiction* itself was to become one of the major themes of Varda's subsequent work—and can be discerned—retroactively—in all of her films.

In 1972 the birth of a son, Mathieu, sidelined Varda's film career, although she took time out from mothering to participate in the demonstrations at Bobigny to protest the French court's guilty verdict in the case of an adolescent girl who had been raped and had the temerity to have an abortion. This event launched Varda into an overtly political relationship with feminism. For the next several years, however, she was a stay-at-home mother. Until, that is, she suddenly found the solution to her restricted life: wrestling with the constraints of motherhood, she had an electric line run from her house to a length of ninety meters. With this "umbilical cord" she managed to interview the shopkeepers and other neighbors in la rue Daguerre and produced *Daguerréotypes*. The film was nominated for an Oscar for best feature-length documentary and won the *Prix d'Art et d'Essai* in 1975.

By 1976 Varda was ready to engage in the sustained meditation about feminism that had been brewing ever since her involvement in Bobigny four years earlier.

Doubtless, the question of feminism is one of Varda's deepest concerns, and centers immediately on the matter of her own identity: "It's difficult to find one's identity as woman," she tells Mireille Amiel, "in one's social dealings, in one's private life, and in one's body. This search for identity has a meaning for a filmmaker: I try to film as a woman. In terms of feminism (even if I was always a feminist, even if I considered myself a feminist in terms of my life choices, my ideas, and especially in terms of what I refused to do) I learned a huge amount about myself and about feminism thanks to the women of the movement, the American radical feminists and theorists, and then the French women after May '68."

What is so invaluable in an anthology of Varda's interviews conducted over roughly fifty years, is the opportunity to understand the evolution of her ideas on this subject. In a first attempt at portraying a crisis of feminine identity in *Cléo de 5 à 7*, Varda noted that "the entire dynamics of the film centers on the moment this woman refuses to be this cliché, on the moment when she no longer wants to be looked at, but wants instead to look at others and becomes the looking subject." To Mireille Amiel she will justly claim, "*Cléo* expressed—and still expresses in my view—a young woman's search for identity and that is always the first step in claiming one's feminism."

From this first portrayal of a crisis of identity in 1962, Varda moved gradually towards a more radical position. In 1974 she admits that "things still weren't so clear when I made *Le Bonheur* (1964) even though I had already read Simone de Beauvoir, and had discussed these things, and had fought for contraception, sexual freedom, new ways of raising children, and alternatives to the usual form of marriage."

In 1975, then, Varda made an eight-minute film about women as a response to Antenne 2's poll: "What does it mean to be a woman?" Instead of addressing the question in socio-historical terms, Varda focused on the body. In the film a group of clothed and naked women of very different ages and body-types look directly at the camera and speak of their experience of their own bodies, of being constantly objectified or mythologized. "My goal," Varda tells Mireille Amiel, was "to be able to talk about the body and to be able to show it in our own way, as an affirmation and not as an exhibition. For me, to be a woman is first of all to have the body of a woman. A body which isn't cut up into a bunch of more or less exciting pieces, a body which isn't limited to the so-called erogenous zones (as classified by men), a body of refined zones." Clearly Varda's respondents in *Réponse des Femmes* (*Women's Answer*) want to change the way they're looked at. And yet, there seems to be no real consensus arrived at in the film, no entirely satisfactory solutions adumbrated, and the question of feminism and its various expressions and "*prises de conscience*" continues to haunt the author of this film.

As she now prepared to make her first "feminist" feature film, *L'Une Chante, l'Autre Pas* (*One Sings, the Other Doesn't*) (1977), she complained, "Even though I can say I am a feminist, for other feminists, I am not feminist enough. But what I have done led me to be a feminist even though I have not made feminist films." In frustration she adds, "I think that each woman should come to understand what she is and her position in the world. But . . . something has to be changed because the image of women in film has been strongly built up by men, and accepted by them, but also accepted by women . . . It's always made me furious, but I haven't up to now been able to change that image."

Although it may not be evident from a first viewing of *L'Une Chante, l'Autre Pas* that she has solved this question for herself, Varda's attempt to come to grips with her feminism is compelling. Her first analysis of what's missing in the cinema, leads her to assert that "you never see a woman relating to her job. You do not see films in which a woman directs things, or about how she does it or how she relates with the people working with her . . . That should be changed. I really think we should prepare ourselves as women and as audience." To this call for films about women in careers worthy of respect, she added the challenge of the problem of maternity: "How can women who still want to have children be sure to be able to have them when they want, with whom they want, and how are we going to help them raise the children. That's the big problem."

What is most consistent in her approach to feminism is Varda's search for a "middle way." As she tells Ruth McCormick, "As feminists, we have to be tolerant, with each other and even with men. I think our movement needs different kinds of women; there shouldn't just be one line, one way. Some women still want children and a home . . . If there are women who feel that they have to live away from men to find their identity for a period, even for their whole lives, who may in fact be lesbians, that's fine with me. Each woman should be able to find her own way."

And so, Varda travelled to Iran in 1976 to film some scenes for her next film. On her return she wrote the scenario for *L'Une Chante, l'Autre Pas*. In this film about two friends, Pomme and Suzanne, each pursues her own way toward happiness. Suzanne's husband commits suicide and she is forced to return home to her family of origin who seem to want to punish her for her situation. Gradually, however, she regains her independence and moves to the south of France with her children and succeeds in marrying an older man. She will find her own identity as a family- planning adviser in a women's center. Pomme, on the other hand, represents the more militant form of feminism, protesting and singing feminist songs. She is married to an Iranian, Darius, but when she emigrates to Iran with him, she refuses to accept that culture's repressive attitude toward women and returns to France, pregnant but free. Of the two, Pomme tends to be more aware of her contradictions as a woman and in her voice-over narration, she becomes a representative for the feminine condition as Varda uses her to provoke her audience to question the role of women in society.

Although *L'Une Chante* is the first mainstream French film to deal explicitly with questions of feminism, its aims seem at times self-contradictory, moving between images of woman's degradation and a final, somewhat dystopic idyllic scene of Suzanne's daughter's family. Varda's interviews on this subject are quite compelling.

Contradictions, it would seem, are, in retrospect, the central idea in Varda's cinema. In reflecting on the evolution of her films she tells Mireille Amiel, "What almost always interests me in my films is the dialectics between public and private, between subjective and general. The cliché and what's inside the cliché. It seems to me that this dialectic, this ambiguity, this contradiction of the clichés of our mental life and the images of lived life is really the subject of all of my films. . . . All my films are constructed out of such a contradiction-juxtaposition."

And perhaps the central contradiction underlying all of Varda's cinema is that between fiction film and documentary. Of any of her documentaries, Varda could say, "It's not just a documentary, right? But it's not a fiction either. I try to break the barrier, break the border, and give freedom to film and allow myself to speak about people, speak about myself, and then discuss, for example, the Cuban Revolution or show images of theater. I'm trying to open the field of cinema, and not to say 'This is that.'"[1] Likewise, of any of her feature films she could also say, "I've never really stopped making documentaries. I'm one of those fiction-film directors who never stopped being a documentarist. I try alternating between fiction and documentary because I believe we never stop learning, and let's say that I learn an enormous amount from making documentaries."[2] And she tells Chantal de Béchade, "For me there's no fiction without its documentary side, no film without an esthetic intent."

In none of her films is this more compellingly evident than in *Sans Toit ni Loi* (*Vagabond*). After founding her own production company, Ciné Tamaris in 1977, Varda had to wait eight years to have the chance to make another feature film. In the meantime, she made a series of short documentaries to "keep her hand in": *Mur Murs* in Los Angeles in 1980; *Ulysse* (1982), a meditation of the lives of two figures in an old photograph; *Les Dites Cariatides* (*Paris's Cariatids*) (1984), a montage of sculptures in the streets of Paris; and *7P., cuis., s. de b.,* . . . (*7 rms, kitchn, bathrm* . . .) (1984), a cinematic rendition of a surrealist play by Louis Bec.

By 1985 she was ready. Varda engaged Sandrine Bonnaire to play a female hobo, who wanders through the wintry landscape of Provence, aimless but fiercely independent. Her encounters with a wide variety of locals (a truck driver, a mechanic, a slum pimp, a manager's wife, an agricultural worker, a Tunisian, a blood donor, a former teacher turned shepherd, a researcher trying to save the plane trees) are narrated "retrospectively" since the entire film is structured as a police inquest after her frozen body is found in a ditch in the opening scene of the film. By beginning her film with the image of Mona's corpse, Varda avoided making a "whodunit" and instead produced a docu-fiction. Each of the scenes involves a documentary-style interview, and yet, as Varda explains, however realistic these appear to the viewer, they were painstakingly and meticulously composed beforehand by the director herself. And, although the scenes of Mona's vagabondage appear entirely unstructured, in fact they are joined through a very carefully crafted series of visual "links," as she explains to Jean Decock: "Tracking shots are connected to Mona's walking, she's only one piece of a landscape that is still there. She's rarely there at the start of the tracking shot, and rarely there at the end. . . . Each of these tracking shots ends with something we see in the next one."

Such meticulous filming and editing makes of this "documentary" an artistic masterpiece and confirms Varda's abiding interest in exploring the contradiction inherent in her belief that "there's no fiction without its documentary side, no film without an esthetic intent." Her film won the Lion d'Or at the Venice Film Festival, the Prix de la Critique Internationale, and the Prix Georges Méliès.

The rest of her remarkable career in film alternated constantly between these two poles. In 1989 she made two feature films: The first, *Jane B. par Agnès V.* (*Jane B by Agnès V*), is a lengthy comic portrait of Jane Birkin seen in many attitudes and seasons and linked to other "Jeannes": Joan of Arc, Calamity Jane, Tarzan's Jane, et al. The second is *Kung-Fu Master*, a love story in which the forty-year-old Jane Birkin falls in love with a fifteen-year-old boy (Mathieu Demy).

In 1990 Varda learned that her beloved Jacques Demy was dying of AIDS. As she nursed him through his final illness until his death in December, she prepared her ultimate homage to her husband: *Jacquot de Nantes*, a "bio pic" in which she explores Jacques' youth through actual pictures of his family and fictional recreations of his life. Three years later she continued her mourning by writing and directing a feature-length documentary about Demy: *L'Univers de Jacques Demy* (*The Universe of Jacques Demy*).

After a ten-year period of relative inactivity, at age seventy-two, Varda created what may be her masterpiece. She spent a year crisscrossing France gleaning material for *Les Glaneurs et la Glaneuse* (*The Gleaners*), a celebration of those who live off of the excessive waste of their society and of those, like Varda, who "harvest" these leftovers into film.

And finally, at eighty-two Varda gave us *Les Plages d'Agnès* (*The Beaches of Agnès*), in which she playfully celebrates a lifetime of photography, filmmaking, and friendships.

As we reflect on this extraordinary lifetime of work "theorized" in this volume in thirty interviews given over a fifty-year period, we can appreciate how intuitive Varda is. She modestly tells Julie Rigg that she's "not philosophical, not metaphysical." Instead, she confesses, "My mind goes on and my work flows in my mind and that's how I think. It's very simple." Rather than philosophy or metaphysics, she tells Hubert Arnault, "Feelings are the ground on which people can be led to think about things. I believe in the importance of reflection. I try to show everything that happens in such a way as to leave the viewers free to make their own judgments." "My real work," she tells Olivier Dazt and Gilles Horvilleur, "is located in this incontrollable zone where the artist's intention (expressed by this or that gesture of an actor, or a certain camera movement, the choice of words) meets the spectator's reception of the film. Where do they meet? What does the spectator feel? The same emotions as I do? Or some other feeling that I stimulate without intending to?"[3]

In the panoply of interviews that you will discover here, we are confident that you will find a wealth of ways to answer her questions, all in service of Varda's core belief that "we never stop learning."

Conforming to the policy of the University Press of Mississippi in regard to its interviews series, the interviews assembled in this volume have not been edited in any substantive way. While this may result in an occasional repetition in Varda's comments, it offers, we believe, more integrity for the scholarly reader. Perhaps more importantly, such repetitions may reveal the director's continuing obsessions or concerns and are therefore quite revealing.

Except in the interviews published in English, where decisions about film titles already existed, I elected to keep the French titles in all of the translations since Varda's titles often contain puns and which may be germain to her discussion of them.

Finally, I wish to thank the following: Phoebe Anderson Kline, Fabien Gerard, and Renée Pontbriand for their excellent work on permissions; Kristen Stern for her work on the bibliography; Verena Conley for her encouragement and ideas at the outset of this venture; Nina Douglass for her unfailing support throughout the preparation of this book; Gerry Peary for his helpful suggestions; Diane Dalmeida of Boston University's Mugar Library for her enthusiasm and expertise; Cynthia Hinds of Harvard University's Widener Library for her remarkable assistance; Flora Billy of the Maison Elsa Triolet-Aragon in Paris *d'une aide très précieuse;* and my students and colleagues for all the ways in which they stretch my mind and imagination.

TJK

Notes

1. Noel Murray, "Interview: Agnès Varda," *A.V. Club*, June 30, 2009 (www.avclub.com/ articles/agnes-varda,29840/).

2. Chantal de Béchade, "Entretien avec Agnès Varda," *Image et son: revue du cinéma*, February 1982, 45. Translated by T. J. Kline.

3. Olivier Dazt and Gilles Horvilleur, "Agnès Varda de 5 à 7," *Cinematographe*, 1985, 22.

Chronology

1928   Agnès Varda is born May 30 in Brussels to a French mother and a Greek father. She is the third child (of five): Hélène, Lucien, Agnès, Jean, and Sylvie. Originally named Arlette because she was conceived in Arles, she will change her name when she is eighteen years old to Agnès. The Varda family lived on the rue d'Aurore until their sudden move during the German Anschluss, to Sète in southern France.

1939   After the move, Agnès begins schooling at the Collège Sévigny in Sète. She remembers that the only classical music she heard as a child was Schubert's "Unfinished Symphony" that her mother played on the hand-cranked record player they owned.

1940   Agnès joins a Girl Scout Choir and travels to the Alps during the summer with her choir-mates. During the summer she spends time in the Pointe Courte neighborhood of Sète where later she will make her film. Family friends, the Schlegels, "adopt" her and take her on vacation. Later, their daughter, Andrée, will marry Jean Vilar of the TNP.

1943   Her parents move to Paris. Agnès attends the Ecole de Vaugirard, then the Lycée Victor Duruy on the Boulevard des Invalides.

1945   Agnès passes the first part of the Baccalaureat on October 1.

1946–47   Her mother buys her a second-hand Rolleiflex camera. While preparing the second part of the "Bac," Agnès enrolls at the Ecole du Louvre for photography courses. During the summer of 1946 she runs away and takes a three-month job on a fishing boat.

1948   While studying literature and psychology at the Sorbonne, Paris, Agnès takes courses with Gaston Bachelard that will influence her later work, though she never dares speak with him. She continues to study art history at the Ecole du Louvre and photography at night school. That year she gets a job at Galleries Lafayette taking pictures of kids with Santa during the Christmas season. Jean Vilar, now the husband of her childhood friend, Andrée, invites Agnès to Avignon to take photos of his theater troupe.

1951   Obtains job as official photographer for the Théâtre National Populaire. Will spend the next ten years working for Jean Vilar, the director, taking portraits with her Rolleiflex of such actors as Gérard Philipe. During this period she moves to the rue Daguerre, to an address she has retained her entire life. Also during this period she meets Alain Resnais.

1954   Thanks to Alain Resnais, Agnès meets members of *Les Cahiers du Cinéma*, Jean-Luc Godard, Claude Chabrol, François Truffaut, Jacques Doniol-Valcroze, and Eric Rohmer, all of whom will go on to (re-)create The New Wave. Writes and directs *La Pointe Courte* which anticipates their work by five years.

1955   Again, thanks to Resnais, Agnès discovers the Cinémathèque, rue de Messine, and sees Dreyer's *Vampyr*. (She had made, by her own admission, *La Pointe Courte* without ever having seen more than three or four films.) Resnais introduces Agnès to the filmmaker Chris Marker. During this period she has a love affair with a man named Antoine who will be the father of her first child, but who will disappear when he learns she's pregnant. Eventually Jacques Demy will help her raise this child.

1957   Pierre Braunberger approaches Agnès and tells her, "I'm going to have you do more films!" The Office of Tourism commissions her to make *Ô Saisons, Ô Chateaux*, which will be selected for the Cannes Film Festival and then the Festival of Short Films at Tours. Agnès travels to China with Chris Marker, invited by Chou en Lai. Their voyage by boat takes two months. Varda's photographs of China are never published since Cartier Bresson had visited the country two months previously and the Paris newspapers had "already done" China when she brought them her work.

1958   At the Festival of Tours Agnès meets Jacques Demy. Later that year, she goes to the rue Mouffetard with a folding chair and a movie camera and films her first uncommissioned documentary, *L'Opéra Mouffe*, which wins several prizes in Brussels and Vienna. The Office of Tourism commissions another film, and Agnès spends the month of August on the Riviera filming *Du Côté de la Côte*, which Godard labels "admirable" in his review of her work for *Cahiers du Cinéma* the following year.

1961   Jacques Demy introduces Agnès to Georges Beauregard, the producer of Godard's *A Bout de Souffle*. Thanks to Beauregard's support Agnès is able to film *Cléo de 5 à 7* in Paris during the month of May. The film was France's official selection for the Festival in Cannes. Her career is launched and invitations pour in from all directions. Much later, when Agnès meets Madonna and Jack Nicholson in Los Angeles, Madonna will ask for the rights to do a remake of the film, but ultimately never does.

1962   Agnès and Jacques Demy are married and purchase an old windmill on the Island of Noirmoutier off the Breton coast. Sadly, Agnès will describe 1962–63 as "nos années difficiles . . ." She meets Bernardo Bertolucci at the Venice Film Festival and the two become fast friends. Later (in 1972) she will help him adapt the screenplay for *Last Tango in Paris*. Agnès is invited to Cuba by the Cuban Film Institute (I.C.A.I.C) and brings her Leica and a tripod. Fidel Castro grants her several hours of conversation.

1963   She returns from Cuba with four thousand photos and spends six months editing them into *Salut les Cubains*. The film wins the Silver Dove award at Leipzig and the Bronze Medal at the International Exposition of Documentary Films in Venice the following year.

1964   Agnès writes and directs her first feature film in color, *Le Bonheur*. She tells Yvonne Baby of *Le Monde* (February 25, 1965), "I was thinking of the impressionists. In their paintings light vibrates and the color corresponds for me to a certain sense of happiness." She also makes a short (seven-minute) documentary, *Les Enfants du Musée*, for French television.

1965   Meets Louis Aragon and Elsa Triolet and makes a twenty-minute documentary of them titled *Elsa la Rose*. During the summer at Noirmoutier, she writes and directs *Les Créatures*, a feature film about the life of a couple on the island and the transformation of the island's inhabitants into fictional characters in the husband's novel. The film will be selected for the Venice Film Festival in 1966.

1966   Agnès follows Jacques Demy to Los Angeles. She meets Jim

	Morrison and they begin a friendship that will be continued when he visits them in France and lasts until his death. Agnès will be one of five mourners at his burial in the Père Lachaise Cemetery.
1967	Agnès contributes her talents to the collective film *Loin du Vietnam*, working with Jean-Luc Godard, Joris Ivens, William Klein, Claude Lelouche, and Alain Resnais. Her own footage will not be included in the film. In California she makes a short film about her uncle, *Oncle Yanco*.
1968	Meets Andy Warhol in New York, who introduces her to Viva (who will play in Varda's *Lions Love*). Some radicals at Berkeley invite her to do a film. She interviews Huey Newton in prison, meets Eldridge Cleaver, and ends up making the documentary *Black Panthers*. The ORTF in France had requested the film, but censors it at the last minute and it was never broadcast.
1969	Meets Max Raab in a café, who invites her on the spot to make a film. Agnès gathers Viva, Jim Rado, and Jerry Ragni in a rented house in L.A. and makes *Lions Love*. The film includes the performance of a play, *The Beard*, by Michael McClure, staged by Rip Torn.
1970	Agnès writes and directs a feature-length film in color titled *Nausicaa* for French TV about Greece. She calls the film a "settling of accounts" with the "fascist" government that the Greek Colonels have established there. Although commissioned by the ORTF, the film is censored and never broadcast.
1972	Son Mathieu Demy is born.
1975	Agnès, wrestling with the constraints of motherhood, has an electric line run from her house to a length of ninety meters. With this "umbilical cord" she manages to interview the shopkeepers and other neighbors in la rue Daguerre and produces *Daguerréotypes*. The film is nominated for an Oscar for best feature-length documentary and wins the Prix d'Art et d'Essai in 1975. The show *F Comme Femme* (*W as in Woman*) on French TV's Antenne 2 proposes a questionnaire: "What does it mean to be a woman?" Agnès produces an eight-minute response that speaks also of "what does it mean to have a woman's body?" French TV was not happy with the result.
1976	Agnès travels to Iran to film some scenes for *L'Une Chante, l'Autre Pas*. This trip forms the basis of a short subject, *Plaisir*

d'Amour en Iran. She writes and directs *L'Une Chante, l'Autre Pas*, which will win the Grand Prix at the Festival of Taormina in Italy a year later. This film was Varda's way of declaring, "Bobigny was more important than '68."

1977   Agnès founds her production company, Ciné-Tamaris. As a "post script" to *L'Une Chante, l'Autre Pas*, she writes and directs a short (fifty-eight minute) video entitled *Quelques Femmes Bulles* for Antenne 2. Varda appears in this film very pregnant with her Rosalie.

1980   Agnès returns to Los Angeles to film *Mur Murs*, a documentary about the murals that proliferated throughout the city, but primarily in Mexican neighborhoods that were decidedly not welcoming to Varda's attempt to film them. This film wins the Josef von Sternberg Award in Mannheim the following year.

1981   Agnès writes and directs a feature film in color titled *Documenteur*, another treatment of Los Angeles, where "smog becomes an allegory" in a young mother's search for an apartment for her and her eight-year-old (Mathieu Demy).

1982   Two short films become the focus of this first year back in Paris: *Ulysse*, an attempt to remember a photograph taken in 1954 of a man, a boy, and a goat; and a second meditation on photography, *Une Minute pour une Image*, for the National Center of Photography in Paris.

1984   Two more shorts are written and produced: *Les Dites Cariatides*, a documentary shot for French TV in January in the streets of Paris; and a somewhat surrealist film, *7P., cuis., s. de b., . . . (A SAISIR)* shot in the Hospice Saint Louis in Avignon during Louis Bec's comedy titled *Le Vivant et L'Artificiel*.

1985   Agnès writes and directs *Sans Toit ni Loi*, which wins the Lion d'Or at the Venice Film Festival, the Prix de la Critique Internationale, and the Prix Georges Méliès.

1986   A relatively quiet year for Agnès in which her single finished work is a three-minute documentary titled *T'as de Beaux Escaliers, Tu Sais* for the Cinémathèque Française on the occasion of its fiftieth anniversary.

1987   The pace picks up again: Agnès makes two feature films. The first, shot in Belgium during the autumn, *Jane B. par Agnès V.*, is a lengthy comic portrait of Jane Birkin seen in many attitudes and seasons and linked to other Janes: Joan of Arc,

Calamity Jane, Tarzan's Jane, et al. Her second offering of 1987 is *Kung-Fu Master,* a love story in which the forty-year-old Jane Birkin falls in love with a fifteen-year-old boy (Mathieu Demy).

1989 Invited to Hong Kong for the Film Festival celebrating *Jane B. par Agnès V.,* Agnès travels with Jacques Demy (invited for his film *3 Places Pour le 26)* and son Mathieu (invited for his role in *Kung-Fu Master*).

1990 As she nurses her beloved Jacques Demy through his final illness until his death in December, Agnès prepares her ultimate homage to her husband: *Jacquot de Nantes.*

1992 As 1992 represents the twenty-fifth anniversary of Demy's film *Les Demoiselles de Rochefort,* the city organizes a huge celebration around his film. Agnès uses the occasion to film a documentary of the town and its love for her late husband.

1993 Agnès's process of mourning continues as she writes and directs a feature-length documentary about Demy: *L'Univers de Jacques Demy.*

1994 Agnès turns from her homage to her late husband to a homage to the cinema and writes and directs *Les 100 et 1 Nuits.*

2000 Agnès crisscrosses France gleaning material for what may be her most influential film, *Les Glaneurs et la Glaneuse,* a celebration of those who live off of the excessive waste of their society and of those, like Varda, who "harvest" these leftovers into film.

2002 It's time to return to the memories of filming and thinking about gleaning as Agnès films *Les Glaneurs Deux Ans Après.*

2003 In a more playful mood, Agnès makes a documentary about . . . her cat!: *Le Lion Volatil.*

2004 From cats to Teddy Bears, Agnès now turns to a documentary about Ydessa's photographs of stuffed animals. She also writes and directs a short documentary on Venice, *Der Viennale.*

2006 While on her cherished island in Brittany, Agnès writes and directs *Quelques Veuves de Noirmoutier.*

2010 In *Les Plages d'Agnès,* Varda celebrates a lifetime of photography, filmmaking, and friendships.

Filmography

LA POINTE COURTE (1954)
Director: **Agnès Varda**
Screenplay: **Agnès Varda**
Camera: Louis Stein
Editing: Alain Resnais
Sound: Robert Lion
Music: Pierre Barbaud
Cast: Philippe Noiret, Silvia Montfort, the inhabitants of La Pointe
Courte
35mm, 89 minutes, b/w
Awards: Prix de l'Age d'or, Brussels, 1955; Grand Prix du film d'avant-
garde, Paris, 1955

Ô SAISONS, Ô CHATEAUX (1957)
Director: **Agnès Varda**
Screenplay: **Agnès Varda**
Producer: Pierre Braunberger, Films de la Pléiade
Camera: Quinto Albicocco
Editing: Janine Verneau
Music: André Hodeir
Cast: Voice of Antoine Bourseiller
35mm, 22 minutes, color

L'OPÉRA-MOUFFE (1958)
Director: **Agnès Varda**
Screenplay: **Agnès Varda**
Producer: Ciné-Tamaris
Camera: Sacha Vierny
Editing: Janine Verneau
Music: Georges Delerue
Cast: Dorothée Blank, Antoine Bourseiller, André Rousselet, Jean Tasso,
José Varela, Monika Weber

16mm, 17 minutes, b/w
Awards: Prix de la Fédération Internationale des Ciné-Clubs, Brussels

DU CÔTÉ DE LA CÔTE (1958)
Director: **Agnès Varda**
Screenplay: **Agnès Varda**
Producer: Anatole Dauman, Philippe Lifchitz, Argos Films
Camera: Quinto Albicocco
Editing: Henri Colpi, Jasmine Chasney
Music: Georges Delerue
Cast: Voices of Roger Coggio, Anne Olivier
35 mm, 24 minutes, color
Awards: Prix du Film de Tourisme, Brussels, 1959

CLÉO DE 5 À 7 (1961)
Director: **Agnès Varda**
Screenplay: **Agnès Varda**
Producer: Ciné-Tamaris
Camera: Jean Rabier, Alain Levent
Editing: Janine Verneau, Pascale Laverrière
Music: Michel Legrand, **Agnès Varda**
Cast: Corinne Marchand (Cléo), Antoine Bourseiller (Antoine), Dominique D'Avray (Angèle), Dorothée Blank (Dorothée), Michel Legrand (Bob), José-Luis de Vilallonga (the lover), Loye Payen (the fortune teller), Lucienne Marchand (taxi driver), Serge Korber (le Plumitif)
35mm, 90 mintues, b/w, brief color
Awards: Official Selection for the Festival at Cannes and Venice Film Festival, 1962; Prix Méliès, 1962

SALUT LES CUBAINS (1963)
Director: **Agnès Varda**
Screenplay: **Agnès Varda**
Producer: Société Nouvelle Pathé-Cinéma
Camera: J. Maques, C. S. Olaf
Editing: Janine Verneau
Music: Michel Legrand
Voice: Michel Piccoli
35mm, 30 minutes, b/w
Awards: Silver Dove Festival of Leipzig; Bronze Medal, XVth International Exposition of Documentary Film, Venice, 1964

LE BONHEUR (1964)
Director: **Agnès Varda**
Screenplay: **Agnès Varda**
Producer: Mag Bodard
Camera: Claude Beausoleil, Jean Rabier
Editing: Janine Verneau
Music: W. A. Mozart, Jean-Michel Defaye
Cast: Jean-Claude Drouot (François), Claire Drouot (Thérèse), Marie-France Boyer (Emilie)
35mm, 82 minutes, color
Awards: Prix Louis Delluc, 1965; Silver Bear, Berlin, 1965; David O'Selznick Award

LES ENFANTS DU MUSÉE (1964)
Director: **Agnès Varda**
Screenplay: **Agnès Varda**
Producer: Pathé Cinéma
Video
7 minutes, b/w

ELSA LA ROSE (1965)
Director: **Agnès Varda**
Screenplay: **Agnès Varda**
Producer: Ciné-Tamaris
Camera: Willy Kurant, William Lubtchansky
Music: Simonovitch, Ferrat, Moussorgsky, Gershwin, Handy
16mm, 20 minutes, b/w

LES CRÉATURES (1966)
Director: **Agnès Varda**
Screenplay: **Agnès Varda**
Producer: Mag Bodard
Camera: Willy Durant, William Lubtschansky
Music: Henry Purcell, Pierre Barbaud
Cast: Catherine Deneuve (Mylène), Michel Piccoli (Edgar), Eva Dahlbeck (Michèle Quellec), Marie-France Mignal (Viviane Quellec), Britta Pettersson (Lucie de Moyton), Bernard Lajarrice (Le Docteur Desteau), Roger Dax (Père Quellec)
35mm, 105 minutes, b/w and color
Awards: Official selection at Venice Film Festival, 1966

LOIN DU VIETNAM (1967)
Collective film directed variously by Jean-Luc Godard, Joris Ivens, William Klein, Claude Lelouch, Alain Resnais, **Agnès Varda**
The episode shot by Varda was not included in the final version of the film, although her name remained in the credits as a participant in the project.

ONCLE YANCO (1967)
Director: **Agnès Varda**
Screeplay: **Agnès Varda**
Producer: Ciné-Tamaris
Cinematographer: David Meyers, Didier Tarot
Music: Yannos Spanos, Richard Lawrence, Albinoni
Editing: Jean Hamon, Roger Ikhlef
Cast: **Agnès Varda**, Jean Varda
35mm, 22 minutes, color

BLACK PANTHERS (1968)
Director: **Agnès Varda**
Screenplay: **Agnès Varda**
Camera: David Myers, John Schofill, Paul Aratow, **Agnès Varda**
Sound: Paul Oppenheim, James Steward
Music: Soul music improvised by the Black Panthers
Editing: Paddy Monk
16mm, 28 minutes, b/w
Awards: Prize awarded at Festival of Oberhausen, 1970

LIONS LOVE (1969)
Director: **Agnès Varda**
Screenplay: **Agnès Varda**
Producer: Ciné-Tamaris
Camera: Steve Larner, Lee Alexander, William Weaver, Rusty Roland
Sound: George Alch and Y Babbish, George Porter
Music: Joseph Byrd
Cast: Playing themselves: Viva, Jim Rado, Shirley Clarke, Carlos Clarens, Eddie Constantine, Max Laemmle, Steve Kenis, Hal Landers, Billie Dixon, Richard Bright
35mm, 110 minutes, color

NAUSICAA (1970)
Director: **Agnès Varda**
Screenplay: **Agnès Varda**
Producer: ORTF France
Camera: Charlie Gaeta
Editing: Robert Dalva, Carolyn Hicks
Music: Mikis Theodorakis
Cast: France Dougnac (Agnès), Myriam Boyer (Rosalie), Stavros Tornes
(Michel), Catherine de Seynes (Simone), Gérard Dépardieu (a hippie)
35mm, 90 minutes, color

DAGUERRÉOTYPES (1974)
Director: **Agnès Varda**
Screenplay; **Agnès Varda**
Producer: Ciné-Tamaris, L'Institut de l'audiovisuel et la ZDF (Mainz)
Camera: Rith Aviv, William Lubtchancsky
Editing: Gordon Swire
Sound: Antoine Bonifanti, Jean-François Auger
Cast: The neighbors of Agnès Varda on the Rue Daguerre
16mm, 80 minutes, color
Awards: Nominated for Oscar for Feature-Length Documentary, 1975;
Prix du Cinéma d'Art et d'Essai, 1975

RÉPONSE DE FEMMES (1975)
Director: **Agnès Varda**
Screenplay: **Agnès Varda**
Producer: Ciné-Tamaris, Antenne 2—Le Magazine F. Comme Femme
Cinematography: Jacques Reiss, Michel Thiriet
Editing: Marie Castro, Andrée Choty, Hélène Wolf
Sound: Bernard Bleicher
Cast: Various subjects reading Varda's declarations
16mm, 8 minutes, color
Awards: Nominated for Césars, 1976, in category of Short
Documentaries

PLAISIR D'AMOUR EN IRAN (1976)
Director: **Agnès Varda**
Screenplay: **Agnès Varda**
Producer: Ciné-Tamaris
Camera: Nurith Aviv, Charlie Vandamme

Editing: Sabine Mamou
Sound: Henri Morelle
Cast: Valérie Mairesse (Pomme), Ali Raffi (Ali Darius)
35mm, 6 minutes, color

L'UNE CHANTE, L'AUTRE PAS (1977)
Director: **Agnès Varda**
Screenplay: **Agnès Varda**
Producer: Ciné-Tamaris, Société Française de Production, Institut National de l'Audiovisuel-Contrechamp
Camera: Charlie Vandamme, Nurith Aviv
Editing: Joëlle Van Effenterre
Sound: Herni Morelle
Music: Wertheiimer and Orchidée, **Agnès Varda**
Cast: Thérèse Liotard (Suzanne), Valérie Mairesse (Pomme), Ali Raffi (Darius), Robert Dadies (Jérôme), Francis Lemaire (Pomme's father), Jean-Pierre Pellegrin (Doctor Pierre Aubanel), the Group Orchidée
35 mm, 120 minutes, color
Awards: Grand Prize, Festival of Taomina, 1977

QUELQUES FEMMES BULLES (1977)
Director: Marion Sarrault
Screenplay: **Agnès Varda**
Producer: Ciné-Tamaris
Editing: Marion Sarrault, **Agnès Varda**
Music: The Orchidée Group
Video
58 minutes, color

MUR MURS (1980)
Director: **Agnès Varda**
Screenplay: **Agnès Varda**
Producer: Ciné-Tamaris, Antenne 2
Camera: Bernard Auroux, Tom Taplin
Editing: Sabine Mamou, Bob Gould
Sound: Lee Alexander
Music: Buxtehude, Carey, Cruz, Fiddy, Healy, Lauber, Los Illegals, Parker
Cast: The people of Los Angeles
16mm, 81 minutes, color

Awards: France's Selection for the Cannes Festival in the category *Un Certain Regard*, 1981; Prize, Festival dei Populi de Florence, 1981; Josef von Sternberg Prize, Mannheim, 1981

DOCUMENTEUR (1981)
Director: **Agnès Varda**
Screenplay: **Agnès Varda**
Producer: Ciné-Tamaris
Camera: Nurith Aviv
Editing: Sabine Mamou
Music: Georges Delerue
Sound: Jim Thornton, Lee Alexander
Cast: Sabine Mamou (Emilie), Mathieu Demy (Martin)
16mm, 63 minutes, color

ULYSSE (1982)
Director: **Agnès Varda**
Screenplay **Agnès Varda**
Producer: Garance, Dominique Vignet, François Nocher and Paris Audiovisuel, Antenne 2, C.D.C.
Camera: Jen-Yves Escoffier, Pascal Rabaud
Editing: Marie-Jo Audiard, Hélène de Luze
Sound: Jean-Paul Mugel
35mm, 22 minutes, color
Awards: Selected for the Cannes Festival in the category *Un certain regard*; César for Best Short Documentary, 1984

UNE MINUTE POUR UNE IMAGE (1983)
Director: **Agnès Varda**
Producer: Garance, Centre National de la Photographie.
170 spots of two minutes each presenting a different photograph each evening

LES DITES CARIATIDES (1984)
Director: **Agnès Varda**
Screenplay: **Agnès Varda,** with poetry of Charles Baudelaire
Producer: Ciné-Tamaris
Camera: Cyril Lathus, Jean-Pierre Albassy
Editing: Hélène Wolf

Music: Rameau, Offenbach
Cast: Caryatids on buildings in Paris
Video
13 minutes, color
Awards: Official Selection at the Venice Film Festival, 1984; Prize for
Best Documentary at the International Festival of Film on Architecture
and Urbanism, Lausanne, 1987

7P., CUIS., S. DE B., . . . A SAISIR (1984)
Director: **Agnès Varda**
Screenplay: **Agnès Varda**, Louis Bec
Producer: Ciné-Tamaris
Camera: Nurith Aviv
Editing: Sabine Mamou
Music: Pierre Barbaud
Cast: Hervé Mangani (the father), Saskia Cohen-Tanugi (the mother),
Pierre Esposito (the older son), Catherine de Barbeyrac (the oldest
daughter), Folco Chevalier (the suitor)
35mm, 27 minutes, color

SANS TOIT NI LOI (1985)
Director: **Agnès Varda**
Screenplay: **Agnès Varda**
Producer: Ciné-Tamaris
Cinematographer: Patrick Blossier
Editing: **Agnès Varda**, Patricia Mazuy
Music: Joanna Bruzdowicz
Sound: Jean-Paul Mugel
Cast: Sandrine Bonnaire (Mona), Macha Méril (Madame Landier), Sté-
phane Freiss (Jean-Pierre, the agronomist), Yolande Moreau (the maid),
Patrick Lepczynski (David), Yahiaoui Assouna (Assoun), Joël Fosse
(Paulo), Marthe Jarnia (tante Lydie)
35mm, 105 minutes, color
Awards: Lion d'Or, Venice Film Festival, 1985; International Critics'
Prize, Fipresci, 1985; Prix Georges Méliès, 1985; César Award for Best
Actress, Sandrine Bonnaire, 1985; Catholic Office of Cinema Prize, 1985;
Best Foreign Film Award, American Association of Film Critics, 1986;
Best Film, Best Director, Brussels Film Festival, 1986; Best Film, Durban
International Film Festival, 1987

T'AS DE BEAUX ESCALIERS, TU SAIS (1986)
Director: **Agnès Varda**
Screenplay: **Agnès Varda**
Producer: Ciné-Tamaris (for the French Cinémathèque)
Camera: Patrick Blossier
Editing: Marie-Jo Audiard
Music: Michel Legrand
Cast: Isabelle Adjani (Isabelle), **Agnès Varda** (narrator)
35mm, 3 mintues, color

KUNG-FU MASTER (1987)
Director: **Agnès Varda**
Screenplay: **Agnès Varda**
Producer: Ciné-Tamaris
Camera: Pierre Laurent Chenieux
Editing: Marie-Jo Audiard
Sound: Olivier Schwob
Music: Joanna Bruzdowicz
Cast: Jane Birkin (Mary Jane), Mathieu Demy (Julien), Charlotte Gains-
bourg (Lucy), Lou Doillon (Lou)
35mm, 78 minutes, color

JANE B. PAR AGNÈS V. (1988)
Director: **Agnès Varda**
Screenplay: **Agnès Varda**
Producer: Ciné-Tamaris with La Sept
Camera: Nurith Aviv, Pierre-Laurent Chenieux
Editing: Agnès Varda, Marie-Jo Audiard
Sound: Olivier Schwob, Jean-Paul Mugel
Music: The Doors, Manfredini, Monteverdi
Cast: Jane Birkin (Herself), Philppe Léotard (the painter), Jean-Pierre Lé-
aud (the angry lover), Farid Chopel (the colonist), Alain Souchon (the
reader), Serge Gainsbourg (himself), Laura Betti (Lardy)
35mm, 97 minutes, color

JACQUOT DE NANTES (1990)
Director: **Agnès Varda**
Sreenplay: **Agnès Varda**
Producer: Ciné-Tamaris
Camera: Patick Blossier, Agnès Godard, Georges Strouvé

Editing: Marie-Jo Audiard
Music: Joanna Bruzdowicz
Sound: Jean Pierre Duret, Nicolas Naegelen
Cast: Philippe Maron (Jacquot 1), Edouard Joubeaud (Jacquot 2), Laurent Monnier (Jacquot 3), Brigitte de Villepoix (the mother), Daniel Dublet (Yvon 1), Clémant Delaroche (Yvon 2)
35mm, 118 minutes, b/w & color

LES DEMOISELLES ONT EU 25 ANS (1992)
Director: **Agnès Varda**
Screenplay: **Agnès Varda**
Producer: Ciné-Tamais, Mag Bodard (Parc Film), and Gilbert Goldschmidt (Madeleine Films)
Camera: Stephane Krausz, Georges Strouve, **Agnès Varda**
Editing: **Agnès Varda**, Anne-Marie Cotret
Sound: Thierry Ferreux, Jean-Luc Rault-Cheynet, Bernard Seidler
Music: Michel Legrand, Jacques Loussier
Cast: Marc Le Gouard (the teacher), Jacques Camescasse (Corvette captain), Ginette Donce (fisherwoman), Jean-Yves Drapeau (traveler)
16mm, 63 minutes, color
Awards: Golden Plaque Award, Chicago Film Festival, 1993

LES 100 ET 1 NUITS (1995)
Director: **Agnès Varda**
Screenplay: **Agnès Varda**
Producer: Dominique Vignet, Ciné-Tamaris
Camera: Eric Gautier
Editing: Hugues Darmois
Sound: Jean-Pierre Duret, Henri Morelle
Cast: Michel Piccoli (Simon Cinéma), Marcello Mastroianni (the Italian friend), Henri Garcin (Firmin, the butler), Julie Gayet (Camille Miralis), Mathieu Demy (Camille), Emmanuel Salinger (Vincent), Anouk Aimée (Anouk), Fanny Ardant (the Star who works at night), Jean-Paul Belmondo (Professeur Bébel), Sandrine Bonnaire (the vagabond), Jean-Claude Brialy (the guide), Alain Delon (himself), Catherine Deneuve (the Fantasy Star), Robert De Niro (her husband), Gérard Depardieu (himself), Harrison Ford (himself), Gina Lollobrigida (Professor Bebel's wife), Jeanne Moreau (the first ex-wife of Mr. Cinéma), Jane Birkin (herself)
35mm, 101 minutes, color

L' UNIVERS DE JACQUES DEMY (1995)
Director: **Agnès Varda**
Screenplay: **Agnès Varda**
Narrator: **Agnès Varda**
Producer: Ciné-Tamaris, Canal+
Camera: Stéphane Krausz, Peter Pilafian, Georges Strouvé
Editing: Marie-Jo Audiard
Music: Michel Legrand, Michel Colombier
Cast: Anouk Aimée, Richard Berry, Nino Castelnuovo, Catherine Deneuve, Harrison Ford, Danielle Darrieux, Jeanne Moreau, Michel Piccoli, Françoise Fabian, Jeanne Moreau, Dominique Sanda
35mm, 90 minutes, b/w & color

LES GLANEURS ET LA GLANEUSE (2000)
Director: **Agnès Varda**
Screenplay: **Agnès Varda**
Producer: Ciné-Tamaris
Camera: **Agnès Varda**, Didier Doussin, Stephane Krausz
Editing: **Agnès Varda**, Laurent Pineau
Music: Joanna Bruzdowicz, Isabelle Olivier, Agnès Bredel, Richard Klugman
Cast: Bodan Litnanski, François Wertheimer
35mm, 82 minutes, color

LES GLANEURS ET MOI DEUX ANS APRÈS (2002)
Director: **Agnès Varda**
Screenplay: **Agnès Varda**
Producer: Ciné-Tamaris
Camera: Stéphane Krausz, **Agnès Varda**
Editing: **Agnès Varda**
Music: Joanna Bruzdowicz, Georges Delerue, Isabelle Olivier, François Wertheimer
Cast: Macha Makeïeff, **Agnès Varda**
35mm, 63 minutes, color

LE LION VOLATIL (2003)
Director: **Agnès Varda**
Screenplay: **Agnès Varda**
Producer: Ciné-Tamaris
Camera: Mathieu Vadepied, Xavier Tauvera

Editing: **Agnès Varda**, Sophie Mandonnet
Sound: Jean-Luc Audy
Music: Joanna Bruzdowicz
Cast: Julie Dépardieu (Clarisse), Frédérick Grassser-Hermé (forutune teller), Silvia Urrutia (first client), David Decron (Lazarus), Bernard Werber (Watchman), Valérie Donzelli (tearful client)
35mm, 11 minutes, b/w & color

YDESSA, LES OURS (2004)
Director: **Agnès Varda**
Screenplay: **Agnès Varda**
Producer: Ciné-Tamaris
Camera: Claire Duguet, John Holosko, Rick Kearney, Markus Seitz
Editing: Thomas Benigni, Jean-Baptiste Morin, **Agnès Varda**
Sound: Christian Börner, Robert Fletcher, Jason Milligan
Music: Didier Lockwood, Isabelle Olivier
Cast: Ydessa Hendeles (herself)
35mm, 44 minutes, color

DER VIENNALE (2004)
Director: **Agnès Varda**
Screenplay: **Agnès Varda**
Producer: Ciné Tamaris
Camera: **Agnès Varda**
Editing: **Agnès Varda**
Cast: **Agnès Varda**
35mm, 2 minutes, color

QUELQUES VEUVES DE NOIRMOUTIER (2006)
Director: **Agnès Varda**
Screenplay: **Agnès Varda**
Producer: Ciné Tamaris
Camera: Eric Gautier
Editing: Jean-Baptiste Montagut, **Agnès Varda**
Music: Ami Flammer
Cast: Women of Nourmoutier
35mm, 69 minutes, color

LES PLAGES D'AGNÈS (2008)
Director: **Agnès Varda**

Screenplay: **Agnès Varda**
Producer: Ciné-Tamaris
Camera: Julia Fabry, Hélène Louvart, Arlene Nelson, Alain Sakot,
Agnès Varda
Editing: Baptiste Filloux, Jean-Baptiste Morin
Sound: Olivier Schwob, Emmanuel Soland
Music: Laurent Levesque, Joanna Bruzdowicz, Stéphane Vilar
Cast: **Agnès Varda**, Laure Manceau (Agnès Varda as a girl), Rosalie
Varda, Mathieu Demy, Andrée Vilar, Jim McBride, Jane Birkin, Constan-
tin Demy
35 mm, 110 minutes, b/w & color

Agnès Varda: Interviews

Agnès Varda from 5 to 7

Pierre Uytterhoeven / 1962

From *Positif*, no. 44 (March 1962). Reprinted by permission. Translated by T. Jefferson Kline.

Pierre Uytterhoeven: Let's talk about *La Pointe Courte*, that you directed in 1954. Do you still think today that the two themes of the film, treated in such very different styles, can't be mixed and shouldn't be?

Agnès Varda: I had a very precise idea when I did *La Pointe Courte* and that was to propose two themes that weren't necessarily contradictory but which, placed side by side, were problems which were mutually exclusive. They were: a couple coming to grips with their relationship and, on the other hand, a village trying to resolve certain problems through a collective process.

The film was divided into chapters, so the two themes were never mixed together but I left open the possibility for the spectator to confront them or superpose them. I've always thought it was very difficult to integrate one's private problems with public issues. In *Hiroshima, Mon Amour* Resnais succeeded beautifully in giving the audience an impression forged from the mixing of these two levels by having the French woman experience a passionate encounter with the Japanese man in Hiroshima. The violence of their encounter resuscitates her memories of her first passion for a German man. In this way the larger social issues are integrated with the private problems of the couple.

PU: But in *La Pointe Courte* why did you choose to separate these two problems?

AV: The construction of the film was inspired by Faulkner's *The Wild Palms*. If you remember, there's no connection in the novel between the couple, Charlotte and Harry, and the old ex-con from Mississippi. It was neither allegorical nor symbolic, just a feeling you get from reading which moves back and forth between these two stories. It's up to

3

the reader to be able to reorganize these feelings. It's exactly like what Resnais is asking of his audience in *Marienbad*.

The need to integrate a private problem with a larger social issue is also a theme in *L'Enclos*. In this particular case, the experiences of the two protagonists are but a detail in the larger picture. What I liked about Gatti's film is that the two characters experience their problem in terms of the camp while at the same time, the camp is thinking about them. But his way of treating the couple and the group is only possible because it is a face-off between two men who are confronted by the same problems faced by all the prisoners in the camp. When it's a question of love between a man and a woman, it's more difficult.

PU: So the couple would have to have resolved their personal problems in order to properly belong to the larger social group?
AV: Yes, but I've already stated this. A harmonious couple, that is, one that manages to resolve their personal problems, can be integrated into a larger collectivity. (There are, for example, happy couples who are union members.)

What I hoped to show in *La Pointe Courte* was the paralysis of the couple who can't seem to shake free of their intellectual and emotional problems, and hence can't manage to think about their affinity to any group. I wanted my audience to understand that there's no connection between social issues and private problems. Of course, there does exist a level of understanding where these antagonisms disappear. But in *La Pointe Courte*, I presented a couple in crisis and not only between themselves, but in terms of their inability to connect with others.

PU: Could you talk to me about the problems of structure in your films? For example, *L'Opera Mouffe* constructed as a series of tableaux introduced by chapter titles . . .
AV: It's a film about instinct, in the sense that an instinct develops according to a logic of its own. I don't mean to say that the film was made any which way, but instead mirrored the panic of a pregnant woman struggling with a serious contradiction. To be expecting implies naturally a sense of hope. Hope of future happiness, hope for the continuation of the race, etc. . . . but on the other hand, there are a bunch of situations in life that are pretty desperate and we inevitably experience some of these in our daily lives. Maybe desperate isn't the right word, maybe I mean an absence of hope; not necessarily a tragedy but . . .

PU: We might say unhope?

AV: Yes, that's it. The word doesn't really exist, but you know the neighborhood around the rue Mouffetard . . .

PU: I live there.

AV: So we could say it's a pretty desperate area which doesn't give us much hope in humanity. On the one hand there are the alcoholics and lots of old people as well, if you've noticed, lots more than in other neighborhoods. Looking at these dregs of humanity (if I may put it that way), you can't help thinking, if you're expecting, that your child might well turn out to be a bum, an alcoholic, an old person. So the film is based on this contradiction. What ends up counting is that the humanity that we see around us produces a certain image of the world. This is the documentary aspect of the film—the virtual woman that sees a certain image of the world around her.

PU: A completely subjective image if you compare it to *On the Bowery*, for example.

AV: I didn't see *On the Bowery*, but I believe that there are no objective documentaries. You'd have to put fifteen cameras in one place and just let them film by themselves for five years; but even then the editing would be subjective. Objectivity would consist in a series of general uncontrolled shots without any editing that would be presented as filmed, scenes from an unmanned camera. So the objectivity would be to record what's going on in the street and even then you wouldn't see everything.

PU: The very act of seeing implies a choice.

AV: Okay, but within certain limits. You're making a choice when you want to hold back. But stand under an umbrella and look at the street and you have a sense of the whole. In the case of *L'Opéra Mouffe*, I pushed this sense of objectivity by adding a specific kind of subjectivity—pregnancy—which is a kind of super-sensitivity which chooses to see the world in a particular way to the degree that the woman's interest in the child she will bear causes her to see the people around her as former babies whom some mother was expecting. No one is obliged to think this way, but you can't help saying when you see a bum: this man was carried by his mother who thought: He'll be a child and then grow up to be happy. There is such an evident disconnect that I felt I had to make a film about it. But when I tell you that this film was made by instinct,

I believe that what I did was so instinctual that it's impossible to talk about structure.

PU: Would you like to return to this subject of having children in a feature-length film? I believe that you think that *La Proie pour l'ombre*, that I know you like, doesn't really deal with this problem.

AV: I wasn't out to criticize *La Proie pour l'ombre*. It's a film I like. I simply meant to say that *La Proie pour l'ombre*, *La Nuit*, *La Pointe Courte* are all films in which the problem of having children isn't really addressed, and even *Voyage en Italie* (although in this film the problem is alluded to by the nostalgia and the desire of the woman to have a child). Of course, love doesn't need children to express itself, but it's evident that once you bring up the problem of the couple, you have to deal with the birth of children. Whether you have children or don't, whether you want children or have too many, the problem of children exists, at least implicitly, for every couple. Also, I don't see why couples' problems should always be presented in social classes where people have the leisure to think these problems through. In other classes, the problem exists every bit as much and people have to work it through. This is one of the most beautiful things about *Le Cri*. A worker encounters a crucial problem in a love relationship. Because of his unhappiness in love, he quits his job. And this in turn affects his relationship. There are three things I love about this film: first the love affair that turns out badly; next the constant presence of a child, a child who is judgmental, a child the woman wants to have with another man; and finally Aldo's relationship to his work which is at least as important as his relationship with the woman. The proof of this is that Aldo comes back to his workplace to commit suicide. Just as an assassin returns to the scene of his crime, the worker returns to the place where he worked. He has a deep attachment to his work. To portray in a film only the loss of love (which is certainly a very tragic subject) would be to deal only in the abstract, which is why *La Pointe Courte* is an abstract film. The characters had neither names nor jobs.

PU: But even so, the man was in his own world and was solidly anchored in that world.

AV: Yes, the film shows the characters' roots. I don't like it when a couple's problems are portrayed outside of their connections to job, community, and children. A couple isn't an abstract thing, but it is nourished by living elements.

PU: Henri Michaux considers that we lead a life of faces, that other people are essentially faces. In your case, why so many faces in *L'Opéra Mouffe?*

AV: The problem for a woman is to understand the mysterious relationship between people and their childhood; and people are first and foremost the faces that one encounters. But also, in the rue Mouffetard I had very precisely a feeling of the press of that mass of people, of the life of the crowd. Making a child is also something that presses. Viscerally, it seems like life is pressing in the womb until the child is pushed out. That's not very scientific. My film is based on instinct. The feelings are neither controlled nor logical. For example there's a whole sequence on tripe. A person who has eaten a lot has a big stomach; a person expecting a child has a big stomach. There's lots of confusion between food and pregnancy. That's why the film is located in a market; the heroine is constantly obsessed by food, vegetables, meat, and tripe. Of course, when you talk about it it's awful. Saying it that way almost dirties the way it's represented in the film. You can't say a pregnant woman is always thinking about eating tripe! It's an awful sentence and an awful feeling. But at the instinctual level, there is this feeling of tripe. Now we have natural childbirth. That's progress, but as always at the beginning of any advance you have to struggle against instinct, the source of fear. I'm for progress, of course, but I also believe that progress must not kill our instincts or ignore instinctive fears. You have to control them, manage to feel them without succumbing to their power, to take them in. Natural childbirth is good, especially if we still manage to safeguard our primitive and archaic instincts. Please don't think I'm retrograde when it comes to science—I've practiced natural childbirth—but I think that we must remain in touch with our ancestral instincts. Women must not lose our sensitivity to these things.

PU: Rilke, speaking of maternity—or creation, if you will, makes a distinction between man and woman, assigning to women the work of childbirth and to men the universe of art. Can you find your equilibrium between your work as a filmmaker and your life as a woman who makes this other kind of creation?

AV: It's really a question of proportions. The problem of maternity vis-à-vis one's work as an artist is the same as my attitude vis-à-vis maternity: it's as though people said, "a woman who practices natural childbirth can't feel the same instincts as her grandmother did." One problem doesn't cancel out the other. Women can be professional artists. I don't feel like an abnormal woman; I live like other women. When people say to me, "Why aren't there more women making films?" I'm astonished. I don't take anything away from my life as a woman to make films.

PU: So, can one say in a general way that having a job doesn't imply abandoning one's husband or lover?

AV: Women haven't been emancipated long enough to have outgrown their suffragette mentality. Women are finally gaining their freedom I'm happy to say; but when some women go from dependence on a husband to the independence of the work place they end up quite dissatisfied. I don't think women necessarily find happiness and equilibrium at work. In a period of transition like the one we're in, the extreme cases are more numerous than the moderate cases. Myself, I'm very moderate in this area because I don't think all women need emancipation and those who do need it sometimes don't find the equilibrium there that they need. It's a question of talent, intelligence, and private life. A woman who gains her freedom from an uninteresting husband is emancipated both from her feminine condition and from her husband. But the more interesting case is that of the woman who loves an interesting man; so if she needs emancipation it's a real need, but it only works if she finds her equilibrium as a woman. If a woman leaves a husband she doesn't love, then it's strictly a couples' problem. There is a lot of confusion surrounding women's questions. And there are more and more confusions as things get more complicated and it's difficult for a woman to get clarity, especially since men contribute to this confusion. Some want women to be able to work; others want to keep women at home; they use terms which only confuse the real issues. But this exaggeration comes from both men and women. Few men consider that a woman who wants to work does so because of a profound need which doesn't necessarily mean she wants to cheat on her husband, become independent, live her life or whatever . . . Each country has its own set of attitudes. In Italy, women who work are despised. People think they're abnormal and can't do otherwise. In France there are certain milieux where people consider that a woman who doesn't work isn't worth much. But all of this is so tricky that we have to work harder to educate women and girls. We have to go slowly on these problems and not get into generalizations about them.

PU: One theme that seems to pervade your work is the theme of nudity . . .

AV: Yes, that's true.

PU: Does this theme have a precise meaning for you?

AV: For me it's the point of encounter between the domain of formal beauty and the domain of moral beauty. It's a privileged domain. A naked body is a measure of beauty. Moreover, a person who is mentally naked, which is so say clear, undressed, without a mask is a moving and beautiful person . . . It's true: it's a theme I always enjoy discussing. The couple I showed in *L'Opéra Mouffe* is a sort of homage to love; it's very pure, not in a puritan sense of the word. There is a beauty in shared love that is phenomenal. The sequence was filmed this way: first the couple is in bed . . . I had a sense at that time that love is a kind of doubling, love is a "transport" as if by a medium . . . You see what I mean? Opium is a transport. Love is one of the ways to attain a reality that would otherwise remain inaccessible. There are people who feel this kind of doubling an impression of a mental landscape. In *L'Opéra Mouffe* it's like the poetic line, "I watched myself watching . . ." It's a little cynical. The girl is in the man's arms, they're happy, they're beautiful. They see their own beauty. At the same time, she sees her own beauty. It's not narcissism: it's through his look that she becomes beautiful. It's the shot where she's lying on the bed outdoors. It's like he has a feline feeling, a caress or fur . . . he can have this feeling without having a vision of a cat. That's why film is a kind of approach. It's always approximate and the image will always be more primary than the feeling. At a given moment, then, they're on the bed and suddenly you see them walking towards each other in the courtyard.

PU: This is one of the most beautiful shots in the film, this walk through a baroque setting.

AV: But it isn't baroque, it's realistic. There's no formal stylization. It's simpler that you think.

PU: And yet *La Pointe Courte* was cinematically very stylized. It was both very linear . . .

AV: Yes, linear like a drawing on a wall, but that's a feeling. In warmer climates maybe you've noticed this. When you are feeling a pain, the head seems to sharpen that pain, dries it out, purifies it, makes it geometric as if it were drawn. So *La Pointe Courte* is made of cold linear images, under a noonday sun. It's not so much a formal essay as it is an essay in feeling. Of course formal concerns always have a deeper level. There's no formalism in the pure state. So even if the film has a formal quality to it, every form expresses a feeling. For the lovers of *L'Opéra Mouffe*, the audience doesn't say them themselves: they're outside or inside, they watch themselves watching, but because of the formal arrangements of the film they get the feelings I wanted to express.

PU: To sum up one might say, with Sartre, that every technique implies a metaphysical position; writing leads us to a universe that could not be revealed except through that medium.

AV: That's normal; writing must witness. What interests me is precisely the silent, secret, inexpressible things that are in people. There are as many things in the domain of the instincts as in the domain of feelings.

PU: If we could talk for a minute about *Cléo de 5 à 7*. Once again the theme of nudity appears in your film.

AV: Cléo is for me typically a character who is not naked. She's a very beautiful girl, but surrounds herself in every situation with screens: superstition, coquettishness, exaggerated femininity.

PU: All of that due to the fear we see at the beginning of the film.

AV: Yes, and also the fear of being taken, of giving herself; the very expression "to get taken," means to be naked and defenseless, a threat to one's sensibilities; every one wears some kind of armor. Of course *Cléo* is a case study; as a woman she's not very accomplished.

PU: Did you feel a lot of tenderness for this character?

AV: No, more like pity. I think it's atrocious that someone should be so unprepared to contemplate death. Cléo is the type of person for whom the thought of death is so surprising that it completely undoes her. She's led to question her entire existence, the musicians, Angèle, her lover, and even her profession as a singer. Cléo finds herself more and more abandoned until she meets the soldier, who's really the prototypical harmless guy. This is no meeting of exceptional beings: it's neither "we were fated to meet" nor "we were meant for each other." Any guy she'd happened to meet at that moment would have helped her understand things better. But it so happens that she meets a guy who is himself somewhat at sea. (I think a soldier is in a difficult position vis-à-vis certain problems.) They both talk about love and he explains his view of things. The problem for Cléo is that she realizes that she's never really given of herself, never felt entirely naked. That's why the guy talks somewhat allegorically and her girlfriend works as a nude model. This idea of nakedness is portrayed visually by her friend posing, intellectually by the soldier, and physically by her experiences of the last hour. Illness undresses her because illness affects the body.

There's a moment at the hospital when Cléo gets to a point of transparency and purity and this is what the film is all about. They're both disarmed, vulnerable. People can begin to communicate when they're in this state. Cléo discovers the way to another existence where other values obtain. Sometimes life opens up a way into another level of knowing. She realizes that there exist other things that she values.

PU: Your film reminded me of *Lola*; a certain lyricism and maybe other things like the musical element . . .

AV: Well it's the same musician but the musical elements aren't the same. The only point in common is the Charleston music you hear in the intermission in the cinema. But Demy thinks a priori that people have access to each other. They live in a natural world where love is considered a natural thing. I, on the other hand, make a cinema full of obstacles, of contradictions. Demy's cinema presents a certain reality—not presented as a problem to be solved—but that you can assimilate naturally. I look for simplicity, not nudity.

PU: I loved the little burlesque of a film that you see in *Cléo de 5 à 7*. But on reflection, it's not funny at all since this burlesque is founded both on an accelerated sense of time and is thus about the approach of death.

AV: In the evolution of Cléo's values, I'd say this is a form of humor, since in this little film we see a hearse, an ambulance (which are after all vehicles associated with death), but when treated in this burlesque fashion they make us laugh. When you can laugh about your own death, it's already a form of lucidity. We could say that among the classes Cléo takes in this "school" this is her class on humor. You see the film, you laugh at it, but it's all the same a form of cruelty to show a hearse and an ambulance; moreover, as you said, the acceleration of time precipitates things. Plus the main character is kind of ubiquitous; when he puts on his sunglasses, he sees everything in black. A black woman is hit by a hearse, okay, that's the dark side . . . But when he takes off his sunglasses, he sees her in white exactly where he had left her. You're familiar with this mental phenomenon: when you see something, between the moment you see it and the arrival of the image in the brain there's a gap so we have the impression of already having seen it. This is a bit like that, because when he puts on the glasses he sees her do something in black and when he removes them, the action is repeated in the same place but in white. So if we start digging around in this little film it becomes troubling. There are two realities, the one negative and the other positive and they are juxtaposed in time, but what's important is that Cléo can laugh at something that horrifies her.

PU: Why is the beginning of the film in color?

AV: My idea was that the life in the Tarot cards is an imaginary life, it's a representation of life, and real life in the film is in black and white. I wanted to separate this representation of life from life itself. Of course it's entirely arbitrary because we see real life in colors. But the perspective of the film, given that it's shot in black and white and that during the credits you hear her story, so the fortune teller predicts her life to her as if she were watching the projection of her own film. Even if the cards announce that she will die, they're just cards.

PU: Let's talk about *La Mélangite*. When I read your description of the project, I thought of Michel Butor's *La Modification*.

AV: I found his novel interesting but not at all captivating. It's cold, very intellectualized. *La Mélangite*, by contrast, will be presented as an adventure story, with lots of humor. When I started out I said to myself: when something happens in the character's head, what would it be like if I illustrated literally what he is thinking? That made me laugh because I'd read Robbe-Grillet's very serious statements where he says, "At the very instant I pronounce the words, *I could go to the seaside* I immediately see rocks, a beach." Robbe-Grillet explains this with utmost seriousness. But when I began to write *La Mélangite* I told myself "this has to be as much fun as a Western." It seems to me that, indeed, our thought moves by leaps, bounds, gallops, and chases; when you think about it, it's quite suspenseful inside a thought which comes and goes, it's quite extraordinary.

PU: So it's to be a film based on our thoughts rather than on reality?

AV: Well, it's both at once. The action is often happening in the mind. For example a character thinks about the future and imagines that he's doing something that can be seen on a screen; that's not original. It's been done fifty times. *La Fête à Henriette*, for example, which is a lousy film, was made like that, about creative imagination.

PU: There's a kind of acting out of metaphor there. When the character is doubled, then tripled, then quadrupled and we suddenly see all four people on the screen.

AV: You have to observe carefully: these four characters are only various incarnations of the first character at different times. I was young (and pure at heart), then impassioned and it wasn't the same; as is often said, we change and he has changed, but since we don't kill off our previous selves there is a dialogue between these characters. People are full of compartments; they confess quite easily "what's good in me . . ." Each compartment represents a character. When you recount this it gets very complex, but when you see it it's clear. A character can be polyvalent very simply and naturally. And language can't really get at this.

Moreover the film is very much about culture. If a thing exists as a common denominator among people, then that's culture. The character in *La Mélangite* is a big fan of Venetian music. He's very focused on a certain form of culture, in fact he's obsessed by it. You have to let yourself go with this film that is structured primarily on associations of visual ideas, on visual puns. You think, for example of the Lyons train station and suddenly you see a real lion in the Vincennes zoo. It will be a continuous play on images the way you have plays on words.

The play on images would include cutting from the real lion to a stone lion, moving from the Vincennes zoo to the Piazza San Marco in Venice.

PU: It makes me think of Vigo and of his image-association in *A Propos de Nice*.

AV: I like Vigo but *A Propos de Nice* isn't like that. I think it's his least successful film. *Zéro de Conduite* and *L'Atalante* are magnificent, but *A Propos de Nice* is his punning, adolescent, not-very-funny-joke, not-always-positive-aggressivity side. It's amusing but a bit primitive, repressed; I've seen it ten to fifteen times (because it was always shown with *La Pointe Courte* when it first opened) and I was surprised by the positive reactions to this film which represents a certain kind of revolt, but very schoolboy and not very well structured. *L'Atalante*, on the other hand is a level of revolt freed of his adolescent humor. You might say that *L'Age d'Or* is also based on instinct, on illustrated feelings. You could really analyze *L'Age d'Or*: a couple making love in the mud, a few yards from an official ceremony, near a monument, what is that? If it's an intellectual idea, then it's merely aggressive and idiotic, but it's a feeling and I believe it, it's so beautiful that the underlying context of the image doesn't really matter. Here you have thought preceding the image, instinct. *L'Age d'Or* is really marvelous in this regard.

PU: Will *La Mélangite* be filmed in color?

AV: Yes, and that's why I have had such a hard time making the film. I've already shot the prelude which is a kind of documentary on the youth of the main character and which would take place in the first part of the program, before the newsreels and advertising, you see. It sets up the important aspects of the landscape of my film. I think people are made up of landscapes. So it's both a documentary about the salt marshes of Sête and on the young man's youth when he lived with his father. It's completely separate from the rest of the film.

PU: You were talking about culture a while ago. Does the film present an attack on this culture or does it constitute an apology?

AV: I'm not sure; I haven't really defined my position on this. I think for some people, culture becomes a second-nature; but to what degree this second nature kills or enriches the first, that's the question the film is asking. Take the example of someone who knows art history. If a landscape makes him think of Poussin, he enjoys the view doubled by the pleasure of Poussin so the painting enriches his experience. But there are people for whom culture replaces emotion and who might say, "Hey, that looks like a Poussin" but who feel nothing about the view—or rather the feeling becomes a formula. It's both a way of learning something about the world and putting up a screen in front of the world. I think that in the case of the guy in *La Mélangite* it's more of a screen; he's so focused in Venetian culture that he can't see anything else. It's an unusual case since the development of our cultural sensibilities should go hand in hand with an increased sensitivity vis-à-vis the real world. Here the opposite is true.

PU: But if culture helps us understand things better, then we can't talk about masks and paralyzing phenomena.

AV: Well this is just a case-study, remember. Initially, my character had a sensitivity enriched by culture. First he sees Venice and then through the acquisition of culture he gets nearer to Venice, understands it better. But there comes a moment when his sensibilities dry up, when his heart doesn't beat anymore. At that point culture has become a form of vice. And there's a moment when this vice becomes necessary to having any feelings. For example, a man loves a woman who resembles a Botticelli. So far so good, he's done nothing more than enrich his amorous appreciation of the lady; but now imagine that he starts looking for a lover who looks like a Botticelli; well that's okay, you'd simply call him a weirdo, but from there to the impossibility of loving a woman who doesn't resemble a Botticelli, well, that's really just a vice.

If the character in *La Mélangite* has stopped loving anything, it's not in order to better appreciate the music and culture of Venice, it's because life has simply stopped. His heart has stopped beating. It's the story of a rapid flowering followed by an equally rapid withering. I sort of like this character, but at the same time I don't feel like I can judge him very well. He's tough to figure out; with each woman a new aspect of his character emerges. He passes through several phases: falls madly in love and then dries up completely. Ultimately you could say this is a very realistic film.

PU: It's like *Cléo de 5 à 7*; I like the very real and visible presence of Paris of 1961 and of the Algerian War that's evoked . . .
AV: Yes, but in *La Mélangite* it will be different in the sense that there's no sense of time passing, it's a purely internal universe; it's a sentimental education.

PU: In your two feature-length films, what problems did you encounter in directing your actors? There seems to be an evident change between these two films.
AV: For *La Pointe Courte*, the *mise en scene* came down to a *mise en place*—just a matter of placing the actors in front of the camera. The characters expressed themselves in a primarily formal way, by their positions in the frame, by their formal relationships; they ended up being marionette-characters. Likewise we didn't have any depth of sound. When the actors are placed at some distance from the camera but their voices sound close up it creates a very anti-realistic effect. In this case the relationship between images, the sight lines, were meant to constitute the very syntax by which I wanted to express things. In *Cléo* on the other hand, the characters were alive, felt things and, even if it wasn't always entirely realistic, their actions were always driven by their *physical* presence. This was very different from *La Pointe Courte*. I adhered very closely to a notion of total realism: no contraction of time, no ellipses; real time, real gestures. When Cléo puts on her necklace, she takes it, puts it around her neck and closes the clasp. Likewise, she takes the time necessary to put on her dress, to try different hats, there's no trickery to the editing . . .

PU: It's almost Zavattini's wager . . .

AV: Yes, I didn't want to hide anything. If there'd been a meal and Cléo had eaten fifteen spoonfuls of soup, I would have shown Cléo eating her fifteen spoonfuls of soup. Her walks, likewise, are in real time.

PU: That's why they seem so long.
AV: Yes, absolutely. A taxi ride takes a long time; at first it's diverting, but then it gets tiresome.

PU: That's subjective time.
AV: . . . which can be felt much more powerfully in objective time. It's a form of *cinéma-vérité*. I think people are defined by their surroundings. In this sense, *Cléo de 5 à 7* is a documentary on a woman. I wanted to make a transparent film, whose form would be clear; objective time gives the spectator some distance on the events. When the time is noted every ten minutes you understand that real time has been superposed on the film's time and this creates a kind of distanciation from the characters. Some people have asked me why I put chapter headings, why I indicated the time of day. Those are the kind of filmgoers who like to get inside the film. I felt this danger already when I began filming *La Pointe Courte*. You always have to be with your characters and, simultaneously, judge them.

PU: Would you like to move toward musical film, something like musical comedy or opera? Something very lyrical?
AV: I don't think so. I like reality too much. *La Mélangite*, for example, is very realistic; the domain of thought is always linked to the visual, and the character's thoughts in *La Mélangite* make up a museum of images. The visual universe is so important that not only does it condition our thought but it provokes it. I think that Resnais is much closer to opera and to music because his form of thought is less connected to reality. He would gladly adopt this approach of mental images. It's evident that *Marienbad* resembles music more than anything else.

Agnès Varda: The Hour of Truth

Michel Capdenac / 1962

From *Les Lettres françaises*, no. 922 (April 12–18, 1962). Reprinted by permission. Translated by T. Jefferson Kline.

Six years ago, well before there was any question of the "New Wave," a young woman, known for her work as the official photographer for the National Popular Theater (TNP), brought the silver screen a rare, singular, and fascinating work. The critics were enthusiastic about *La Pointe courte*. There was a lot of talk about the *"cinéma d'auteur,"* about "personalized" cinema in the wake of Alexandre Astruc's *"camera stylo"* (the camera-as-pen). But the public, for its part, reserved judgment. The originality of Agnès Varda's first film, her style which was later seen to be a precursor to the New Wave, seemed to be an isolated event, more private and marginal than popular.

Following in the footsteps of Alain Resnais, Agnès Varda reaffirmed her enormous talent in a series of short films, each more brilliant than the last, each of which won prizes at various film festivals: *O Saisons, ô châteaux, Du Côté de la côte,* and *Opéra Mouffe.* In these films, documentary seems to burst the bonds of realism, reaching into the realm of the fantastic, the unexpected, the poetic. In this vast field of exploration where Resnais and Chris Marker had brought their probing and inventive cameras, Agnès Varda established her own domain and forged her own very original path. Attentive to the most subtle forms of beauty, she was able to reveal social and psychological truths captured in mid-flight with an infallible prescience and instinct. However, while a group of hotheaded, noisy young auteurs were easily finding the backing for their feature-length films, Agnès Varda had to settle for her more refined and meticulous approach, the precious and passionate artistry that earned her the esteem and admiration of the cinéphiles but only modest and less visible successes and not the popular acclaim reserved for her brothers in film.

Now Agnès Varda has another chance at reaching the audience that she deserves, and this chance is her second feature-length film, *Cléo de 5 à 7*, a surprising and delicate film, a profound and penetrating incantation against death and fatality, a film that the world of cinema has been anticipating and discussing for several months now, and which is going to burst forth with the spring like a blossom on an exotic tree.

Michel Capdenac: Agnès Varda is a demon of vivacity, vivacity made woman and accompanied by perpetual movement, and yet this vivacity, which is focused in her cat-like eyes, is accompanied by a quiet reserve and modesty that are not in the least affected. Agnès Varda speaks of the past with a tranquil lucidity but not without some bitterness: *La Pointe courte* turned out to be a financial disaster whose repercussions she felt for a long time.

Agnès Varda: After that I wanted to make another feature film entitled *La Mélangite*, an idea suggested by my producer, Georges de Beauregard. La Mélangite is sort of this century's malady: a mix of confusions. It was to be a sentimental journey of a habitual liar, who moved back and forth between Sète and Venice.

MC: And with *Cléo de 5 à 7* weren't you trying to portray our century's other malady, our sense of anxiety, not the metaphysical kind, but the kind that's produced by our modern, very real and fatal plague, cancer? The feeling of panic that takes hold of us when we believe—or know— that we're condemned?

AV: I knew first of all that I needed to situate the film in Paris, in order to convey a certain feeling of confusion, of chaos, the climate of fear that infects our lives. This contemporary anguish seems to be more insistently and deeply felt in a big city like Paris where there are so many people.

MC: What's strange is that you've chosen to express this through a character who seems to embody the absolute opposite of anguish: a beautiful, frivolous popular singer whose every moment might seem imbued with grace and joy, yet whose terrible vulnerability you've revealed so abruptly.

AV: I needed a somewhat frivolous character to highlight this sudden transition from coquettishness to anxiety. The film is principally the story of the growing awareness of an internal evolution and that's why chronology is so important. I absolutely had to show the difference and contrasts between objective time and the subjective time experienced by the character. In the cinema we don't believe in objective time; the time of the cinema is fictional, outside of real time. In any case there is no "reality" of time. So the film is divided into chapters, slices of time that mark contractions and distentions of time. Five minutes can seem to last an hour at a given moment of existence. For someone who knows she has only one or two months to live, the rhythm of life changes completely. There is in my film a "minute of truth": it's the scene in the song that suddenly crystallizes this fear and this sense of the fragility of things that Cléo has been bottling up inside of her and which suddenly and violently burst out of her. She tears off her wig as if it were a mask . . . From this moment on, her anguish leads her to discover others and the people she discovers mirror back the image of her anguish.

MC: The fear of death plays the role here of truth teller even though it's difficult to admit at first that this stunning beauty is but a dead woman allowed but a brief stay of execution.

AV: But we're all surrounded by the dead! There are people who live with the idea of death, who have in some way prepared for it. Cléo, on the other hand had never thought of it before, and her idea of death is of a strange and violent enemy. The contrast is all the more brutal since she's so beautiful, so vigorous, and so apparently healthy. You can imagine her posing for Renoir. And suddenly her beauty and good health come face to face with a notion of Death who attacks her body and penetrates her entire being. She thought she was the center of the world and suddenly she's lost her footing. It's a well-known story: the discovery of solitude and of the need for others. This hidden malady makes her feel suddenly open, cut off from all her familiar ways of doing things and from then on, she becomes progressively naked, stripped of everything. She takes leave of herself, and gradually tears away her masks. So it's this kind of detachment (literally!), this discovery of herself that seemed to me so exciting to portray. And also this new way of seeing the world.

MC: Indeed, what's extraordinary in your film is that it succeeds in communicating to the viewer this feeling of vulnerability overtaking Cléo, so powerfully that we end up seeing through her own eyes, her fear, her feeling of being shipwrecked, abandoned to a world where everything's changing meaning and color—streets, things, people . . .

AV: Cléo belongs to the category of people who ordinarily don't really take in what's really happening around them. And suddenly she begins to look, to really see the people she passes in the street, the state of things around her, a guy eating frogs, the art-students in the studio. The more she enters into the life of the people around her, the more she finds herself at a loss. She's looking for an answer. And the answer comes in the person of the young soldier she meets.

MC: He too is a future victim—not of cancer but of the war, at least that's what we can expect. It's a striking symbol, but how are we to interpret it?
AV: Every story like this leads us inevitably toward a more general idea; anxiety about death leads us to some more general anxiety. But I wasn't out to make what you might call an ambitious film, just the meeting of two people at a moment of acute crisis. This guy is just any guy, another dead man walking, a soldier on leave who can state very simply that it's silly to die for nothing, who has a romantic vision of the world and who latches on to Cléo, talking to her about things he knows best, his studies, gardening . . . He's also adrift, he is, like Cléo, open to whatever happens, but for different reasons. And so Cléo allows herself to engage him in a real dialogue—the kind she's never had with anyone else before. With his sincerity, he upsets all her previous ideas about things. Ultimately he's an essentially good person who's not interested in himself, and who in a completely natural way takes on Cléo's death. Indeed they seem to exchange deaths and she feels intensely relieved since she needed someone who could share her anguish. In this sense, the human intentions of the film go way beyond its esthetic intentions.

MC: And yet, judged by the sumptuousness of the film's images and its plastic inventiveness, the esthetic intentions are hardly negligible!
AV: For me there's no fiction without its documentary side, no film without an esthetic intent. But I wanted the film's esthetic side to be entirely at the service of the natural emotions presented. Maybe it's a film that offers a set of refined images, but in the main it's about very simple and clear notions. There's no ambiguity: what you see is what it means.

MC: I noticed in *Cléo* a use of light and of lighting that conveyed not only objective states, but also emotions, subjective states . . . For example, Cléo's immense studio, bathed in white light.
AV: What I'm interested in, in fact, is what light can communicate. For Cléo, this overwhelming brightness is already a sign of her dissolution into nothingness, a pale death, a white death, like in a hospital. That's

why the musicians who accompany her dress up like nurses. Here death isn't associated with blackness, but with light. You see, photography is a vocabulary in the cinema just as much as framing or editing is. I had to make the spectator see and yet allow him to keep his distance and to judge. I didn't try to play on the spectator's emotions. Ultimately every creator is an intermediary who takes on the task of transmitting to his customers this natural product of life and instinct that we call emotion.

MC: Emotion is linked here to a tragic phenomenon: cancer, about which a sort of legend and aura of horror has formed. Why choose this precise illness to illustrate your point? Were you dealing with personal memories? There seems to be a meditation on cancer which focuses not on the scientific aspect of it, but rather the moral aspect . . .

AV: There is a veritable psychosis about cancer whose effects I've seen in people I've known who were entirely conditioned by this illness. I spent a lot of time documenting this phenomenon in hospitals, and in some cancer clinics that I visited. I met more than a hundred people, some who were coming in for their first examination, who arrived completely stressed out and abject; some who were in treatment . . . It's terrible. Then I realized, after having talked with all of these patients, that I risked turning my film into a medical reportage. So instead I focused my attention on the thing that had originally struck me the most: this feeling of fear and anxiety, suffering and panic like the reactions people had to the plague in the Middle Ages. I also noticed that, overwhelmed by these emotions, the sensitivities of many of the patients were sharpened and they began to see and understand things they didn't normally comprehend.

MC: In Corinne Marchand, you found a wonderful actress to play Cléo, with whom the composer, Michel Legrand, makes an unexpectedly wonderful appearance. This chance encounter is one of the most successful moments of the film. How did this come about?

AV: I knew Corinne Marchand from having seen her matched with Bourvil in *Pacifico*. She also had a role in *Lola*. I wrote the role of Cléo for her because I believe in creating roles for specific actors. Without modifying the major lines of a film, you should nevertheless chose certain characteristic details, certain speech patterns in harmony with the personality of the actress who will play the part, gestures and words that belong to her in real life. As for Michel Legrand, I have to admit that I hadn't thought of him for that role. But when he was rehearsing some of the songs with Corinne, I realized that he was very gifted and had a marvelous personality, exactly right for this role.

MC: And now, Agnès Varda, what are you going to do. What are you preparing?

AV: I have several projects in mind, including *La Mélangite*, that I really want to do. I've also had discussions about directing *The Life of George Sand*. A historical film would be interesting. I intend to base it on historical documents and not get too far from existing archives. I will try to recover the real historical events of her life and stick quite close to these and to the personalities of George Sand and of Musset in order to express what they meant to their own times.

A Secular Grace: Agnès Varda

Jean-Andre Fieschi and Claude Ollier / 1965

From *Cahiers du cinéma* 165 (April 1965). Reprinted by permission. Translated by T. Jefferson Kline.

Fieschi & Ollier: Let's begin at the beginning: with photography . . .

Agnès Varda: I was a photographer and I've remained one. It's like a way of seeing. I worked as a photographer for years, but not any more. You lose your touch but you never lose your eye. Now I mostly take photographs for my search for film locations. It's a better way of seeing things and settings on beautiful 18 x 24 prints laid out on a table. I find it helps me write my scenarios. There's even a sort of natural linkage in a series of photos where you can "read" things and I find it very inspiring.

F&O: You have the distinction of having started out in the cinema with a feature-length film. How did that happen?

AV: There's a mystery to *La Pointe Courte* that I've never been able to explain: what ever drove me to make a film? I knew nothing about the cinema, first of all because I never went to the movies; by the age of twenty I'd only seen a maximum of about twenty films. Nor did I live among people who were in any way involved in film. I really believe that I undertook *La Pointe Courte* the way you write your first novel, not caring whether it will be published or not. Of course I was an avid reader at that time so you can discern the imprint of literature in my film: the film was directly inspired by Faulkner's *Wild Palms*. Not in its story line but in the way it's constructed: you know, the way it alternates between the story of the couple and the rising waters of the Mississippi. I loved this feeling of suspension, somewhat annoying as you're reading but which feels quite extraordinary in retrospect. In France it was a time when we were beginning to talk a lot about Brecht's theory of distanciation. I hadn't yet read any theoretical writings on this but I was fascinated by this attempt to interfere with the spectator's identification with the film's characters.

F&O: This is a constant in your films . . .

AV: Not exactly. In *Cléo* this invitation to step back from the action doesn't happen in such a voluntary and arbitrary way. The spectators could, if they wanted to, identify with Cléo, or they could simply tell themselves it was the story of a beautiful young blonde who dies and be moved by that. On the other hand I voluntarily created distance by cutting the film into chapters with the time of day indicated. In this "objective" time measure by the clock there was the desire to remind the viewer: only forty minutes left, only twenty minutes left, etc.

F&O: To come back to *La Pointe Courte*; was there in this film some degree of improvisation?

AV: *La Pointe Courte* was carefully designed, shot by shot, before we started filming, an approach made possible by the fact that I knew the place really well, having spent weeks and weeks there talking to people, walking around, observing the inhabitants of the place. It isn't really a documentary, but the relationships are authentic: the parents really had a daughter and didn't want her to get married. I heard such stories from the women in the village while they were peeling carrots or doing their laundry. And, as in the film, the fishermen were trying to get together and form a union to struggle against the unjust restrictions that had been imposed on them. These problems were explained to me by the men while they were repairing their nets in their huts. So that part of the film was intended as documentary. As for the dialogues spoken by the couple, I wrote them to complicate the style of the film while at the same time simplifying the characters. The idea is to make the couple abstract: we don't really know who they are or what they're doing, or where they'll go afterwards. That wasn't what interested me.

F&O: Tells us about how the film came together.

AV: One day Anne Sarraute introduced me to Carlos Vilardebo and his wife, Jane, two very nice people who were working in film and who'd already made a short. I told them about my desire to make a film and explained the subject. I'd never even seen a movie camera and Carlos told me: "You've got to find someone to help you get started with the technical side of things." He volunteered to do this for free and to have his wife work as continuity check. So he put together a team of people he found in various studios who had some free time and were intrigued by the challenge. That's how our little cooperative was assembled where everyone had specific shares based either on monies contributed or work provided by the team. We spent about seventy thousand francs ($14,000), which is really not very much, but ten years later this money hasn't been entirely reimbursed.

F&O: The public's reaction at the Studio Montparnasse was very favorable.

AV: Exceptionally so. But the film didn't get released until 1956, even though it was shot in 1954. Resnais, who edited the film, and also a member of the cooperative, told me at that time, "You absolutely must show this to the two people in Paris who 'feel' the cinema more than anyone else, André Bazin and Pierre Braunberger." So we organized a showing for them. Braunberger found it interesting, because he has a nose for anything new: he was happy. Bazin told me that I absolutely must show the film at Cannes and I followed his advice. I left for Cannes, left the reels at the baggage check in the airport and went to find Bazin at the "Palace" and he provided me a list of people to invite to the screening. Well, I was lost in the land of the Zulus! None of these names produced the faintest spark of recognition. Nevertheless I went and dropped off the invitations at various hotels and rented the usual hall on the rue d'Antibes. On the day of the screening there were lots of people. Afterwards there were several reviews, notably from Bazin and Doniol, who said really interesting things and talked about a new cinema, etc. Back in Paris, Chéray offered the film a moving career of five weeks and we attracted a total audience of about twelve thousand. I had an extraordinary press book. There were a lot of people who spit on *La Pointe Courte* when it came out, but three quarters of the critics were pretty struck by the evident political position of the film, which is what it is, but you couldn't argue that it was just any old film made any old way. It's a film "to read" which makes more of an impression retrospectively than while you're watching it.

F&O: Besides Faulkner are there any other influences on *La Pointe Courte*?
AV: There were references to painting; particularly to Piero della Francesca that are visible in particular in the choice of Silvia Monfort with her round face and long neck with that low cut neckline. I was also very preoccupied at the time by Bachelard's courses at the Sorbonne on the "imagination of matter." When I see the film today I'm mostly surprised by its daring.

F&O: A lot has been said, whether as a reproach or as praise, about the literary quality of the work.

AV: This aspect of the work is obviously open to debate, but it's what interested me. And yet, in the dialogue between the couple, I wasn't trying to be pointedly literary but instead systematic. (They were analyzing the future of their love, physical love, and their knowledge of each other.) On the other hand what I sometimes regret, when we were dubbing the film, was not avoiding the redundancy of insisting on theatrical diction when the text was already pretty theatrical. In part that had to do with the actors themselves: I didn't know how to tone down the natural theatricality of Noiret and Monfort, because directing actors for the first time is extremely difficult. Now I think I should have made them speak the text more naturally. The film's message wouldn't have suffered, and the film would have been more enjoyable.

F&O: Yes, but this theatricality fits in with the message of the film.
AV: Yes, but I think of it as a kind of youthful mistake. Distanciation doesn't necessarily imply aggressiveness. The truly "distanciated" works of Brecht are not stiff and aggressive. In other words, distanciation doesn't consist of beating people on the head and shouting "Wake up!"

F&O: There's a camera movement that flies closely over the stony beach and then enters a wicker fishing basket and comes out the other side. Was that in the scenario or not?
AV: It's funny how people always grill me about this shot but it's the only shot that I didn't choose. The only one. That was a valuable lesson for me: You should always make the film the way you want it and not listen to others. But there's no point on dwelling further on it. The rest of the film, as I said, was very premeditated.

F&O: There are many points of convergence between *La Pointe Courte* and *Voyage in Italy* . . .
AV: Obviously I hadn't seen *Voyage in Italy*. But indeed it's pretty troubling even though my film is made from an entirely different perspective than Rossellini's, without his Christian side. Indeed quite the opposite is true. I remember a formula I often used, saying, "Marriage is a secular sacrament." And it's funny because that's the same formula that I've been using for *Le Bonheur*, saying "Happiness is a secular grace." For any subject you can find a Christian and a non-Christian treatment. And while we were on the subject of similarities between films, Resnais kept saying to me while we were editing the film, "Hey, that reminds me of *La terra trema*" or else, "Here's a shot that reminds me of *Chronique d'un amour*."

After seventy times, that kind of thing began to get on my nerves. It's not that he found the film derivative, but when you're editing you have time to really look at the shots and naturally various associations come to mind. I ended up thinking that maybe I should go see what he was talking about and I started going to see films at the Cinémathèque, to see first-run films, and reading film journals. So I really discovered the cinema after the age of twenty-six . . . while editing my film! I got a ridiculously late start and don't really feel that I've ever caught up. I also realized that I wanted to be a filmmaker.

F&O: So you've "entered the system"?

AV: Exactly. I thought it would be a pity not to make any more films, and the situation seemed unending and made me impatient. Then Braunberger called me and told me, "I'm going to have you make a film." "Terrific." "The Office of Tourism has asked me to produce a film on the châteaux of the Loire valley." I wanted to punch him! I thought, "wow, he must really despise me! I've made *La Pointe Courte* and he wants me to make a film about the châteaux of the Loire valley!!! Which I hate. Such decadent architecture. After Romanesque art there's nothing else . . . etc." But then I asked my friends what they thought and I learned that it's better to get into the system through the usual channels. *La Pointe Courte* was a beautiful film and all, but no producer was going to give me a cent to make a film after that. By making short subjects, on the other hand, you try your hand, you get into the "milieu," you get to know people.

So finally I set off to visit these chateaux with a heavy heart. These awful ruins, this is disgusting, I thought. The weather was awful. I told myself, "I'm going to have a rotten off-season!" But it turned out I had a sublime off-season—drowned in golden sunlight . . . I was completely won over by the sweetness of the banks of the Loire. And if the film is full of the melancholy of a long-dead era, there's no special hatred of the chateaux. The film is even quite didactic on an architectural level. People always say, "How charming!"—it's twenty-two minutes long with only seven minutes of chateaux and fifteen minutes of fun, of gourds, hats, and other things. But if you listen carefully to the seven minutes of discussion of the chateaux there's an excellent explanation about the evolution in architecture from the Loches keep to Chambord. It's neither wrongheaded nor crackpot on the subject we were commissioned to film. Worthy of a student of the Louvre Art School.

F&O: So what was the reaction of the Office of Tourism?

AV: Great! They were overjoyed! "Encore!" they said. "Let's do a film on the Côte d'Azur!" "Yeah, right," I told myself. "Next they'll want a tour of the Limousin, Périgord, who knows?" But I'm getting ahead of myself. After *O Saisons, ô chateaux*, I made L'*Opéra Mouffe*. I was so annoyed to have made a film for the Office of Tourism that I consoled myself by making a 16mm film for myself. For the first few days Sacha Vierny helped me out, but after than I managed by myself. I went everyday to the market on the rue Mouffetard armed with an iron folding chair that I could stand on and watch the crowd. I placed my chair in the middle of the rue Mouffetard, which, as you know, has a fairly steep incline, and filmed from slightly above the crowd. No one noticed me since I was there all the time and after a couple of days I became as much a part of the décor as the baker's or the lemon merchant's stands. I filmed to my heart's content for a month. I used chapter titles: pregnancy, desires, alcoholism, etc. While filming I knew which of the categories each particular segment would fit into. It was like large melodic lines. Some mornings I focused on drunkenness, others on tenderness. I made my choices according to whatever I felt I wanted on a particular day. Obviously with such a method I had a huge job of sorting things out afterwards.

L'*Opéra Mouffe* is my favorite one of my films. It's the freest. I'm interested in this line between modesty and immodesty. Perhaps I was able to enjoy that state of grace of pregnant women, fully into "a scrim of women." I enjoyed capturing in the middle of the Mouffetard markets the confusion between a stomach heavy with child and one of food. And so many contradictions! A pregnant woman watches the waves of people, especially older people, on a steep incline and she thinks: "They were all newborns once; someone sprinkled fresh talcum powder on them and then kissed their little behinds." That's the kind of thought that pushes our gaze to the fine line that separates cruelty from tenderness. I had the feeling that I understood lyricism on the basis of miniscule feelings. Delerue really captured this feeling in his music; it's both a bit painful and happy. For the second film I was paid to shoot, *Du côté de la Côte* (*Along the Côte d'Azur*), I wanted to make an essay on tourism. Why do people go to the Côte d'Azur rather than somewhere else? It's not obvious.

F&O: Did you start with a very clear idea of the colors you would use?

AV: In both the commissioned films I did there is a strong feeling of color but I didn't really have any preconceived ideas about color. In *O saisons . . .* there is a mix of the deadness of the stone and the vitality of the gold, that's all. In *Du côté de la Côte* the use of color is very baroque. But I wouldn't say they are films about color.

F&O: Does doing a commissioned film permit you to use irony?

AV: I don't make ironic films. I like to laugh (I thought of calling the film *Eden-toc (Eden-tical)* but irony implies that we're making fun of others. When you accept to do a commission, obviously you don't want to end up being bored, but you should use gentle humor rather than irony. The people who saw *Du côté de la Côte* had fun with it, but it isn't really funny. The film belongs to a genre of observation which is very indulgent as indicated by the film's voice-over. The idea is that the people are looking for a kind of Eden which they feel they have a right to because they're so tired. It isn't really their fault if the Eden that the Côte d'Azur offers is so tacky. But whatever the reason, this tacky Eden alludes to another, greater idea of Eden—the idea of rest for the weary which is a beautiful idea, a fundamental idea. You have to be indulgent while watching the people in this film. You laugh at first but then you get it.

F&O: Can you tell us about one of your favorite projects, *La Mélangite?*

AV: Well, in simplest terms it's the sentimental education of a young man. The film covers a period of ten years and the character changes. When he falls in love, for example, he undergoes physical changes and each time he changes another actor takes over his role. So it's the story of a character played by five additional actors. In the beginning he's alone, then he's two, and at the end he's multiple. It's a way of resolving the problem of the monologue in the cinema: you see five "vitelloni" (from Fellini's film, meaning callow youths, literally "big calves") who stroll around the wharves of Sète or who sit around pontificating in outdoor cafés. The main character monologues with the voices of the multiple personae inside him. There are five of him. Things get very complicated when he gets involved with women, as you can well imagine.

F&O: So there's addition, not replacement.

AV: Right, what's so funny is this coexistence. I don't like having to change actors or send the others off to bed. They have names. The first is Valentin-#1; the second is Valentin-crazy-for-love. But we don't spend our whole life in crisis: we can be crazy for love intermittently. The third is The Actor, and the last is The Last Valentin (since they're all named Valentin), the residue and sum total of the others. The others co-exist in him as a matter of principle.

F&O: So this is all on a purely objective level?

AV: No. François, the character in *Le Bonheur* is a typically unified character. For me people can be one or many, they can be many or few according to their capacity and complexity. And Francis is not a "many" character, which is not the least bit pejorative on my part. It's not another self that falls for the second woman, not at all. It's to the degree that the character in *La Mélangite* is capable of being several that things get complicated in his relationships with women. He has it in him to meet a certain woman, but a second self is incapable of accepting this woman, and a third self aggressively rejects her. That's what I call *la mélangite*. At a given moment there's a process in which the five Valentins question everything, come to a crisis and must find a solution.

F&O: Is this a transitional film for you?

AV: It's like *Le Bonheur*, I make some films while waiting to make other films. I sometimes have the impression I'm going to make a career of waiting for Godot. These are films I've made not exactly out of a sense of frustration, but nevertheless while sitting on the fence. I shot *Cléo* to prove to Beauregard that I could make a film for less than 50 million francs, and I really enjoyed making it. I went up to the Park Montsouris at ten in the morning, or at eight in the morning or at five in the morning until I got a white deliquescent light on the lawn that I wanted. It's this sort of thing, like the connection between light and feeling in a certain locale that I work a lot on.

F&O: *Salut les Cubains* is neither a commissioned work nor a work of transition. It's just a film you enjoyed doing?

AV: That's right. It's an homage to Cuba. I was invited there by the I.C.A., the Cuban Film Institute. I brought a Leica, some film, and a tripod since I had this project in the back of my mind. I really found the Cubans extraordinary and the form of their socialism surprising and joyful. They are the only Latin socialists. When I'm in Moscow I feel like I belong to another race from the Soviets. I have to work to understand them. In Cuba things were easier. I felt like I was Cuban and could understand. And then I laughed a lot. The folklore of their revolution, the rhythm of life, the heat . . . I brought back over four thousand photos and spent six months editing about fifteen hundred of them but it was worth it: in Cuba they say that it has the "sapor" (flavor) of a Cuban film. And for them, to get the flavor of something is to *be* Cuban. They do programs with my films and call them "Salut Agnès" ("Hello, Agnès!")

F&O: The reaction of the people who have just seen *Le Bonheur*, whether positive or negative is always very passionate.

AV: Yes, people seem to have very violent and very contradictory physical reactions. Some men leave the theater as happy as anything, feeling relaxed and very peaceful . . . Others feel all beat up almost unable to walk . . . There are women who come out crying, or else feeling really rotten. As for me, I only begin to see my films when they're completed. It's only now that I've been able to begin to ask myself questions about *Le Bonheur*. What's for sure is that I didn't make the film thinking about what peoples' reactions would be and their reactions have been pretty difficult for me. I started out with very minimal impressions, very small feelings: family photos. In one you can make out a group of people sitting around a table under a tree, their glasses raised, smiling at the camera. When you see the photo, you say, "That's happiness." It's the first impression. When you look more closely you get an uneasy feeling: all these people, it's simply not possible, there are fifteen people in the picture, old people, women, children; it's not possible they could have all been happy at the same moment . . . Or else you wonder, what *is* happiness since they all look so happy? The appearance of happiness is also a form of happiness. And these impressions which are connected to the related pleasure of making a home movie, you know, a blurred close-up of a kid's face who has just entered the frame, are the source of my film.

Happiness is also a play of mirrors: I'm happy, I say I'm happy, I want the other person to be happy because I say that I'm happy . . . Because even if it's a notion that one can have all by oneself, it's always much stronger if it's shared. Like at picnics, this kind of collective joy when all the families get along well, when there are kids frolicking on the grass and others are lying down under the trees getting ready to take a nap . . . It's all related pretty closely to a feeling for nature. The film is first and foremost a mix of emotions in which the plot is secondary.

F&O: What strikes us, indeed, is the refusal of both psychology and moralism.

AV: Psychology doesn't interest me; it's not the subject of the film even if you can use it to explain the characters' behavior. As for the absence of moralism, I understand that the absence of any sense of guilt in the film bothers some people. And yet, there is nothing to prove that the woman has committed suicide, even if no one in the audience doubts that she has.

F&O: To be sure.

AV: Why don't they—or I for that matter—doubt it? We are conditioned by an entire classical and Christian tradition of guilt. I think she killed herself, and yet I also have my doubts.

F&O: The male character seems to have the "secular grace" that you were talking about earlier.

AV: What I try to understand in this film is: what does happiness really mean? Is there anyone allergic to happiness? To what point can one introduce unhappy incidents in a life and continue to be happy? I didn't ask myself, "If I make his wife die will he still be happy?" But deep down I asked myself, "What is the meaning of happiness, this need for happiness, this aptitude for happiness? What is this unnamable and slightly monstrous thing?" It's like in science-fiction novels; there's this thing there and all you have to do is get away . . . And this "thing" gilded with happiness, where did it come from? What form does it take? Why is it there? Why does it leave? Why can't the people chasing it catch it? And why can some other people catch it? Why is it that some people who have everything don't have this? Why do some people who have nothing going for them have this? Why doesn't it have anything to do with merit? This sense of well-being and of happiness seems to have little to do with anything physical, spiritual, ethical, or anything else: there are just some people who feel happy.

F&O: Our first reaction as we left the theater was that the film took place on another planet.

AV: Because the characters are so uncomplicated that they seem stiff. They are like robots with some vital force. You can't pigeon-hole them into categories, sub-categories, divisions, or other social sets. The only exception might be François whose sense of family is so strong that he can't imagine happiness outside of the home—and whose sense of fraternity is also very strong. These are his only social instincts. The rest just belongs to his five senses.

F&O: It seems strange that François doesn't seem to have any affiliation with unions or social or political groups.

AV: He's an artist. If he were a worker in a Renault plant, whether or not he had an aptitude for union activities, he would have been involved in it and I would have had to approach the problem differently. I intentionally chose the only social class where people are neither really bosses nor workers.

F&O: Still, he might have had concerns about increasing his material wealth?

AV: Why should he since he's happy? In this respect, everything seems to indicate that he doesn't spend his time sighing, "Oh, if only I had a T.V." . . . He doesn't need to own a car, he can borrow one. François just looks simple, in reality he's a wise man. There are people like that. I know people who aren't acquisitive, people for whom bettering their situation isn't everything.

F&O: So the idea of maximizing one's wealth is replaced by maximizing one's happiness.

AV: Yes. Instead of investing money to make money, here people invest in happiness to increase their happiness. Well to some extent anyway. He doesn't try to increase his stock of happiness; he receives it as a gift. And the character gets to the point where he knows no limits. Where would the limit be? Who'd be able to tell him where the limit is? Let's come back to the image that I've been criticized for so many times, the apple orchard. François says, "It's a perfectly square field." At least he possesses a sense of form and can imagine this space in abstract terms. Except that the notion of an apple tree includes the notion of sap, of something in excess, a kind of wart on the bark, an excrescence. So what's happening? He's portrayed after all as a guy who's not a ladies' man, who doesn't need to be having affairs. It's clear that his relations with his wife are perfectly sufficient. It was important to show that the categories of "wife" and "mistress" are not the subject of the film. They really belong to the same category.

F&O: You communicate a sense of fear as the film speeds up after the accident, which leads to the substitution of the second woman for the first. They look a lot alike.

AV: They look more and more alike. I thought about that. What troubles me about happiness is . . . well, if you ask people in the street if they're happy, in general they'll tell you it's because of another person, a unique person. We have the impression that everyone is unique and that we love them because they're unique, and that what's beautiful in love is that ultimately this unique person could be anybody. The more the person is unique in the eyes of the other the more they represent all women, or all men, virtually anyone could be the significant other.

F&O: Hence the idea of interchangeability.
AV: Oh, no! That's not an idea we could call a practical proposal. No, it's really a tragic element that occurs within happiness. It's an idea that's both cruel and intellectually satisfying. Like the seasons of cruelty: the cycle of the seasons is both satisfying and perfectly cruel.

F&O: It's possible that the substitution of one female character for another gives rise unconsciously to the notion of the doubling of the masculine character. This person we've seen as unique throughout the film in opposition to the women is suddenly perceived in the last few minutes as double and it's a different self that walks away at the end.
AV: Well, no, I think you're projecting that on the film. In any case it reminds me of a funny story that's related to this reasoning by inversion. In *La Mélangite* other than my "quintupled character" there were two important women's roles. I asked Monica Vitti to play the role of the Italian woman who meets Valentin in Venice. She answered, "Well, it's a pretty small role. Why not have me play both women since the same character is playing five different men?"

F&O: To speak a bit simplistically, we might distinguish in the film "a life side" and a "death side" from beginning to end, in constant interplay.
AV: Rivette told me pretty much the same thing. He saw the "death" element as embodied by Marie-France Boyer with her steely blue eyes and her pallor. Once she appears, death makes its way, effects its substitutions right through to the end. I was surprised and delighted by this interpretation. It's as though someone gave me a kaleidoscope: I didn't write the film with this in mind, but it's definitely there in the film and I like it . . . Resnais, on the other hand, said he felt the presence of death in the music of Mozart.

F&O: Maybe it wasn't clear before starting the film, but when you do these shots of white sheets . . .
AV: White is such a fascinating color, and very much part of my vocabulary. Just as there are writers who privilege certain words, I have word-images that appear in all my films. So everything linked to love tends to be expressed in white, white sand, sheets, walls, or paper. Or snow, or

the morning light on the grass in *Cléo*. This dissolve into white is for me love and death. It's not symbolic or systematic. It is images that are awakened individually in me, which force themselves on me. In *Cléo* white is tragic. It's not obscurity that invades life but a kind of brightness which dissolves existence.

F&O: *Le Bonheur* describes a process of absorption.
AV: Of death as well. And love. It's also there in *Cléo*. Each time we feel a profound sense of death, each time *Cléo* is "buffeted by death," she experiences a kind of white-out. In the scene in the park, with Antoine (which we shot at six a.m.) all of sudden the grass exploded with white light.

F&O: One could argue that in *Le Bonheur* your repertoire of signs is very well organized.
AV: But there's nothing symbolic there. You were talking to me about the color purple, but it's simple, purple is the shadow of orange. That's a feeling that brings us back to the idea of painting. The Impressionists discovered that colors are complementary, that a lemon had a blue shadow and an orange a mauve shadow, which isn't really true in reality, but which feels nevertheless like the right idea, the right feeling. In *Le Bonheur*, gold (the color not the symbol) evokes the color purple because there is no color without shadow. It's also because purple is a color I adore, a color I wear and that speaks to my eye . . . It's as if you asked a painter to justify all of his color choices. He doesn't necessarily think about which colors are complementary or how they are combined. As for me, I'm more likely to make choices based on feeling rather than reflection since I have a very strong sense of color.

F&O: For the film's spectator, all that gets pretty easily organized into a system of signs: so from the beginning purple is right away associated with the character of Emilie, and after the death of the wife, this color spreads: in her bedroom Marie-France Boyer wears an undergarment of purple, the flowers are mauve, and even the cover of the paperback . . .
AV: The shot you're talking about poses an unusual problem which came up during the editing. I had filmed a first version of this shot where the girl, wearing her mauve bathrobe, was knitting a pink sweater. There were some books on the table, a bunch of paperbacks, and so you had a pink theme going. When we projected the scene in the auditorium to work on the sound track, there was a chorus of technicians gasping,

"Hey, she's pregnant!" I finally realized that when you wear a bathrobe and you're knitting something pink, it's necessarily for the baby . . . I replayed this scene for other people and got the same reaction. But if she were pregnant that would be too big a change in the meaning of the story, so I had to reshoot the scene. In the final version Emilie is reading a magazine whose entire page is gold colored, which confirms what I said about the complementarity of purple and gold. You want to use your own vocabulary, trust your feelings, and end up bumping into other people's preconceived ideas of things. That experience bothered me so much that I took out the improvised parts of the film.

In another scene Marie-France Boyer is lying on her bed and closes a book. This is another scene I had to redo. I'd taken a random book off the shelf: it was Moravia's *Conjugal Love*. At first I thought it was funny, but while we were doing the editing, I realized it looked as though I'd planned it. So I had to reshoot the scene with another less interesting title. It's terrible how meaningful images are . . . Here's another typical case: it was toward the end of *Cléo* in the scene in the bus. The bus slows down next to a delivery van in front of a florist's shop. There were flowers on the roof of the van. Antoine grabs a daisy and hands it to Cléo. But right next to the flower shop there's a funeral parlor and by chance a pregnant woman was walking by right at that moment. I loved it! So I yelled to Bernard Toutblanc, "Quick, catch that woman and get her to walk by again!" Toutblanc rushes into the flower shop, buys a bouquet of flowers, and tells the lady, "Madame, I'd like to present you with these flowers . . . and might I ask you to walk by the shop again?" This is a typical moment in improvised scenes. But there wasn't an audience member who didn't tell me, "You made the bus slow down on purpose in front of the funeral parlor." But why didn't anyone say, "in front of a flower shop where a pregnant woman was walking by with a bouquet of flowers?" So that's how it is: there are highly planned sets of images that we need to organize and then this kind of happening that the practiced eye latches on to.

F&O: But didn't the image of the pregnant woman walking by the funeral parlor risk giving a kind of closure to your film?
AV: Not at all! It's just a pregnant woman walking by a funeral parlor, just happens by at that precise moment, what's the big deal? . . .

F&O: Was *Le Bonheur* written quickly?
AV: Yes it was quite an experience in the sense that I don't think I've ever

worked to quickly. I wrote it in exactly three days. I just suddenly had the urge to know what it would be like to just dive in and write and then film . . . And I realized I was entirely comfortable: working on a scenario composed in the heat of inspiration was very stimulating. I threw myself into filming without a worry and derived a lot of pleasure discovering these "respirations" on the run. I knew that I needed two long takes from five to six minutes, one with the wife and one with the mistress. I needed two long "breaths." When I started out, however, at the time I was making *La Pointe Courte*, I was so scared that I thought I should never trust my inspiration . . . but Queneau was right: it's in writing that you become a writer. And it's in filming that you become a filmmaker.

Interview with Agnès Varda

Hubert Arnault / 1967

From *Image et Son* 201 (January 1967). Reprinted by permission. Translated by T. Jefferson Kline.

Agnès Varda: I don't much like talking about people's work before it's finished. You know I intend to make more films and to try more and more to see my way clear in all this. I don't particularly like classifications either. I've only made four or five films.

Hubert Arnault: Well that's a good start. There are certain problems that you like to tackle. At least that's the impression your viewer gets.

AV: Not so much problems really. I'm interested in certain questions. What I believe is that the viewers who get the chance to see my films which might otherwise be considered simply diverting, sometimes need the film to be more than just a story, want the film to raise questions or challenge them in some way they feel the need to be challenged. Ultimately I believe that people have a taste for reflection. They have a taste that leads them to reflection. I often think of my public as a mass of people whom I really like, but just because we have a friendly relationship doesn't mean that we can't talk seriously or lightheartedly about important subjects. It's really on the level of feeling that this connection interests me. I believe that ultimately people have a lot in common but that they don't have a lot of opportunities to think about this or act on it. So I want my films to act as revelations. This is what interests me. There are questions that I personally find intensely interesting and which I'd like to find answers to. I try to ask these questions with enough clarity and enough ambiguity to get my viewers to ask them for themselves.

HA: Are your films aimed specifically at the viewer's feelings?

AV: When I talk about feelings it's because it's through feelings that we can capture the attention of the audience and then engage their minds.

You can't have one without the other. There would be no point in making a thesis-film first and then turn around and make a film about feelings. No, what I'm saying is that feelings are the ground on which people can be led to think about things. I believe in the importance of reflection—not so much during the film perhaps, but often afterwards. Take for example the film entitled *Le Bonheur*. It's very evident that most of the people who saw this film (and there were about 150,000 of them) were asking themselves as they left the theater serious questions about their own ideas about happiness or were discussing the situation in the film and their reactions to it; thus it's a movie that elicits an active response from its viewer. It's the kind of film that provokes the viewer's interest well after it's over. People didn't go home and say, "Wow, what beautiful colors" or "what pretty flowers." As they left they were beginning to say: "Men . . . women . . . happiness. And what if the guy were a worker, or, what if the guy were middle class?" Which means that the film provoked people to think and I think it's great that people ask questions about happiness. It's a really important subject and even if they had a negative reaction to the film, it's not like they could walk away saying, "That was awful. Forget it!" Some people had negative reactions to some of the characters in the film but still they talked about it so it provoked them to have a reaction, to think about things. This is what interests me in making films.

HA: Speaking about *Le Bonheur*, don't you think the subject came to a halt with the drowning of the legitimate wife? Wouldn't it have been interesting to play out how their ménage à trois might have continued?
AV: That's another subject. I also asked myself that question. I was asked, "Why didn't you continue to follow their three lives?" But that wasn't my subject. This isn't an interesting illustration of what a man's life would be like with two women. That's not at all the subject of the film. The subject of the film is really that a guy who is constitutionally drawn to happiness both because of his love of nature and his other aptitudes, and for lack of any outside pressures (whether religious, political, etc.), well, for a character like that, you notice that any person so focused on happiness supposes and requires that he will have to invent some ethical position. It's a film about the invention of ethics as a moral problem that sooner or later will come up in our relationship with others. It just so happens that in this film the guy pays dearly for his awakening, plus, since his nature is more positive than optimistic he will tend to be pretty logical in the sequence of events that confront him. It's not because his

wife dies that he would give up on happiness or end up unhappy. That's the attitude of someone with a more negative personality. This is a guy who, when suddenly wounded, thinks that he has to try to continue being happy. It's really up to the audience to understand this nuance, the difference between his present happiness and the former one. These are nuances, but life is full of nuances. The film presents this particular situation. It should be evident that each spectator must draw his own conclusions and judge the character according to his own personal criteria. That's perfectly o.k. In any case, the characters who continue into the second part of the film are, in my view, quite courageous. Because, the young woman could cave under the weight of her guilt, and, my God, how many women her age are there who could forge ahead and care for the happiness of two children who are not hers . . . These characters are very courageous within the limits of their particular problems that are quite restrained, but the characters are nevertheless very brave. People often say, "this woman who commits suicide . . ." but I find it's a terrible cowardice to commit suicide when you have two children. You should at least try to resolve your problems before you abandon your kids. It's too easy, too cowardly a solution. She comes across looking terribly weak. As for me, I avoid making moral judgments about my characters. I feel a great deal of sympathy for the three characters, and I really tried to show them in a particular situation. I wasn't interested in showing "this one is good, that one is bad." I tried to show everything that happened in such a way as to leave the viewers free to make their own judgments. Of course it's a fairly unusual subject. In this end, this film doesn't resemble my other films very much.

HA: Well, *La Pointe Courte* also treats in its own way the problem of a couple. Isn't there some continuity there with *Le Bonheur?*
AV: Well, yes, but it isn't the same thing. *La Pointe Courte* was *also* about a couple, but it was also and especially a film that showed them in the context of a village in crisis and it was the contrast between these two worlds—their life as a couple and the collective life of the village—that was the real subject of that film.

The Underground River

Gordon Gow / 1970

From *Films and Filming* 16 (March 1970).

Agnès Varda has brought with her to cinema a richness of awareness and a talent to provoke and delight. In this interview with Gordon Gow, she explains her approach to directing, life, and happiness.

California sunlight beats against the glass of a big window above a bed, making the room too bright in the early morning. So the people who sleep in the bed must try each night to remember to cover the window, because it has neither shutters nor blinds. They choose for the purpose some brightly colored material, through which the dawn light filters gently, touching them with gold and other kindly hues. In this way, they are enabled to rouse themselves to whatever lies ahead in the waking hours; to begin the day, at least, with a glimpse of beauty. On the other hand, if they forget to cover the window the night before, the hot sun on their eyelids will be cruel and the day will start badly.

These elementary yet strangely potent qualities are to be noted in *Lions Love*, the film Agnès Varda made in the United States. She is not by any means the only director who relates characters and environment, and stresses the tactile value of inanimate objects. In her case, the tendency is just a bit stronger than usual. One feels it more. And she is inclined to speak of her films in terms which reinforce this response: "The girl in *La Pointe Courte* is associated in my mind with steel. Because she's from the city, you know, and that makes one think of trains and the railroad. And the man is associated with wood, because his father was a ship's carpenter. *Le Bonheur* is about trees: I mean it's about other things, too, it's about fucking and it's about picnics. But it's also about trees. Because men behave like trees. And if you watch trees closely over a period of time, you will notice that they change, like men. Everybody is replaceable, people say, and that's true but only in terms of a person's function, because each single person is unique. And so is each single tree. Unique, and subject to change. That's what nature is.

"The reason I think like this is because of a professor of philosophy who had a very great influence on me when I was studying at the Sorbonne. My idea then was to become a museum curator, which I didn't. But this professor, Gaston Bachelard—he's dead now—he really blew my mind. He was a very old man with a beard, and he had this dream of the *material* in people: a psychoanalysis of the material world related to people, wood, rivers, the sea, fire, wind, air, all these things. Not only in nature itself but in dough, for example; if a woman is making pastry and enjoying what she is doing, the relationship and the psychology are there in the woman and the dough. He taught us to study writers not only by the stories they told but by the material things they mentioned."

Before this influence there had been already an inherited predilection for at least one of the elements, the sea: "Because my father was Greek. And I really need the sea. I need the smell of it."

Although born in Belgium (in 1928), she went to live at Sète quite early in her childhood; and there to the west of Marseilles in the Gulf of Lions, the ozone apparently heightened her enchantment. Her eventual studies at the Sorbonne were followed by a period of four years at the Ecole du Louvre where she acquired a formidable knowledge of art, which contributed to her success as a photographer. At about the age of twenty she was appointed official photographer to the Théâtre National Populaire, working initially in Avignon and later in Paris. The TNP's director, Jean Vilar, was also from Sète: "He was the first to introduce the theories of Brecht to France. Before then, the theater had been decadent and bourgeois. The company was very strong, too: Gerard Philipe was there, of course, and Jeanne Moreau, Philippe Noiret, Charles Denner. And the experience increased my interest in theatre, which had already begun while I was at the Sorbonne, although at that time I didn't have any enthusiasm for the movies.

"When I made my first film, *La Pointe Courte* in 1954, I knew nothing about the rules. I wasn't like Truffaut and Godard, watching movies all the time. In fact I had only seen five movies in my entire life: one was Walt Disney's *Snow White and the Seven Dwarfs*, another was the animal film *Bring 'Em Back Alive*, then *Quai des Brumes* and *Les Enfants du Paradis*—and I didn't even know who Carné was, I'd never heard of him—and the fifth one I can't remember.

"Yet they still call me the grandmother of the *nouvelle vague*." She gives a kind of squirm as she recollects the familiar description, which sprang from the fact that Alain Resnais was her film editor for *La Pointe*

Courte (by which time he had already made a couple of shorts himself) and that the initial Varda essay in cinema has been regarded as the precursor of the first Resnais movie of feature length, *Hiroshima, Mon Amour*, which emerged about five years later. For *La Pointe Courte* Varda returned to Sète, using the known environment as a background for her study of a married couple and their personal problems, in juxtaposition with the economic and social predicaments of local fishermen. "I had not intended originally to make a film of this subject. What I had in mind was a novel. But I drew pictures by way of an outline and I showed these to a man who was an assistant film director. He suggested to me that cinema might be the ideal medium. And so I went ahead, with some money that I had borrowed."

Afterwards she went to China to do a pictorial magazine feature; and then came a succession of short films, *O Saisons, O Châteaux* (1957) in which the eloquence of mannequins in fashionable gear was set against the ageless beauty of the castles of the Loire, *Du Côté de la Côte* (1958), and *Opéra Mouffe* (1958), which had to do with the thoughts of a pregnant woman as she walked through the Mouffetard area of Paris in a perambulation to be echoed subsequently in *Cléo de 5 à 7*.

The second of these three short films is worth some attention. For a start it epitomizes the Varda inclination towards the precepts of Bachelard, evident in all her work, as distinct from the Brechtian influence of Vilar, which is not especially apparent until *Lions Love*. If the juxtaposition of the human and the inanimate had been simple in the study of pretty girls and timeworn castles, the wry historical observation of the Riviera in *Du Côté de la Côte* gave more subtle indication of the Varda touch. One recalls the flimsy scarf, alarmingly intertwined with the wheel of a horse-drawn carriage, while the commentary spoke of Isadora Duncan's accidental death; an image less accurate but far more evocative, in the bland Mediterranean night, than the stricter versions of the occasion as reconstructed later in the TV film by Ken Russel and the film by Reisz. There is also the bringing together of nature and tactile objects and the human element, as the camera prowls across warm sand to observe abandoned sandals and eventually comes to rest upon the naked flesh of a man and woman basking in the sun.

When Agnès Varda went to the Tours Festival with *Du Côté de la Côte* in 1958, she met her future husband Jacques Demy who had gone with his own short of Cocteau's *Le Bel indifférent;* "Neither of us won a prize." But one can assume that an influence was established, because Varda's *Cléo de 5 à 7* (1961) is intermittently redolent of her rapport with Demy. Chiefly perhaps, because of the optimism of its latter phase, but also on account of the casting in the title part of Corinne Marchand, who had impressed Varda by her interpretation of a minor character in Demy's *Lola*, and the incidental appearance of Michel Legrand who composed the music for *Lola* and the Demy movies that followed it.

Cléo de 5 à 7 takes place during a late afternoon in Paris and is centered upon a small-time singer who is awaiting the result of a medical examination which will reveal whether or not she is afflicted with an incurable disease. The period of anxiety heightens her perceptions, giving her a fresh awareness of the everyday world around her. Walking through Montparnasse, she observes each place and incident minutely: Varda throws in a queasy fragment in which a street performer swallows a frog and ejects a stream of liquid from his mouth. The mood is suspended deftly between the documentary idiom and the poetic strain, reaching a mildly sentimental apotheosis when Cléo meets a young man in the park of Montsouris, who advises her that love can be stronger than fear. It is all quite neatly done, but has been overpraised and barely stands up to a second viewing. Perhaps its most telling effect is Cléo's abrupt removal of her wig, disclosing hair of another color underneath. This comes as a surprise, after the film has been in progress for quite some time, and the action lends the character a certain vulnerability as well as strengthening the impression that delusions are being abandoned in the face of reality. A similar thing occurs in the opening phase of Losey's *Secret Ceremony*, where the impact is sharper.

Following another short, *Salut les Cubains*, Varda made *Le Bonheur* in 1964. With the possible exception of *Lions Love*, it is her best achievement, coupling her own visual sense with some elegiac camerawork by Jean Rabier, who had also been director of photography on the monochrome *Cléo*. It is a tone poem, attuned very closely to her affinity with nature and the material world. She describes her own work and its motivations as "an underground river of instincts," and the definition is very apt. The young Carpenter (Jean-Claude Drouot) in *Le Bonheur* is related emphatically to wood: he is a creature of good nature and of calm, quite happy in his working hours amid the wood-shavings, cycling home in childlike pleasure as he weaves his bike around trees, and mildly accepting the bounty of an extra-marital love affair as equivalent to a proliferation of apple-trees which burgeon side by side.

This is clearly in line with Varda's analogy between men and trees: "I love being under trees myself. Sitting there in the shadows. And I love picnics, too—Jacques doesn't, or at least not so much; I find it hard to persuade him to come on picnics. So that's why I put the picnics in *Le Bonheur*, I guess: to relieve my frustrations."

Despite a basic difference of attitude in their work, Varda does seem occasionally influenced by Demy's precepts, as in the park scene of *Cléo* and in the color scheme of *Le Bonheur*; the things people are wearing are matched to the settings against which they move, and the fronts of houses are painted in dominant tones. The fades between scenes are not to blackness as usual, but to white, or blue or red. The sexual passages are frank and warm. And again there is a major effect when the husband lifts the dead body of his wife and the action is repeated several times over; a moment imprinted upon the mind. This kind of repetition had been used before by Resnais, in *Marienbad*, but it was Varda's employment of the effect within a romantic-dramatic context that elevated the repeat-image to its full value and made it part of the language of cinema. The notion was parodied quaintly by Richard Lester in *The Knack* when he had repeat-images of Michael Crawford shutting a door with emphatic finality.

Mutability is a primary theme of *Le Bonheur*, carefully stressed in the autumn sequence at the end, when the leaves of the trees have changed color, still agreeable but perceptibly upon the verge of decay. Likewise the carpenter, maintaining the outward show of continued happiness, has fog on his breath when he speaks, white and cautionary against the deceptively warm tints of the woods around him.

Death is another of the Varda themes; already noted in the Isadora scarf, the apprehension of Cléo, the drowned wife in *Le Bonheur*, and the forewarning of winter as the carpenter's lips give forth that gentle mist, less disturbingly but not less meaningfully than the street performer's emission of frog fluid. This darker strain was to become more apparent in *Lions Love*, but meantime in 1965 Varda made *Les Créatures*, in which Catherine Deneuve played a young married woman deprived of her speech after the shock of a motor accident. This aspect of the movie stems from a dream Varda had: "I had it three times over, this dream that I was mute and couldn't speak any more. And it was strange, because I'm a woman who likes to speak. But it wasn't a nightmare. In the dream I simply didn't want to speak. I remember it clearly, because I had it three times and it was a very long dream. Jacques was in it and so was our daughter, and the old lady we'd engaged as pediatrician when our child was born. She was in the dream explaining to me that I should bring myself to speak—but I didn't want to."

There are times in her waking hours, in fact, when Varda is content to go for days without speaking. But these periods are spent with her husband in the windmill they own on the island of Noirmoutier: "There we can live and work in silence. He'll be writing something, and I'll be writing as well, and we never discuss our work with one another. That is satisfactory, because we both believe that men and women are able to communicate without words. It's a thing that is natural to us. If you love somebody, then you should virtually *be* the other person, and in that case there is really no need for speech. Talking in such circumstances would merely be playing the game of family life."

Les Créatures was filmed on Noirmoutier, which stands just off the Brittany coast, facing out towards the uncharitable Bay of Biscay: "It is beautiful in the winter. I got to know it through Jacques, because it is not far away from Nantes where he lived as a child, and it is the only part of Brittany that reminds me of Sète." Joined to the mainland for a couple of hours each day at low tide, the island is otherwise isolated; and in *Les Créatures*, while Catherine Deneuve remains charming in her mute expressions of love and also of apprehension as the plot thickens, her husband (Michel Piccoli) roams the island in mental quest for material he can use in a novel. The wife grows increasingly pregnant, and simultaneously the varied people encountered in their restricted neighborhood are incorporated into the husband's inventions until reality and fantasy are intermingled.

The engaging monochrome photography, deriving full value from the locale, is by Willy Durant, who also contributed later to the visual felicities of *The Immortal Story* (Orson Welles) and *The Night of the Following Day* (Hubert Cornfield). His aptitude would seem to have merged very nicely with Varda's concept. There are intrusions of red tinting of different intensity according to the mood of a given moment, pointing up the fantasy which at times becomes pretty wild. There is a little too much about a local inhabitant who is elevated in the novelist's mind to the stature of a crazy scientist with fiendish power over everybody including the pregnant wife. This conceit gets rather out of hand, in my opinion, but nimble trick photography makes something quite beguiling of a game of chess played between scientist and novelist with the sundry characters of the island standing as chessmen to be manipulated in their relationships and fortunes. In such details, relating humans very closely to inanimate objects, as well as in the continual atmospheric reminders of the sea air, Varda's preoccupations are manifest: "My only regret is that I didn't have the guts to make it all more abstract."

It was a couple of years after *Les Créatures* that Varda embarked upon the American experience which would yield up *Lions Love*. Demy had gone first, in an exploratory frame of mind, while she was busy in Paris; but he had not been in San Francisco for more than a week or so before he wrote to her, indicating that he wanted to stay and that she should join him. She was there within the month, and they stayed and worked in the USA until well into 1969.

Varda's first essay was a short film about the Black Panthers, much in line with her occasionally straightforward political pieces (in addition to *Salut les Cubains* she had been among the French directors, including Resnais and Godard, who made *Loin du Vietnam*).

Then, having taken measure of the California scene, she proceeded to *Lions Love*, a film which has the power to exasperate and charm, according to the nature and disposition of individual spectators. A series of impressions, she describes it as a collage. We find the hallucinatory Viva, famed already in the Warhol oeuvre, sharing a rented Hollywood house with Gerome Ragni and James Rado, the coauthors and lyricists of *Hair*. The three of them also share the wide bed beneath the sun-gold drape that masks the window; and they are given to disporting nude in the blue waters of a swimming pool in the grounds—the men getting wet, while Viva stays dry and alabaster-smooth upon a giant inflated bauble that drifts across the surface of the water. Since they refer to one another as Viva, Jim, and Gerry—and since Shirley Clarke, who joins them after a while on a venture into the underground type of filmmaking which might possibly gain commercial backing in a changing Hollywood, is addressed as Shirley—we can take it that these four principals are representing, to some extent, figments of themselves. But at the same time, they lend their personalities freely to Varda's thoughts.

She has made a great deal of the environment. Evidently the smell of the sea was near enough to keep her happy; but we catch only a glimpse of the Pacific, in an newsreel insert when police charge down upon a beach to clear it of hippies whose potential love-in has been blighted by a fringe element of violence; although voices that accompany the sequences inform us irritably that the trouble was started by the police themselves. The almost casual way this is thrown into the movie, a swift scurry of action followed by a desolate and sad expanse of sand and water, is typical of the collage approach. The rented house is minutely explored by Varda's instinctive eye for tactile values; "I rented it myself for the purpose, and it is quite typical of rented houses in Hollywood. Somebody told me that Elvis Presley lived there at one time, but I don't know." When Shirley Clarke arrives from New York, the boys show her around her temporary abode: "this is a genuine plastic weeping willow," says one, "and there's a real weeping willow outside that belongs to Katharine Hepburn." Thus, having made her customary oblation to trees, Varda peruses the texture of other objects, and of bodies. There is even a camera-prowl accompanied by a song called "Inventory of a Rented House."

The film has begun, abruptly, at a Los Angeles performance of Michael McClure's *The Beard* as directed by Rip Torn, with the small theater audience turning its attention momentarily from "Jean Harlow" and "Billy the Kid" and their four-lettered conversation on the miniscule stage, in order to applaud the late arrival in their midst of Viva and her companions. Later, Viva herself and one of the *Hair* guys are moved to entertain a party of children by doing *The Beard* themselves in the drained swimming pool of the rented house. Varda was reproached in California for this scene, because the children not only chortle with delight at what they see and hear, but also pass a cigarette from hand to hand: "My own daughter was among them, and the others were the children of friends and neighbors. And they were not smoking marijuana, as some people assumed. But they *were* smoking. So did I as a kid. I used to smoke leaves from eucalyptus trees. When *Lions Love* was finished, I showed the whole movie to an audience of children, aged about twelve or so, and they loved it."

Much of the film has to do with love, and the quest for happiness. Darting from point to point, making witty use of two authentic conversations about the financing of a movie in America and the moral and monetary complications involved when a director claims the right to have the ultimate say in the cutting room, Varda brings her thoughts to something approaching a plot when Shirley Clarke, depressed by the strictures imposed upon her as a creative artist, is driven to attempt suicide. In a Brechtian diversion, Varda has retained the footage she continued to shoot while Shirley Clarke stops in mid-spate, declaring that she cannot play the scene because it has no truth for her: if she were going to commit suicide, she says, her method would not be an overdose of pills. Whereupon Varda enters the frame herself, swallows whatever they are using to represent the lethal pills, and lies down upon the bed, remarking that this is all she wants done. So, imitating the same actions, Shirley Clarke does it. The alienation is curious, even in the context of such a defiantly jigsaw movie; and perhaps more remarkable still is the involvement that follows when Shirley Clarke is in hospital, recovering slowly, while Varda receives news that Andy Warhol has been shot in New York (as he was, you may recall—but not fatally), and also, by a little poetic juggling with time, the television set gives forth protracted reportage concerning the assassination of Bobby Kennedy.

Viva says, "I can't stand it. Shirley, Kennedy, Andy—everybody's dying. When is it our turn?" She doesn't cry. Her face is blank, and there is a numbness about her, which was the way Varda wanted it: "It's as if she has experienced an earthquake and has the feeling that no place is safe."

Reactions in the small household are varied. "Pope John's dead too." "Don't make fun." "Who's making fun? TV-death. It's a national pastime." And so it would seem as the catch-as-catch-can documentation of the Kennedy death pours forth continually from the television set in a sequence heightened by Varda: "I just bought the footage from the TV company, and then overlaid some of the vox pop reactions they'd obtained from people in the street, so that these voices could be heard while we looked at the visuals. It wasn't a direct repetition of the way they actually did it on TV."

In fact it proves quite pungent; and reminds one that Varda employed a TV insert from Jean Renoir's *Le Déjeuner sur l'Herbe* in *Le Bonheur*, with implications both painterly and physical, although on that occasion nobody in the cast paid the slightest attention to the television set, whereas in *Lions Love* the watchers are intermittently heedful. Death is heavy in the air. But, at another time, fitting casually into the collage, the television set in the rented house provides a ray of hope. Frank Capra's *Lost Horizon* (1937) draws fitful interest: Viva and the others talk as they watch, as people will, but when it comes to the line "I believe it because I want to believe it," Viva tells them: "That's the message."

Equally affirmative is the entire matter of the children's party, through which Viva wafts rather helplessly but is always eager to please: "I made them fruit salad. Fresh. Which they didn't touch. All they wanted was French fried potatoes and ketchup." That and, presumably, *The Beard*. Varda supports her permissiveness in respect of the children quite firmly: "They are the space children of the future, you see. We say that in the movie. And so they are."

Lions Love is arguably the best of Varda's work, free-ranging and perhaps self-indulgent, yet filled with concern and with spontaneous emotion, despite the alienation effects. In this film her "underground river of the instincts" is running fast and deep, and her responses to the American scene, both critical and affectionate, are typical of this remarkable woman, who brought with her to cinema none of the conventional training but a richness and a talent to provoke and delight.

Lions Love

Andre Cornand / 1971

From *La Revue du Cinéma* 247 (February 1971). Reprinted by permission. Translated by T. Jefferson Kline.

Filmgoers and cinephiles who loved the short films of Agnès Varda, then *Cléo from 5 to 7, Le Bonheur,* and perhaps also *Les Créatures,* may be disconcerted by *Lions Love.* And yet it would be misleading to say that America changed the director. Behind a new cinematic structure, we can discern tendencies and preoccupations that were already Varda's in *La Pointe Courte* in 1954 (the contrasts of differing worlds, the play of contradictions), then in 1957 and 1958 with *O Saisons, O châteaux,* and *Opéra Mouffe* and *Du Côté de la Côte* (her taste for subjective documentary). We also rediscover in *Lions Love* the problem of freedom in love that Agnès Varda had tackled in *Le Bonheur.*

But, just as her short subjects and those of some of the other directors who began "the new wave" brought us so much that was good, *Lions Love* seems to me to be an accomplished work which brings together so many of the different currents of the modern cinema (both the young French cinema and the Underground American cinema). In this sense, *Lions Love* opens potentially new avenues for the Seventh Art. Agnès Varda herself has said that it's as much a collage as an inventory. We prefer the term collage here because the various aspects of this film aren't so much added one to another or juxtaposed as they interpenetrate and imbricate themselves with each other.

Lions Love is a meditation on Hollywood, on its past, its myths, a documentary on its Underground super stars, a reflection on American attitudes, a study of the passage from adolescence to adulthood. It's occasionally a psycho-drama and especially a reflection on the way cinema, television, and the mass media mix fiction and reality.

Agnès Varda tells us she abandoned herself to a "description of a baroque world using the reserved approach of an inventory: stationary

shots, long camera movements, use of the most natural lenses." Beside—
or beyond—this lucid intelligence, we find in *Lions Love* other characteristic traits of our director: perspicacity, humor, nostalgia, poetry. But
rather than offering a long analysis of the work it seemed to us more interesting and more useful to ask the director about her film.

Andre Cornand: Tell us about the meaning of the title.
Agnès Varda: The original title was *Lions, Loves and Lies* but the actors
found it too long, too heavy, and too explicit. The clapman simply wrote
Lions love on the take numbers, so the title stuck. It's a combination of
two words that in French could mean "Lions as lovers," "Love in the
manner of Lions," "Lions and Love," "Lion-Love" or just "roaarrr!" The
original title "Lions, Loves and Lies" summed up the three themes of the
film. a) Lions: Actors are like lions. Indeed, they used to be called lions.
My three actors should have had manes. What does this new generation
of actors headed for Hollywood look like? Who are today's stars? Are today's politicians the best actors? Are they the true stars? Are they lions?
b) Love: The three major characters love each other. How will they manage their lovers' triangle? How does the post-hippie generation conceive
of married life? c) Lies: Are actors liars? What about politicians? Who's
lying to whom? What does it mean to lie in Hollywood? Is making a film
about new stars in Hollywood fiction or documentary? Is it dishonest
cinema?

AC: What's the subject of your film?
AV: I could give you twenty different answers that would all be more or
less true and more or less limited. I wanted my film to express two great
currents in America: sex and politics. But the film is very chaste and the
star politician, Bobby Kennedy, is more victim than star: his casket looks
like a television.

The film, which I'd prefer to call a collage, is about:

Stars: The new stars on the Pop scene. Nostalgia for the stars of yesteryear and, as I've already said, the political stars.

Making a film in Hollywood: This subject is about Shirley Clarke, who
is a director in real life. But, since I'm the real director of *Lions Love*, the
subject is really about my attempt to make a film in Hollywood. Since
this film becomes part of the story, we wanted, here and there, to have
shots of filming and to allow the actors to wink at the spectator, to act or
not act as they saw fit.

Liberation and Quest: The three actors live freely, but it isn't so much sexual freedom they're after, but a certain mysticism, the mysticism of the hippies.

Hollywood: It's a magical city with its typical streets, enormous boulevards, and enormous studios. Everyone who comes here has, at some point or other, to test his private life against the "Hollywood thing."

The End of Youth: The characters are no longer flower children. They're too old to be hippies, too young to be adults.

Contradictions: Between political events and private life. On the one hand, a tragic event reduced to a tiny image in a box; on the other hand, three characters in bed and their reactions as they eat breakfast.

The Assassination of Robert Kennedy that continues the Shakespearean history of the Kennedy family.

To sum up: The film's subject is stars, films, free love, freedom of editing, California trees, television, the end of youth, plastic flowers, political heroes, swimming pools, red glasses, rental properties in Hollywood, coffee, and who has to get up first to make it.

AC: What's the play we see at the beginning of the film?
AV: It's a play called *The Beard* by Michael McClure. It had runs in several cities including New York and Los Angeles and had provoked a big scandal. The actors went to jail, the author too and there were lots of demonstrations outside the theaters by conservatives. Ultimately in L.A. the theater was burned down. The playwright gave his two American folk heroes, Jean Harlow and Billy the Kid, some pretty audacious, gross, and funny lines. I saw the play in Hollywood, cradle of the star system. This play about stars who were lost in a futile eternity convinced me that I wanted to do a film about stars. On the other hand, by beginning *Lions Love* with a play the three actors were attending, I allowed myself several levels of play. The actors are exaggerations of us and certain major events—political dramas, national tragedies—can lead some people to behave like actors. That is, to "act" can sometimes become a psychodrama the way it did for Shirley Clarke in this film. The world can sometimes be a huge theater full of noise and . . . well just reread the classics!

AC: When did you shoot this film and how long did it take?
AV: *Lions Love* was shot in March 1969, in a rented house. Work with the actors took about four weeks. I also spent about two weeks on the documentary work.

Mother of the New Wave:
An Interview with Agnès Varda

Jacqueline Levitin / 1974

From *Women and Film*, nos. 5–6 (1974). Reprinted by permission.

Jacqueline Levitin: What has your experience been as a woman film-maker in France? Were you involved in the women's movement?

Agnès Varda: When I started to make films, which was nineteen years ago, there was no women's movement in France. There were women doing things here and there—in writing, in painting, and music. But there were very few women making films. I didn't ask myself if it would be difficult for me as a woman to make films; I must say I didn't start with an inferiority complex. I just thought I would like to make films, so try. Years later, many girls came to me saying they would like to make films, would I write a letter for them because it is so difficult for a woman to make her way in this society of men—which is sometimes true. But I always respond that, though it may be true for society, you should not think like this yourself, but rather, "you are a human being, you want to make films, is it difficult or not." That's the point. If society is anti-women, let's face that little by little. But that shouldn't be your starting point of view. And I say that because I never thought of myself as a limited human being because of being a woman. I never thought I was "half a man." I never wanted to be a man.

I was a photographer. I had started with stills of whatever I could find—children around me, family, marriages, banquets, whatever could make money. Then I became a photographer for the Theatre National Populaire. Nobody came to me saying, "You are a photographer and that is something because you are a woman." When I was too small, I would take a chair and stand on it—that was the kind of problem I would have being 30 centimeters shorter than any one else. Now everybody would like to say that people were paternalistic, because now in the feminist movement one has to say that even women who have made it were treated as "little things." I didn't think that. I just did what I had to do—in the midst of men and women, and I felt good.

And when I made my first film, *La Pointe courte*, I never had any problem such as the cameraman saying "Look, I can't listen to you because you are merely a woman." I would say, "I like that shot, or that distance, make it sharper, or more contrast," or I would argue about the depth of field, but it was technical conversation. When the film came out I had good reviews, even though it never made back the money it cost to produce. But no one said, it was a minor film because I was a woman. Instead they said, "You are perhaps changing something in the French cinema and it's good." So I never suffered any alienation as a woman in my work.

JL: How did you begin making films?

AV: I had written the whole script of *La Pointe courte*. It was finished, on paper. I thought I would never shoot it. I thought I would put it in a drawer and look at it three years later, saying, "Yes, at that time I was thinking about making a movie." And then a friend came to me and said why don't you do it? I said with what? How? They said it's easy, let's make it. The problem was to find money, to get a crew, and to find people able to help me do it. We were all very young, and had very little experience. But we lived together in a rented house. Everybody had to stay there and eat there because we had no money to pay individual expenses. We had to organize ourselves as a collective. And then we shot.

From the point of view of production, it was really something revolutionary in 1954. I didn't even have the right to be a producer. We have a professional hierarchy in France in which it's necessary to pass through the ranks, do five apprenticeships before making a film. And the same for the technicians. I didn't ask for my card. (It's very funny after all, because I only got my card entitling me to be a director thirteen years after my first film.) I didn't bother with laws or unions, or get official authorization. It was a way of eliminating the "taboo" of Cinema, of the closed world of cinema and its hierarchies. That's how it became a real film. I was so sure that it was a one-time thing—I never thought of myself as a filmmaker—I went back to photography after that, making money since the film didn't make any money. But, years later, someone asked me if I wanted to make films for the tourist office and I thought yes, it was another way of making money, and maybe later I will make other films. That's how I did the shorts—*O Saisons, O chateaux, Du Côté de la côte,* and then *Opéra Mouffe*. Then the desire came to make other movies; then I became a "filmmaker."

It took me seven years to make another feature, *Cléo de 5 à 7*—because I could not find the money, because I had no time to write scripts. I was taking stills, not because I was a woman, but because I was writing the kind of films that are difficult to set up financially. When I did *Cléo*, which is about a woman, I really had in mind to make a film about a woman facing a great fear, and that fear makes her think about herself. She discovers that she is a little doll, manipulated by men, a little girl who makes no decisions, who sees herself only through other people's eyes. And in that hour and a half she starts to relate differently.

I thought all my films as a woman, because I didn't want to be a "false man" making films. I was trying to make films about what I knew. When I was pregnant, I made a film about pregnancy, as I wanted people to share it with me (*L'Opéra Mouffe*). In *Le Bonheur* I tried to understand the sense of innocence.

Little by little the feminist movement built up and a lot of women started to think about their position in society. And in the last five years, it has become not only something very strong and good, but very fashionable as well—which is the worst part of it, because it is "in" to speak about women. Ten years ago it wasn't "in" and maybe in ten years, even though the movement will be growing, maybe society will have another topic to be excited about. Right now we are in the middle of it. So women come to me and say, "*Le Bonheur* is shit. It's not a film for women made by a woman. Society got you and you betrayed us, etc." But when you have in mind to show the clichés of society—and that is what *Le Bonheur* is all about—you have to show the clichés. You don't have to say, "Because I am a woman I should absolutely make feminist films because the feminist point of view is not generally exposed." It is true that I can now see my own films with a new vision because of things which have happened, because of books which I have read, because I did a kind of self-education on feminism, which we all do now, because we have opportunities to do so. Things are clear now. But they weren't so clear ten years ago when I made *Le Bonheur* even though I had already read Simone de Beauvoir, and had discussed these things, and had fought for contraception, sexual freedom, new ways of raising children, and alternatives to the usual form of marriage. I agree with the new generation of women, even though I think they are wrong to have a point of view even before starting anything, and want only to express the desire to change themselves and to change the image of women in society. I think they are right, and I am myself willing to do the same. But I don't think it means we have to forget that whatever women have made previously, for or against women, has been a way for women to promote themselves, to come up enough so that other women could speak from a feminist point of view and make that point of view clear. So I can say I am a feminist. But for other feminists, I am not feminist enough. But what I have done led me to be a feminist even though I have not made feminist films.

JL: Do you think now that you would like to make a feminist movie?
AV: Yes, I would like to. But it would never be my only aim. I would never think that I was born only to express what women suffer and what women have to change in society. I am a human being and some things can be understood as a human being. You don't have to emphasize all the time that you are a woman. For example, Women's Film Festivals. Maybe one or two were necessary just to show what has been done by women. But in another sense it is really segregation, and racism. Women can be as wrong as men about women and some men can be better. I believe that Bergman, for example, knows more about women than a lot of women. Even though the identification of women has to be made by a woman, it exactly parallels the problem of the Black Panthers; when black people started to raise their consciousness, white people spoke for them, were conscious for them. Then little by little, they thought they should think for themselves. That's what women are doing now. And they are right. But it doesn't mean some men have not understood. I don't think we should put so much importance on the sex of the film-maker, but on what he is saying about women and how.

JL: Some feminist filmmakers think that it is not only a question of re-vealing the psychology of women, but of presenting a "heroic" picture of women, women who conquer the condition of being a woman in a male-dominated society and come to a self-consciousness. Do you think that this is the type of film that should be made?
AV: I think that each woman should come to understand what she is and her position in the world. But if you only consider that aim you will produce the kind of films they are making in China. They are raising consciousness, for sure, but what a bore! It's the same stupid thing as Westerns in which there are good guys and bad guys and the good guys should be the winner and the bad guy—you will explain how bad he was. But what is the point? I think it is brainwashing in the same way. I realize

something has to be changed because the image of women in film has been strongly built up by men, and accepted by them, but also accepted by women—because as women we have accepted that women should be beautiful, well-dressed, loving, always and only involved in questions of love, etc. It's always made me furious, but I haven't up to now been able to change that image. In films the only thing we are able to accept in a woman is her relationship with love—is she or is she not in love; has she been in love or will she be in love. Even if she is alone, she *has* been in love or she should be or she would like to be in love. Men have another position in films. You have films where the man relates with his work, films of male friendship, films where he must struggle and fight. But you never see a woman relating to her job; you cannot accept that the subject of the film would be a woman doctor and her difficulties with an operation, her patients, etc. You do not see films in which a woman directs things, or about how she does it or how she relates with the people working with her. If a woman has a job, it is usually as a decorator, or as a secretary, or she works in a post office. She has a job but it is never the main theme. In most films the main concern is a woman's relationship with love. And that should be changed. I really think we should prepare ourselves as women and as audience.

JL: Is that self-criticism?
AV: Yes, sure. But I couldn't do otherwise because I couldn't have been able to make a film. I wrote a script, I remember, years ago about a woman teaching New Math and having to fight because it was the beginning of New Math in France. They had to fight on all levels—the parents, because the parents would not accept the program, because they did not understand New Math and didn't want to lose the power they had at home helping the child with his work. It was the story of a woman facing the parents, giving lectures, fighting the old methods of teaching math. I would say that her private life played a very small part. I could never raise the money to make the film.

JL: Producers want you to make love stories because you are a woman?
AV: No. Not because I am a woman but because they only want women to be involved with love in a film. They say nobody will be interested in a New Mathematics teacher. But things have changed because I remember the American film *Up the Down Staircase*, in which the main concern was the woman's relationship with her job. It was good on that level. But that kind of thing is rare. It's difficult to raise the money. And if I

could make *Cléo* about femininity and fear of death, it is because the girl was beautiful. If you told the same story about a fifty-five-year-old lonely woman, who would care if she were dying of cancer and who would come to see the film? Here you come to another point—what the audience wants to see. Do you think they want to see the truth? No, they don't. Why should they see what they see around them all the time? If you do a film about union problems and a worker getting up very early—you think people want to see that on a Saturday night? No. They want some entertainment, good looking people, a dream. They accept to have their consciousness raised about something, but if it is in the context of some entertainment. We shouldn't forget that the movie is a popular art; people go to movies to have a good time. They don't want to be taught all the time. That's why we have to change the image of women, but we have to be careful not to become such bores that no one wants to listen to anything.

We all live with an illusion—of beauty, of love, of one's career, of power, etc. I don't know if the aim is to make people lose their illusions, see what it is all about and how they could handle it. I sometimes think that, like in *Le Bonheur*, these people with their illusions are much happier in fact than other people who know and can't face it. The point is, are movies made to make that illusion continue, maybe pointing at times that it is not enough, or can they be made to show people what is around them and what it means? I cannot answer because I cannot forget that movies, because they involve so much investment that must be made back, feature films (not documentaries, super-8, or video where you can do social work) are a mass art. Can we find a situation in which you do not fool the audience and still entertain them? For example in *Le Bonheur* I was trying to make the shape of the film so lovely and nice that if you don't want to face what it means you don't have to. You can see the film as a beautiful bucolic picnic painting and enjoy it as it is saying, "He's a little selfish but life goes on." You can also start to think about what cruelty of Nature means, what is the function of a woman, how can she be replaced so easily—so what is the life of a woman about? Does it mean that ironing and cooking and putting children to bed is enough, and that any blond woman can do it for that man? But you are not obliged to read the film at that level. So I was trying to make a movie clear enough—I was trying, I really didn't succeed well in *Le Bonheur*—but my aim was to make a movie entertaining enough so that people could see sort of a love story with a little affair, a little drama, but not too much, a feeling that life can be beautiful, etc., and on another level, if you want to read it, and make up your mind about what it means to be a

man, what it means to be a woman, what cruelty it involves if you want
to be happy, how someone must pay for you, at what age you can give another mother to children—all these questions can be raised after seeing
the film. But it still looks like an entertaining film. That's what I wanted
to do. That's why it's so smooth—but I overdid it and it's not really
good—I tried to make it like a beautiful apple you want to eat. Because
I believe if you make a very serious film to raise consciousness, people
leave. Most people go once or twice a week maximum to the movies, and
because they are tired and want to forget what their life is most of the
time, and they just want to see a lot of nice things, or violent—because
they don't dare to have so much violence in their lives. So one should be
clever enough to manipulate the needs of the mass audience but in a way
that would not be meaningless and empty.

JL: Do you generally work with women, do you think it is your role to
promote women in filmmaking?
AV: It's not my role but I like to do it. I get along very well with women,
and with men. I don't think, "Well I've made it and they'll just have to
make it their own way." So I had a lot of assistants when I was a photographer, which means I taught them in two or three months and then they
became photographers, some very famous now. And in films I always
had women editors, and assistants. If I can have a woman I take her. If
there is a man who does the job better I take the man. It's in terms of
needing good people to make movies. If the woman is the same or better
I would rather take the woman to help her. But she has to train herself
to qualify. Competition exists in movies. It's difficult to make a film; you
really need good people. But I don't write my scripts with women. The
only film I worked on with women was a film about women that I wrote
two years ago, but which I couldn't shoot.

JL: The abortion film?
AV: The abortion film about women in France. I needed a lot of information and I knew some women sociologists, doctors, etc., who could help
me a great deal to bring to the film information and strong feelings that
I didn't have. But I worked with them two or three months and then I
wrote the script alone. I enjoyed working with them, because a collective consciousness raises itself more clearly when women work together.

JL: Has the situation for women in film evolved significantly in France
since you began?
AV: Yes, enormously. I was almost the only woman filmmaker at the

time. So, you might say I was fortunate, if it's fortunate to be almost the only one. Men have had the tendency to think of me as a "little phenomenon" because I was a bit the pioneer of the New Wave. But it was a case of circumstance and education. In other words let's say that the identity of women is not tied particularly to the fact that I succeeded a little in doing something in this profession.

I think that one can begin to speak of women and film when 50 percent of filmmakers are women, since 50 percent of the population is women. There are two problems—the problem of the promotion of women in all professions in equal number to men, and the problem of society: how can women who still want to have children be sure to be able to have them when they want, with whom they want, and how are we going to help them raise the children. That's the big problem. It's no use to think I'm going to do this or that and then be completely blocked if one still wants to have children. A woman has the right to think that her biology will permit her to have children if she wants them. If she wants to have three or four children (even if it's a mistake from the point of view of ecology) she shouldn't have to think, "With these three children, what's going to happen to my career." These problems of the place of women in society are very important. In the meantime there is only one solution and that is to be a kind of "super-woman" and lead several lives at once. For me the biggest difficulty in my life was to do that—to lead several lives at once and to not give in and to not abandon any of them—to not give up children, to not give up the cinema, to not give up men if one likes men.

JL: I remember when you spoke of making *Les Créatures* you said you had been happy with yourself for including a fight scene. Was it a kind of proof of status in the male world of cinema?

AV: I was impressed because I thought it was always said that a woman couldn't make a fight scene, or war films, or things like that. And I never wanted to make war films or fight films. But for certain details of the scenario it was necessary that two men fight, and actually I had the inferiority complex that perhaps I wouldn't know how do do it and I hired a specialist to help me. And when it was done I thought, "Oh, it's terrific; I've made a scene where two men fight." But after, I thought it was stupid because it was useless.

So I had a slight inferiority complex that I had a limit. And after, not only did I get over this complex but I realized that this complex was silly because the role of a woman is not to prove that she can do all that a man can do or knows how to do. On the contrary, the role of a woman is to do what she feels she should do as a woman. And if she wants to do things that are different from what men do then all the better.

JL: How do you prepare the actual filming of a script? Is the choice of images precisely worked out before you begin filming?

AV: Quite so. There is a part which is improvised. By that I mean that there are two stages, the stage where the film begins in my head—often it's a place that inspires me: for *La Pointe Courte* it was truly the village of La Pointe Courte, for *Lions Love* it was truly Hollywood, and for *Cléo* in a way it was certain streets of Paris. And when all the production details have been settled, when I know I'm going to make the film, I go often to the site which will be the setting of the film. I try to really understand the arrangement of things, so that I can integrate (the character) as accurately as possible into an environment which explains him, justifies him, attacks him, or contradicts him, so that one understands the dialectic between the character and the environment. On the other hand, I take notes to find a personal line of narration. Narration is not only important to develop the plot, it is essentially composed of my choices as narrator. And these indications—I try to feel them, to not make a mistake in how I interpret them. For example, for the material in *La Pointe Courte* I remember this particular detail: I had an idea of a dialectic between wood and metal. I had the feeling—I don't want to explain it in symbols—that the main character who was the son of a shipbuilder, he who was born of the village, who had his roots in the village—I linked him with the feeling of wood, that he felt at ease when he saw branches, when he saw ships made of wood, when he touched wood. And she, with her way of grinding her teeth, this furious, aggressive character, who questioned not only her marriage, but her position and identity as a woman in relation to him—I always imagined her as related to metal, with iron, with rails, with iron fences, iron wire. One can't justify this in logical terms; it was the feeling that I had. And I tried to use it discreetly, but use it in the story so that one can feel physically the opposition between iron and wood.

JL: It seems to me that one can divide *La Pointe Courte* into the part that concerns the village where a warmth pervades and the part that concerns the couple where one senses the photographer.

AV: Yes. But you feel all the more the presence of the photographer because there is no warmth. I mean by that that I was perhaps as much the photographer in one part as in the other, but it is evident that I was attached to the village and to the villagers. And I wanted to show that their life and their vital problems of survival were very dear to me. On the other hand I purposefully gave a literary style and a stiff cold manner to the couple because I wanted to fight against the tendency of film to always create dramas. When a man leaves a woman in a film it is generally because he loves another woman. When a woman leaves it is because she has another lover. It was very rare, at least in 1954, to question the idea of the couple. It's a philosophical or moral problem—however one wants to call it—not of this specific couple, not if he had done this or that but of the couple—their conversation was almost abstract. And asking them thus to neither be particularly real, nor kind, nor sentimental, nor physical, nor sensual, automatically I didn't make it easy for the spectator to identify with them in a "warm" way. Thus the coldness is the distance that I wanted between them and the audience. And one senses the photography since when one feels distance he becomes a voyeur and one looks at the image itself.

JL: Did you learn much from your experience of working with Resnais as your editor for the film?

AV: Yes, when he edited the film he made me realize that the cinema existed, that it had its own long history, that there were some beautiful films, and that there were things that I had naively thought to invent and which already existed. The idea must be accepted that *La Pointe Courte* is a naïve film, in the sense of someone who writes his first novel thinking he is going to renew literature and then is told, "But Beckett has already done this, and Ionesco that and Joyce . . ." So I wasn't pretentious. When he said that several things were inspired by Visconti—one can't say inspired because I had never seen a Visconti film—which resembled Visconti, I said to myself that now I would begin to reflect upon what I could do that would be more specifically personal.

JL: Have you developed your own style for directing actors?

AV: No, I don't really feel that I am a good director of actors. Perhaps it is because of my idea that the setting and all the other things express a great deal which is perhaps not as well expressed in the acting. It's the opposite of theater. I always thought that the theater was so tied to the work of actors that the cinema should turn away from the work of actors and involve itself in what was left. When later I directed actors, I tried to prepare them, but not by speaking in psychological terms. You have to speak to them instead in concrete terms, saying "the person you are playing is awkward, he puts on his shoes like this . . ." To indicate the difference between eating slowly or fast, the manner in which one picks up his fork, helps an actor portray his character.

JL: You have often spoken of the desire to make your intentions understood clearly by the audience. Is it important for you to make a film *for* an audience?

AV: It's a question that I've often asked myself: do I want to make the effort to make a film for the fishermen of the village of *La Pointe Courte*—I take this example because the villagers are people I really love. (It's not from a political ideology.) And I have answered "no." No, because they have too far to go between their clichés and strangely enough, bourgeois alienation, which numbs the fishermen the most. It's the workers who have a bourgeois outlook very often. Often they dream to get what the bourgeois have. It is they who often have a narrow outlook in morality because they want to identify with the bourgeois class, which itself tries to become free morally. It's something very well known. And it is on this level that I argue against Jean-Luc Godard's politics. I am not militantly political enough to say from now on I am going to make films for the fishermen of La Pointe Courte and for the workers of the Renault factory so that they will enjoy it, but also recognize themselves and identify and think that it really concerns them. I am not modest enough. And not militant enough. And too egotistical. I still participate in a bourgeois culture in which a film is made by an artist.

Agnès Varda Talks about the Cinema

Mireille Amiel / 1975

From *Cinéma 75*, no. 204 (December 1975). Reprinted by permission. Translated by T. Jefferson Kline.

Mireille Amiel: Since *Lions Love* we haven't heard much from Agnès Varda. She has been working on *One Sings and the Other Doesn't*, so I thought getting her to talk about her work would be now or never. I set out for an interview and came back with a long monologue from the author.

Agnès Varda: *Daguerréotypes* is a sort of dual project. It's partly the work of a documentarist (which I like being) and the work of a feminist (which I like being). It's a film about my neighborhood. La rue Daguerre is a strange street, inhabited by normal people who don't have a lot of money and a lot of artists who were attracted to this so-called poor neighborhood which has remained quite folksy despite recent attempts to gentrify it.

It's my neighborhood. These are my shops and I've always been interested in them. Especially one of them, "The Blue Thistle," a sort of dress-makers, bazaar, and perfume shop all in one. It's the only place I know where you can get twenty grams of rice-powder or thirty centiliters of eau de Cologne (you bring your own bottle). It's the owner himself who makes the eau de Cologne—he's an extraordinary man and his wife is even more extraordinary. She's amnesic and is thus a captive of this closed world of the store and in this street. She's the phantom of the small business world. She has always fascinated me.

Last year German TV offered me a chance to do a film—carte blanche. And here's where I connect up with my second project, feminism. You see, exactly one year before I'd had my second child, Mathieu. It's not easy to work when your child is still a baby, even if you have help. More than just changing diapers and the fatigue that comes from no sleep, a child requires his mother's presence and attention. Plus the time you want to spend loving him and enjoying him. You can't always "forward" your child to yourself on a trip or during a shoot. I'd already experienced this with my first child, Rosalie, sixteen years before. But at that time I was making *Du côté de la côte* for a couple of weeks on the Côte d'Azur in the summer. And even then it wasn't easy.

So this time there was no question of going anywhere. I had one year to complete the project. I was a bit stuck at home. So I told myself that I was a good example of women's creativity—always a bit stuck and suffocated by home and motherhood. So I wondered what could come of these constraints. Could I manage to restart my creativity from within these limitations? Ultimately this didn't strike me as so very different from dealing with other kinds of limitations, such as the constraints of making a commissioned film. (I made *O Saisons, O Chateaux* and *Du Côté de la Côte* for the French Ministry of tourism.) This time I would come face to face with a limitation that must be confronted by many other women.

An Entirely Day-to-Day Approach

So I set out from this idea, from this fact that most women are stuck at home. And I attached myself to my hearth. I imagined a new umbilical cord. I had a special eighty-meter electric cable attached to the electric box in my house. I decided I would allow myself that much space to shoot *Daguerréotypes*. I could go no further than the end of my cable. I would find everything I needed within that distance and never venture further. That gave my film a special meaning for me in addition to its documentary aspect.

At every level. First of all at the level of the picturesque, which exists everywhere. Next and especially at the level of society. We say "the silent majority." And it's true. It's a term that best describes these workers who are, as they say, valiant, who have no truck with politics, who have no time for it, who just want nothing to change since they're so focused on the (enormous) problems of just existing, surviving.

When they talk about political issues (The Montparnasse Tower, The Supermarkets), they don't even know they're being political. The Revolution or simply the evolution of society are considered personal threats to their store. That's why they're called the "silent majority," because they don't do a political reading of events or else they think these things just aren't their problem.

And I don't believe it's my role or anyone else's, given the conditions of making this film, to judge these people or their behavior. Even if we know that they're at least partly responsible for our society, they're just like us, exactly like us.

So my intention wasn't to make a political film. I don't go ask these people, "What about the economy? Taxes? The future? Do you want things to change? So how will you vote?"

I tried to make my approach entirely match the daily life of the neighborhood. Just tried to capture their way of living, their gestures. Because you know there's a complete gestural language among small business people and several things fascinate me about it.

A Relationship between Silence and Strength

First of all let's look at some of the clichés of the business world. And by "cliché" I'm not referring only to language—"How are you? What's the weather going to be today?" Etc.—but also to more subtle behaviors. For example the art of waiting. Everyone knows the merchant has to wait in his shop. Sometimes that wait can be very long. The merchant obeys the whim of his clients. But as soon as the client comes in, the minute he enters the store, he's the one who has to wait. Even if it's for the simplest thing, he has to wait a while. There's a ritual . . . I wouldn't go so far as to say of vengeance but of "give and take." So a sort of sizing up is immediately set in motion. Inside the shop (and contrary to the saying "the client is king"), it's the merchant who's king. This silent struggle and careful sizing up is what a simple documentary can portray.

And when I say "simple," I'm talking about another aspect of feminism. To film simply the simplicity of everyday life was my approach.

Maybe not in the first degree, since, indeed, I could have made a film about myself: cooking, nursing my child, trying to write. But I preferred to bear witness to the world that is open to women, to a woman who goes shopping.

So, the first point was, what do we know about the life of merchants.

Another point: the kind of work merchants do: and for starters the fact that they work as couples, where the most often it's the woman who sells the products that her husband has made or prepared.

This feminist reflection on the "woman-as-assistant-to-her-husband" wasn't covered in my film, but it's one that fascinates me.

The butcher's assistant, the tailor's assistant, all these women bound in close solidarity—and complicity!—with their husbands.

So, the third point of this documentary from a feminist point of view: how can you make a film that isn't a form of rape?

Okay, the term *rape* is maybe a little strong. But you know there's a whole race of documentaries that I would qualify as voluntarily aggressive.

I wanted to avoid the approach: "Okay, we've got them where we want them, we've got them trapped." It's like they're hunting down documentation and I don't like hunting.

You know these films where the zoom seems to have Parkinson's disease! They consist of going fishing in quest of a shot of clenched hands that denote anguish or a shot of someone scratching his head in a way that suggests he's got lice. Of course, this type of documentary is not without interest. But I simply refuse to go there.

Understanding Gestures

Let's agree on one thing. Of course we want to show a maximum of things in our films, and I'm not saying I'll never film people without their knowing it but I would do so in the framework of a pre-established complicity.

So what I did was to ask the merchants for their consent that I could morph from a client into a filmmaker, and told them that I was interested in trying to understand their gestures, the pace of work, their solution to the art of waiting. I talked to them about the film. To be honest I have to admit that I didn't discuss my hypotheses about their immobility. I didn't (couldn't) tell them that my goal was to understand the notion of the "silent majority."

How could I say, "You are the silent majority and you fascinate me because I don't understand you at all?" It was easier to tell them the other side of that truth: "We know each other and I like us to understand each other better so I will never betray you in my film but will simply try to film as much as I can."

From this perspective, my cinematic technique was of capital importance: it had to serve the goal of my filming and submit to the spirit of the film.

And in that respect, I had the luck to work with a remarkable woman, Nurith Aviv, my camerawoman. She shot practically the entire film, very quietly with the camera on her shoulder. She shot only by hand, but it was calmly done.

The general idea was to have the camera running all the time, flexible, discrete, a bit mute, somewhat immobile. Sometimes Nurith would stand there immobile for ten minutes ready to shoot, but not shooting, just waiting.

The only moments at which the camera was stationary were the "daguerreotype portraits."

As for zooms, there are almost none in the film. Zooms are an atrocity! Obviously they're practical because they allow a lens change in the middle of a gesture or movement, but they really must be kept to a minimum.

The thing is, that if you're going to approach someone, you must do it gently. Slowly in physical terms and slowly in moral terms as well. Any zoom-ins on the characters should be as gentle as possible, following their real movements in as organically and biologically correct ways as possible. If the camera moves it should follow the rhythm of the film—in this case a very slow rhythm. We must try to forget the cyclothymic jumps that accentuate rapid evolution.

I have a lot of admiration for Nurith Aviv's camera work: her images affirm her deep respect for her subjects.

A Somewhat Surrealist Bit of Luck

We shot a first version of the film in ten successive days. We began with the fiesta at the café, which we didn't use all of, but used effectively. We weren't quite sure what was going to happen or what days the illusionist was going to propose. We decided to limit this part to two visits and ask the merchants on that street to attend if they possibly could in order to light up the evening. In the illusionist's number I decided to film only the pieces that had some connection to commerce: the manipulation of money or of objects, rice, liquids, and I tried, when filming the audience, to focus on the married couples among the merchants.

Sometimes chance intervened in an almost surreal way. I found it fascinating, for example, that it was the barber who accepted to be put into a trance in exactly the position his clients assume when being shaved, head back and "Don't move! I don't want to cut your throat!"

After the fiesta we filmed each of the shops, one after the other. We just watched the people and their gestures and occasionally asked a question or two, such as: "Have you lived here long?" "Where were you born?" or "When did you meet?" Then we stopped shooting and I began the editing. It was really hard to structure all of this material. The first edit took more than two months. I tried to find the ideal balance between the fiesta and the shops. For example, it became clear that the slow and patient presentation of the shops had to come at the beginning. Once the show was underway with the accelerated rhythm of Mystag the audience couldn't have tolerated the slower pacing. So I decided to open with the sad world of commerce, introduce the gala at the café and then set up a system of parallel edits that brought out the points of reflection.

From a Dreamless Sleep to Death

Then we continued alternating between a couple of days of shooting and then editing which allowed us to see what things needed to be put in relief. Shots of hands at work, for example. Then, a little later, I asked this question about dreams which turned out to be so important and which justifies the underlying continuity of the film: the passage from the daguerreotype to sleep, and from a dreamless sleep to death. Everything comes back to the central subject of the film: immobility—the immobility of sleep but also the immobility of thought which rejects dreams, assumed to be the agents of disorder and troubles. Dreams are rejected in the same way movement is. By means of this simple question the discourse became more political.

The closer I came to this world (which is really not mine), a world whose politics I vehemently reject, the more difficult and less approachable it was. The invisible stubbornnesss of this world takes the form of a refusal to answer questions. In the midst of a high degree of general politeness and apparent openness that never diminished in the least during our entire shoot, in the midst of all this simplicity, I realized more and more that their answers to my questions were "off the mark."

My relations with my neighborhood are necessarily ambiguous. I've been there a long time, I know everyone and everyone knows me. That undoubtedly helped. But at the same time, I'm marginal, an "artist" and my life doesn't resemble theirs in the least. Neither my private life— or rather what they see of it—nor my professional and public life—or what they know of it through magazines, TV, or the demonstration on abortion.

But now for the first time, we had a working relationship. Not just because they were the subject of my work but also because, suddenly, they discovered that editing is a process that can take months. All of a sudden, the fact that they get up at dawn and I at 8:00 or 9:00, that they're imprisoned in their shops—took on a different meaning when they saw the patience necessary in my work.

Now when they see me carrying film canisters (even though they'd seen them before), not only do they know they might be on the films in these canisters but also how much time and work it takes to make the films.

Film Is a Kind of Dream

In July we showed the film to our neighbors. We did a kind of "summer cinema in the street." First we showed the film (everyone had brought a chair) and then drank some rose wine together to discuss it. But frankly the discussion didn't go very far. What was immediately clear was the joy they had seeing themselves on the screen. But my commentary and my reflections and the montage I'd created of their gestures, their statements didn't lead to any commentary whatsoever. I'd be tempted to conclude that in the cinema the sound track affects people much less than the images.

The discussion with these people, who were after all the protagonists of the film, was never very open. I felt the same quiet refusal that I'd observed while filming. A refusal to go beyond clichés. The unconscious idea: we are clichés of shopkeepers and she's a cliché of a filmmaker. Not one of them seemed to have felt that their lives had been questioned to any degree whatever. Not one of them had any desire to learn anything whatsoever about themselves. They refused the film in the same way they'd refuse the reality of their dreams. Film is a kind of dream, and meets with the same resistance.

It's said that French film is bourgeois and deals only with the bourgeois. Many of us feel the need of a cinema that speaks of the others. But it's really hard and the example of *Daguerréotypes* proves it. This film could conceivably be considered a study of the life of the neighborhood, but hardly as a collective questioning of this life. Of course, some filmmakers have different experiences, for example, Karmitz in *Coup pour coup*.

By filming women at a moment of crisis and asking them to take advantage of the occasion to talk about their crisis he did them a huge favor, helping them (and eventually their audience) to see themselves more objectively.

I Made a Film-Testimonial

When I've presented *Daguerréotypes*, I've occasionally been reproached for not having been useful since I confessed I hadn't been able to mobilize those people who the film presented. Of course, that's a valid argument. But I would answer that my film was a kind of witnessing of what was there, an archive whose object was to understand a phenomenon at a particular historical moment, a document belonging in a cinémathèque or a library: it's a document about a certain way of life in a certain year in a certain cluster of houses.

In 1954 I attempted a somewhat different experiment with *La Pointe courte*. In that film, a couple (Silvia Montfort and Philippe Noiret) are trying to understand each other in a very precise context—a fishing village. Now, the livelihood of these fishermen was threatened. The so-called pollution caused by powerful industrial competitors made their work impossible. What interested me in this particular situation and what almost always interests me in my films is the dialectics between public and private, between subjective and general. The cliché and what's inside the cliché.

I believe that this is true for all of my films, even for *L'Opéra Mouffe*, which tells how one can be at the same time pregnant, blessedly happy, and yet also aware that life is also about misery and aging, which are more than anywhere else omnipresent in the Rue Mouffetard. The contradiction fascinated me all the more because it was so unavoidably evident.

To come back to *La Pointe Courte* we have the contradiction between a couple who are trying to understand what's happening to them from within and what's happening outside in this geographically and politically specific environment. The film was created for and with the fishermen. I used what they told me, and what I understood from their preoccupations and their language. And the staged meetings that I created specifically for the film enabled them to discuss the need for a water-treatment plant that could be obtained through their unions. All things which ended up happening a few years later. I can't claim that the film was the unique cause of these developments, but it certainly precipitated these things.

On the other hand, a few months ago, I was asked by the people living in the "Pointe Courte" neighborhood and their children to organize a showing of the film. The twenty-five-year-olds who attended were the babies in the film. And the reactions I heard, however sympathetic, were nevertheless the kind of thing you'd hear if you were looking through a family photo album.

A Magical Not Political Power

They talked about themselves, about getting older, told stories about those times, but no one talked about the water treatment plant or the union. The images they saw had a magical and not a political power. The major theme of their discussions was the passage of time and how the image can bring back the past.

I think that for *Daguerréotypes* we'll see the same phenomenon. Maybe what I'm doing is called author-as-witness cinema . . . I believe that I do *auteur* cinema, but I don't really like the word *auteur* if it's given too limited a meaning. In any case I always insert myself in my films, not out of narcisssim but out of the desire to be honest in my approach.

Before leaving for the U.S. in '67, I wrote a fictional story based on my feelings about the putsch of the Greek colonels in April '67 (I'm half-Greek). I proposed this scenario to French Television, but they took two years to respond to my proposal. Their letter of acceptance arrived two weeks after my return to France. We shot the film. The principal young actresses were Myriam Boyer and France Dougnac. But in 1970 France sold a lot of Mirage planes to the colonels, so . . .

The Woman Filmmaker Scares People

The film was never broadcast on French TV. There were invitations from festivals, but the film was never sent. No one ever wrote to me about its status. When people asked, the TV people answered, "not finished, hasn't been shown, later." They paid me. But I didn't have the rights to the film (even though they never paid me for the scenario since the film wasn't broadcast). Now the film is completely out of date . . . naturally . . . because it was so topical at the time.

That was the only time I've been politically censured. For the past several years, my feminist opinions have caused a few difficulties in my work. Before, there were no problems. I didn't excite fear as a filmmaker. Now feminist filmmakers scare people.

I don't see my being a woman as a problem so much as a fact. A fact that has, for many years, become a way of thinking, though perhaps not always in terms as clear or filmable as I might wish.

It's difficult to find one's identity as woman: in one's social dealings, in one's private life and in one's body. This search for identity has a meaning for a filmmaker: I try to film as a woman.

Between *Cléo de 5 à 7* (1961) and *Réponse de femmes* (1975) there has certainly been a considerable evolution in my work.

I learned a lot in fourteen years—that's normal. And in terms of feminism (even if I was always a feminist, even if I considered myself a feminist in terms of my life choices, my ideas and especially in terms of what I refused to do), I learned a huge amount about myself and about feminism thanks to the women of the movement, the American radical feminists and theorists, and then the French women after May '68. But none of that has caused me to disavow *Cléo*. For *Cléo* expressed—and still expresses in my view—a young woman's search for identity and that is always the first step in claiming one's feminism.

From the Looked-At Object to the Looking Subject

Cléo started out basing her entire sense of self on others' looks; she was their cliché (and consequently their thing). Cléo is a woman-cliché, tall, beautiful, blond, curvaceous. So the entire dynamics of the film centers on the moment this woman refuses to be this cliché, on the moment when she no longer wants to be looked at, but wants instead to look at others. She tears off the attributes of her cliché (wig, feathery dress, etc.) and leaves behind those who define her in this way (her lover, her pianist, her assistant), walks out into the street dressed fairly normally, and starts looking. She looks at other people. From the looked-at subject she becomes the looking subject. And right away, when she encounters the soldier (whom she wouldn't have noticed before and considered a nuisance) she establishes a dialogue.

This is huge: the discovery of a male-female relationship that is not based merely on eroticism, a struggle for dominance, a social game, or a sexist comedy!

This is for me one of the ultimate goals of the feminist revolution. It's also why I maintain that there's no break between *Cléo* and *Réponse de femmes* even if there has been a huge evolution.

Réponse de femmes was initially a sketch written for a program on Antenne 2 called "W as in Woman." The question "What does it mean to be a woman?" was posed to some sociologists, lawyers, historians, etc., but also to three women-filmmakers, Coline Serreau, Nina Companeez, and me. We had seven minutes to answer. As for me, I answered, "We're always talking about the feminine condition and the role of women, but I want to talk about the woman's body, about our bodies."

So I demanded to be able to talk about the body and to be able to show it in our own way, as an affirmation and not as an exhibition. We went back and forth with the show's directors on whether we could show a close-up of the woman's sexual organs. Okay, but . . . ultimately the close-up was cut before the broadcast. But I was able to get permission to reconstitute and finish this cine-tract after the show and to distribute it commercially.

I would love to see *Réponse de femmes* in theaters shown before a

Belmondo or Delon film or any of these men's films where the female characters are always shown to lack any spine (when not actually whores or hangers-on).

We Must Take Back Desire!

For me, to be a woman is first of all to have the body of a woman. A body which isn't cut up into a bunch of more or less exciting pieces, a body which isn't limited to the so-called erogenous zones (as classified by men), a body of refined zones . . .

All you have to do is imagine a woman who likes to be caressed under her arms and who says so only to have her lover complain that he's not her physical therapist! Our women's voluptuousness, *our* desire must be reclaimed!

Along with many other privileges, for example, to choose whether to be pregnant or not. It's a privilege I will protect and want to see given its true value outside of any questions about family or nation. To be pregnant is a marvelous and terrifying thing. Progress in techniques of natural childbirth (*accouchement sans douleur*) have their limitations and risk making childbirth into something aseptic and almost a non-experience. They tell you, "Breathe! Push! Blow! It'll be easy! Tranquilize yourself, take some valium, sleep, take some Mogadon, etc. The last-month prescriptions are a total aberration! (I threw my prescriptions in the waste-basket. I wanted to live my life and sleep badly if it came to that. So what if I experienced fifteen to twenty sleepless nights while my baby was pounding my stomach from within, it's pretty amazing to say the least!).

Anyway, I've already made a little film where some of these socially incorrect impressions of pregnancy are portrayed. *L'Opéra Mouffe* is the notebook of a pregnant woman unafraid to show what pregnancy really looks like.

In 1958 I was already focused on the contradictions (my favorite subject) between the hope a pregnant woman feels and the hopeless spectacle that surrounds her in the Rue Mouffetard.

The Contradiction Between Cliches and Images

It seems to me that this dialectic, this ambiguity, this contradiction of the clichés of our mental life and the images of lived life is really the subject of all of my films. *Cléo from 5 to 7* is subjective time vs. objective time.

Le Bonheur is about the suave clichés about happiness vs. the cruel reality of happiness as a cruel structure that organizes everybody's activities. What really upset a lot of women and even certain feminists was that behind the soft colors and pretty formulas of happiness (according to the iconography of the media, the ad agencies, and the beautiful images we used to enjoy), we discover the very cruel idea that the woman/wife can so easily be replaced by another woman/wife as long as she performs the same functions as her predecessor: cook the meals, take care of the kids, water the plants, kiss her husband, and let herself be fucked, etc. . . .). So despite the pleasure of making this film, enjoying the picnics, the kids and the trees, the pleasure of showing all of this with a certain voluptuousness, I didn't lose sight of my subject.

Le Bonheur is not a psychological portrayal of an egotistical man torn between two blondes. Rather, it's an extremely detailed almost maniacal exposé in images and clichés of a certain kind of happiness. It focuses on gestures and the function of gestures with such insistence as to provoke the very explosion of their meaning.

It's a film that irritated lots of women, and I understand them. Just as I understand their discussions about sexual and professional discrimination in the cinema.

But I say: I didn't have any particular problems because I was a woman, I had no more or fewer problems than, say, Rozier, Rivette, Resnais, or Rohmer (just to name men whose names begin with R). But I refuse to get yelled at because I was an *alibi* assuaging the consciences of the men—even if it's a bit true. As long as I was "little Varda," "little Agnès," the exception in the generation called "the New Wave," I didn't get in anyone's way and I was even helped out, supported, and appreciated by my "colleagues" and companions.

Risking Your Man

But things have changed. They changed when a lot of women decided to make films and when I myself proposed other, more radically feminist subjects. I discovered that the former darling of State-funded films and liberal productions wasn't the darling anymore. We're not in 1954 any more when I made my first film. I learned that I needed to develop a new language of film, not just my style. Even if I was lucky enough to be "naturally" feminist (as measured both by my refusals and by the energetic choices I made to confront every constraint), even if I was lucky enough to be recognized for my work in film before the movements of the sixties,

I still belong to "the movement" in both my thinking and work. All that began for me in '67 in Hollywood where Denise, who taught me California slang, talked to me about the sociology course she was teaching: Woman and her Image. So I began reading theory: Sulamith Firestone, Kate Miller, and Germaine Greer.

I remember some of the more powerful ideas that were circulating at this time: the Americans said that a woman doesn't begin to be a feminist until she puts her relationship with her man at risk. Both the man and the life of the couple—however exciting, funny, fantastic, and rich it may be—has to be questioned.

There can be no feminist movement without putting one's relationship at risk.

Summing Up '66 to '72

When I came back to France in the summer of '69, women on the left were beginning to contest their dependence in the struggle and so "the women's movement" was born and was developing. I struggled in my own way. I went to demonstrations when they needed bodies. I shouted at Bobigny when they needed voices. I went to a few meetings but I didn't devote a whole lot of time to the movement. I have too much to do to be able to manage my double life as a professional and private person.

Since '66 I've written a bunch of scenarios (scenarii) that I wasn't able to produce: *Christmas Carole, Hélène in the Mirror, Viveca, the Wise Woman.*

Nothing was working. I spoke, I wrote against the clichés of our time. I also worked with several women and did research and read a lot in order to write *My Body Is Mine.*

The State Financing people refused to fund this project any more than my others and no contracts were forthcoming. That was in '72.

I was, however, able to make *Lions Love* in the U.S. in '69 and two shorts, *Uncle Yanco* and *Black Panthers*, and had also written a scenario, *Peace and Love.*

Back in France, I made *Nausicaa* for French Television in 1970 (it wasn't broadcast), which was politically censured. So I didn't accomplish much between '66 and '75.

I confess I was discouraged. I was also feeling the contradictions of my feminine condition.

Mathieu Demy, whom I'd waited so long for, was born in '72 and, despite my joy, I couldn't help resenting the brakes put on my work and my travels. I was unhappy that I couldn't do "my" films even if I could always bear a child.

One Sings, the Other Doesn't

The feminine condition of a filmmaker is concrete and immediate and that's what brought me to *Daguerréotypes*: this experience of making a film while attached to an umbilical cord, a stay-at-home-mom film . . . that we talked about.

And I began work on *One Sings, the Other Doesn't* (finally a scenario that received State Funding) and that I'm going to produce and shoot in the spring of '76.

It's the story of two fifteen-year-old girls: their lives and their ideas. They have to face this key problem: do they want to have children or not. They each fall in love and encounter the contradictions work/image, ideas/love, etc. They're two terrific characters, two very different girls—to begin with because one sings and the other doesn't. Yes, there will be songs in the film. It's a feminist musical.

The three male protagonists in the story are all marvelous. That didn't prevent one producer from writing me to inform me that he wouldn't invest one red cent in a movie in which men were made fools of. When I asked him what he meant, he said that the men in the film were okay, but they didn't have enough screen time. Now that's true. In the life of a woman, a man (even a man who's loved, however extraordinary he may be) takes up only 5.1 percent of a woman's time. She has her job, her children, other friends, her social life. All men's films have no problem with the inverse relationship: how many Westerns portray women more than 5 percent of the screen time? How many cops and robbers films have a silhouette of a woman cross a room from time to time? How many psychological dramas? Apparently men are not ready to have the tables turned on them. Yes, *One Sings, the Other Doesn't* has women as its principle subject. It also has no object! So we'll see some interesting stories but not necessarily HIS stories.

L'Une Chante, l'Autre Pas: Inteview with Agnès Varda

Jean Narboni, Serge Toubiana, and Dominique Villain / 1977

From *Cahiers du Cinéma*, May 1977. Reprinted by permission. Translated by T. Jefferson Kline.

Narboni, Toubiana, & Villain: We read the press-book of the film and thought it was really well done, the way it talks about the shooting. Now we'd like to ask some questions about before and after, by that we mean the composition of the scenario, for example . . .

Agnès Varda: With Claire Clouzot, I tried to put together a press-book of information and notes about the shooting and the team we worked with. Because for this film, the subject and the relationships between my audience and me are more essential than the writing. I've been tagged as an intellectual and that's a cross to bear . . . and false. This little book is not theoretical and in that it resembles the film. Has the same tone.

N, T, & V: We saw *Daguerréotypes* and *One Sings, the Other Doesn't* and really like your way of writing and talking . . .

AV: The two films share the fact that I do a commentary in each. *Daguerréotypes* was about my neighborhood, but not so much about "my best friends, my good neighbors" you know, a populist film about the past. As a matter of fact my neighborhood was pretty allergic to me for a long time; but as time went on things worked out and I became a kind of institution; I was there and got accepted simply because I didn't move away. I wanted to get some distance, and understand the terms of this distance both in terms of politics and in terms of options. And also to witness the kind of vague tenderness that exists between people who live on the same street. So I couldn't really use any one else to do the commentary— it would have been dishonest to speak from a "distanced" position and not from a "sympathetic" position as well. I am the one who is engaged in this connection, I'm the one who lives near "my" shopkeepers even if they represent for me a kind of "immobilism" and neutrality. It's the same issue in *L'Une Chante*: I am involved in the story of women and in women's laws and women's images . . . I wanted to be a part of it. At least my voice.

I probably wouldn't have wanted to provide commentary for a love story despite my own sentimentality.

As a filmmaker I wanted to add my voice to the imaginary dialogue between these two girls, to speak of their friendship since it concerns all women and our contention that we have the ability to get along. So a vocal trio seemed to me to be the right solution—musically as well. And then the voice-over of the narrator gives the story a romantic side except that the usual subject of such a story is a bit different since the subject here is not love with a capital L . . . but rather the question of woman's identity. The relationship of these two women to maternity (which they experience lovingly to be sure, but also experience as a refusal—or a desire—or an exaltation, etc.). Also their relation to their work and to women's solidarity. And then love, their loves, mixed in with all these other feelings. I didn't intend the voice-over to be the intrusion of an omnipresent author-narratrix . . . It's just me in the film, with them, accompanying them.

N, T, & V: There are two characters whom one might term strong personalities but the film isn't really a naturalist film.
AV: It's true. I tried in any case. Strong personalities with lots of character. "Real women," I would say. Not just to be realistic but instead so that the allegory would be believable. So that the somewhat theoretical design of the film won't be too visible. The trajectory of Suzanne (the design) is that of a victim who's spent fifteen years de-victimizing herself. As for Pomme, her element (color) is a matter of temperament: a rebellious nature who rattles her cage, is full of sounds and fury which take on melody and form. In the scenario the two women emerge into their femininity by living through the classical moments in the lives of women: love/work, maternity/friendship/involvement, etc.—each in her own way, while around them the history of French women from 1962 to 1972 is evolving. The subject of the film requires this double focus, moving between documentary and fiction.

As for the people, the women undergoing this evolution, I've been working on this for a long time: taking notes, observing the incremental changes, the words, whether from my own or from my friends' experiences, from couples who are close or not so close, from people I listen to, from the things I see and hear in all these places where I'm studying "the feminine condition."

I know all kinds of bits and pieces both of Suzanne and of Pomme, of relatives who experience authority the way they do, of artists who take on neither wives nor children, of foreigners in France, of women who laugh, cry, etc.—one sings, the other doesn't, it's me and me with others. But I also felt the constant need to take off from a too-naturalist approach: both through commentary and through images of space and water, through the dream-like quality of the film, through the songs which dreamily articulate feminist thoughts, through images of feelings (like those of the "woman-bubble") or images of children's books, like the little Zorro, the comedian, son of a son-father with his tiny bundle. I needed to mix these images with images of real women in the Toulon shelter who spoke with us and taught us their slang and ways of talking. *L'Une Chante, l'Autre Pas* is a dreamy documentary, a docu-dream.

As for the friendship of the girls that is foregrounded, there's nothing theoretical about it—it's vital. I've also had friends who've been very important in my life. And in this film I've told their story as if it were a novel (the genre "they met by accident, ran into each other again at the mayor's ball, then she got married while he was travelling. The separation was exactly what they needed. He sent her messages and when he returned" . . . etc.) Except that this is about friendship. They become friends briefly during the problems of 1962. It's nice and they seem to understand each other. Then the drama. They get separated. It always works: if people are separated after a brief but emotionally intense encounter, the feelings remain. Along with the desire to see each other again. When they see each other at Bobigny (in another very emotional situation, the demonstration), they're only together for ten minutes. Very frustrating. They want to talk to each other some more. It's like in Stendhal, their friendship begins to "crystallize" into feelings. And then the cards . . . with just a few words thrown in . . . so they tell each other the rest, in an imaginary dialog . . . etc. And the groundwork is laid for the joy of seeing each other again . . . etc.

N, T, & V: You say this is not about love, why?

AV: Friendship is a powerful connection that can produce jealousy, nostalgia, "exquisite moments together." When it's love, things go even further, when people get to the point of wanting to touch each other . . . In my story, this physical connection is unthinkable. I never imagined it.

I really wanted to revalorize friendship between women as a feeling that incorporates violence, tenderness, coherence, solidarity. The vagaries of crystallization and its sequellae. Something vital and alive. And then the associated joys of, for example, running into each other at a demonstration . . . at Bobigny.[1] They'd come to shout slogans, to be part of the crowd. And suddenly you feel that you're not just happy to see this person, you're very happy that they're *here*. Which means you're fighting for the same ideas and perhaps more prosaically, you're involved in the same way. Deeply moved, excited. Together.

And it's the same thing at the end of the film. One is now married, the other no longer. But they're feeling the same things: living true to themselves. There are images, the lake is meditation, flowing water when it stops, a pause—a sort of magic light that evokes the waking dream. There, on this day, at this moment of their lives, they can feel this total sense of friendship without a trace of ambiguity because they all live in an extended open family, a place where this friendship really has its place. In institutional families friendship between women has no place, even if it exists. Women tend to meet each other in the game of social acquaintances and sometimes become friends. But "deep" friendships only get lived out in the margins of women's lives.

N, T, & V: So from the beginning, this has been the history of women's friendships?

AV: But not as strong, no, in the beginning there were two or three women characters who met by chance . . . but their friendship wasn't so precise or so vital. It happened all by itself. I asked myself why such parallel lives as we see in Vera Chytilova's film, *Something Else*, why this kind of modesty, why this distance? They're different but I want to portray what they have in common.

N, T, & V: There was always the part that takes place in 1962?

AV: The first version of the scenario takes place entirely in 1962. It was called *Women and Children First*. I wrote it in almost one burst. It was very different from the film. It was sad . . . I had fallen into a trap. This first attempt had a side "report-on-what's-going-wrong-for-women-with-men-children-and-society." I told myself that I didn't want to fall into that particular trap, there's no reason for this. I've already made films and I'm not reduced to telling myself I have to express what's in my heart. A

lot of women making their first film need to make this sorrowful com-
plaint. These are often very beautiful films, these sorrowful complaints.
What's in our hearts . . . it's okay at first . . . I'm just as much interested in
what's in my heart as the next woman. A little spring that bubbles along
among some stones. This silly but tenacious optimism that is my form
of happiness. Or of perseverance. An urge to laugh . . . I set about writing other versions thinking about all these women I know, women of
the movement, women on the move towards living well. And thinking
more about myself. I worked a lot on all of these versions, on the words
of the songs, on the secondary characters, on the incomprehensible and
contradictory drives that we feel, on facing our marriages and facing our
children.

I tried to take account of all of this, with humor. And it isn't black humor. Especially when we talk of our own time, from '62 to '72 and to '76.

N, T, & V: There are films which seem entirely evident when we view
them and then afterwards we feel as though there was some sort of
short-circuiting, intended or not. When you say "between '62 and '72"
we immediately think of the events of '68. But in your film there's nothing about '68.

AV: There are a couple of reasons for that. First of all, I wasn't here in
'68. I was in Hollywood. I read everything about it and heard all the stories, observed the consequences, etc., but in this film which is about the
collective and personal lived experiences of women, I wouldn't have
known how to integrate '68 and wouldn't have dared to invent what it
was like living through '68. On the other hand, '68 meant a lot to the
two characters. Suzanne says, "I worked for a gynecologist, but he was
too manipulative and after '68 I dared tell him what I thought of him
and left to found a Center for Family Planning." As for Pomme, she talks
about meeting the *Orchidée* group in '68 and went busking with them,
and from her mini-starlet solo status went on to become a singing member of the group. This is a huge change inasmuch as she begins writing
songs both for herself and for the group. The other reason for having
"skipped" '68 is the subject of the film. If there is a struggle going on in
this film it's the struggle for contraception, for the liberation of women's
sexuality and women's bodies. In the history of this struggle, Bobigny is
more important than '68.

Of course Bobigny is very much a result of '68. And the style of demonstrations, the slogans, the tone, all that had evolved after '68. But
this struggle dates from way back. I would have felt as though I were

perverting my subject, of making it "chic" if I'd based it on, or connected it with '68. My film is a woman-filmmaker's look at the history of feminism in France from '62 to '76, focusing on two women who have different personalities, tastes, and social origins. It's a limited subject. And I kept myself strictly within the limitations of the subject. It was tough!

N, T, & V: What really works in this film is the differentiation of the various time periods: '62 the end of the Algerian war, and after '72 a period deeply marked by the spirit of May '68.

AV: '62 already seems like another time. We tried to capture not only the allure of the girls, their style and the very tense and dramatic feel of the time (it was the period of a kind of collective hysteria about cancer . . . among other things; remember *Cléo*?). And we women were discovering how terrible the laws were regarding women's rights. Problems of authority and the authorities. Already since '55 I'd been demonstrating against these laws.

After '72, after Bobigny (and other less spectacular demonstrations) things really changed. In the film I took great pains to portray the evolution of Family Planning centers, for example, and how the MLAC [Movement for the Liberation of Abortion and Contraception] worked in depth with thousands of women. When "consultations" gave way to collective debates.

For many women, feminism was experienced intensely yet subtly. There are all kinds of feminists. For those who love men it's perfectly obvious that there's a problem that is sometimes dialectical and sometimes contradictory and sometimes horrific. Between groups at work where they're listened to and their private lives where they're hardly or not at all listened to, there's a big gap.

A gap between a utopic ideal that they glimpse outside the home and something indefinable and sad that they discover at home in their non-dialogue with the man they love. So there are variations. For other women there's little gap or none at all. In *One Sings* the two girls chose to be coherent. That's why Pomme "abandons" her child—or rather "gives it up" if you prefer. It's pretty courageous of her. When you think about the social pressure that's brought to bear on cases like this! "Maternal instinct" is always brandished to make women feel guilty. One distributor told me, "The minute I see a woman capable of leaving a man or her child, that's it, I want nothing more to do with the film. It no longer interests me." And he looked at me, this *woman director*, with such hatred. The bastion of maternal love is sacrosanct, it's so degrading, it's terrible.

That's why I had to take on this subject: an all-out attack on maternity. Access to abortion freed of guilt. Giving up children for adoption. The horror of parental authority. Love of children, others' children as well. Contraception. New laws. Sex ed. Love of men. The desire to have a child. Paternal tenderness. Broken families. The beauty of pregnancy. The right to one's identity with or without children. It's no longer a film, it's an encyclopedia.

N, T, & V: So it's a militant film without a militant discourse.

AV: Militant? That's blah-blah. I put everything in the songs. A tactical decision. No one listens to "discourse." No one reads an encyclopedia. What's lived, sung, felt . . . I thought that this would make a stronger statement, more effective.

I cut the scene where Pomme and the Iranian are struggling over the child and she says, "in general it's the mother, etc." and he answers, "why?"

I didn't include the discussion. I showed how much their decision is about love, truth, pain, and nostalgia. I love "heroines" like that: when they attempt to live their various beliefs, morals, and femininity in a coherent way.

It's the bodying out of all of this that interests me. When the girl tells herself, "I can no longer have sex in a certain way . . . or with that guy," or "I'm going to have kids and if we can't discuss the upbringing of our kids in such and such a way then I've chosen the wrong father for my children." I loved the woman in *La Cecilia*.

N, T, & V: We find the idea of pregnancy in all of your films, right from the beginning.

AV: How could I not have fantasies or favorite images? Pregnancy is an idea, a mental image, a bizarre form, a superb scandal. It's a very rich theme. I loved being able to have children and make something of them. It's both extraordinary and very day-to-day. There's a lot to re-invent on this subject, in images and movements. But when I treat pregnancy in the cinema it's because of the contradictions that arise. When I was pregnant with Rosalie, I made *L'Opéra-Mouffe*. Whatever your brilliance, your pessimism, your thoughts about existence, the answer is always . . . Life. It's not a dialectical idea, it's a lived contradiction. Gramsci said, "We have to be pessimists in our thinking and optimists in our actions." Those aren't his exact words but that's the idea. That's also the idea of pregnancy. A vital and magnificent drive riddled with contradictions.

All my films are constructed out of such a contradiction-juxtaposition. *Cléo*: objective time/subjective time. *Le Bonheur*: sugar and poison. *Lions Love*: historical truth and lies (television)/collective mythomania and truth (Hollywood). *Nausicaa:* history/mythology, the Greeks after the coup and the Greek gods and there, as in *L'Une Chante*, there was a mix of dream and documentary.

I'm really trying to write for the cinema Lumière/ Meliès. To use this superb element of the cinema which is made up of real faces of people in real situations, not surprised or spied on, no, people who agreed to be filmed for a project they didn't create but which they choose to participate in. Like the peasants in Allio's *Pierre Rivière*. Or the workers in the toy factory where Suzanne is employed. And also to use the dreamlike imagery of the cinema all this bric-a-brac or this iconography, depending on the situation, of our mental world. And forms. And colors which attach themselves to words written in the early hours of the day we are shooting, but already determined one or two months earlier. The inner music when we're filming is the tempo.

N, T, & V: In the film the system of postcards is not just a matter of letters, but works like a musical variation, almost a fugue.

AV: Yes, its both novelistic and musical. Post cards punctuate the imaginary dialog. It's a postal movement, very light and colorful. It transforms old timey cute images into fresh emotions. And it works with the rest of the film's notes (notations) and responsive chants. The postcards are launched in '62 when Pomme buys one in Paris to convince her parents that she's gone to the Abbey of Senanques. Then there's the meal shared by Pomme and her parents. Suzanne experiences this later in Auvergne with her family. We discover the family of women in a lunchroom in Amsterdam, the other in the lunchroom of the factory. One has a dramatic abortion all alone, the other a more comfortable one in the company of friends. In their relationship to men there is also the counterpoint figure when Jerome refuses to accept his children whereas Darius completely accepts his, or when Pomme has her crisis in Iran and wants to flee her touristic marriage at the very moment Suzanne is tempted by a married man . . . These itineraries are not parallels but fugue-like, with unison cadences like the family of women or the final sunset.

Music seems to be the only way to convey what isn't evident and/or feelings that lie beyond the characters' decisions: a momentary sense of grace, an internal difficulty, the feeling of being inexplicably stuck, little failures, unexpectedly sweet times. It must be the indulgence that comes with age that allows us to feel better. Before I might have said, "oh we might as well . . ." And I would film that way too. Now it seems to me I'm more attuned to these silences between the images, the white noise between the sounds. My own complications have cleared up . . .

N, T, & V: In films like Demy's, there is a luminous aspect, like a post-card, but also a streak of shadow, of anguish . . . In *Cléo from 5 to 7* and in *Les Creatures* there's pregnancy and cancer—one might even say that pregnancy is a cancer that turned out well.

AV: Nice definition! But I don't associate anguish with shadows. The shadows have all kinds of colors in them. Anguish is not one of them. The shadow can even be colored violet, as in *Le Bonheur*, a complementary color to the yellow sunlight, the golden hues of summer.

I made a short film about my Uncle Yanco, this father of my dreams that I discovered very late on. He was fabulous and tender. He spoke eloquently of the colors in his paintings, and said, "between the desire and the painting there is a little bitterness, a passing shadow." I found that very touching. There's no light without shadow and the shadows are very beautiful. I seek out lighted shadows . . . a delicate shadow, even though I focused so much on a kind of purifying sunlight in *La Pointe Courte*. But to come back to your idea about pregnancy; the child conceived in shadows becomes light. We say in French that to bear a child is to "give daylight to" it. I say in the voice-over, "she gave daylight to her baby in the noonday sun . . ." At various moments I like to provide such little personal observations. And when I think about it, I had an experience of childbirth that was wonderful, at noon, and another at night that I didn't enjoy. I'm not a night person. But midday shadows are another thing altogether. As for cancer, it's a pregnancy gone bad (Orchidée sings my lyrics for the bubble-woman: a studio of molecules, a beautiful ovulation, a cell factory, a huge fish.) Cancer is a cell factory run by Ionesco gone crazy.

N, T, & V: What about Demy? He also has a "where do babies come from?" side. He's the only film director who's made a film about the urge to be a father.

AV: It was while we were expecting Mathieu. I was pregnant. He wasn't. Maybe he was jealous, but jealous in the nicest of ways. Or else it was his way of experiencing this with me. With humor. Jacques has a very private side. He's incredibly discrete. Maybe it was his discrete way to celebrate *the most important event* . . . etc. I've read Goddeck's *The Id* and liked it; it made me laugh. Because of "the look." It's a very visual concept. His reflections on men who suffer from pregnancy come from his observations of men who lead with their stomachs . . . What an eyeful!

When you come across an example of this, what a laugh! When I saw in Iran all these penis-minarets and breast-domes, this sexualization of architecture displayed in the most sacred places is really sublime. I wanted to use this look to express indirectly in pure form the delights of love. That's why Pomme falls in love with an Iranian. In order to be able to show their love and Pomme's humor like that. Blue breasts on an azure backdrop. In those stone penises from which emanated the muezzin's melodies.

That's not very serious of me. And oh so politically incorrect.

Nurith Aviv asked me a bunch of moralistic questions like, "Are you sure you want to keep the scenes of Iran? Maybe we should cancel the trip?" But I dug in my heels, eventually talking about Pomme's trip as the avatar . . . The whole thing about phallus=capital, the imperialism of sex, but I think they end up being fairly useless pirouettes. Iran is a disgusting country but I saw and filmed scenes of real sensual pleasure. At least it's a variation on cinematic scenes where the heroine relaxes her hand to indicate her excitement as he stares at her breasts.

Anyway, I made other kinds of trips in this film. Like the several collective abortion trips we made to Amsterdam that were really hard, even for me and even if we laughed a lot . . . Certain of the women who were there talked with me and we exchanged addresses. And afterwards I went to see them in France. It was very moving to meet up in another context with, for example, a young woman who was the fifth of twelve children and who, already at twenty-two had two children of her own. She and the other women talked about their abortions, whether they suffered or not, shared confidential stuff with each other and all, then all of a sudden you see her at home, having dinner with her mother, with the TV going strong, fourteen people in the kitchen, and her husband arriving home on his bike and joining the clan . . . What a trip!

I'd still like to make lots of other films, not about problems but constructed out of the lives of people who experience these problems. And then the ideas, proposals, openings, active utopias . . .

It's a bit because of this that since the release of *L'Une Chante* I can't talk about the cinema without talking about the people whose lives made up this film or about its origins or about the team of people I worked with. I could go on and on about the beautiful photography of Charlie Van Damme, about the 40 lens and the nearly always precise space he created around the characters of the film in which we avoided close-ups and single shots.

I could also talk about the discussions I had with Jöelle van Effenterre during the editing, discussions about connections between scenes, musical overlays, a thousand thoughts on how to get just the right tone. And cuts.

I seem to remember that one of the interviews I did for *Cahiers* ended with "It's in filming that we become film directors." I still think that. Except that now, because of the evolution between language and culture I'd say, "It's in film that I've become a film directrice."

Note

1. In 1972 at the Bobigny trial, a working-class mother, three of her colleagues, and her underage daughter, a rape victim, were tried for procuring the daughter's abortion. Their trial became the focus of a massive protest that eventually saw the overturning of the law banning abortions in France.

Agnès Varda

Gerald Peary / 1977

From the *Real Paper* (Boston), October 15, 1977. Reprinted by permission.

Agnès Varda, whose thrilling *One Sings, the Other Doesn't* opens the 1977 New York Film Festival, is as pesky as she is petite: compulsively sharp-tongued, opinionated, borderline rude. Shoes kicked off and bare feet slung up on her New York hotel couch, this five-foot Left Bank lily in a purple peasant dress readies for a quarrel. Varda can't fathom that this film critic has seen little of the work of her favorite woman director, Hungary's Marta Meszaros. "She has already done six films and three of those are great. It is strange therefore for you to be talking as a 'specialist.'" And she ridicules the two movies she's seen of my favorite, Dorothy Arzner. "I hated them. I thought she was a man! I'm not interested in seeing a film just made by a woman—not unless she is looking for new images."

Varda reacts heatedly to my rather impolitic, obvious question, about her *Le Bonheur* (1965). "Let's not go back to that," she bristles. "That was more than ten years ago." For the thousandth time, someone has asked Varda how she could make a film showing a wife drowning herself in a lake so that her husband can hang out freely with his mistress.

"Some people understood *Le Bonheur*," she replies disdainfully. "Women have become upset and asked, 'How could you replace a woman with another woman?' That's what life is about. A man is replaced by another man in war. A woman is replaced by another woman in life." Another point of contention: Varda cannot tolerate puritanical responses to *Le Bonheur*'s conclusion, where the husband blissfully marries the mistress. "If his wife committed suicide, and he wants to feel good with another woman, he has the right! Do you think he should cry for twenty years?"

One Sings, the Other Doesn't catapults Varda back into the front-line of overtly feminist directors. But she can't forgive those who have looked elsewhere in recent years, like to Ingmar Bergman. "He's spent ten years in clinics, you know. Between each film, Bergman lies down like a corpse—and then he makes a beautiful picture in which the woman is filled with anxiety." Robert Bresson too. "Bresson is a genius, but his women have to carry all that shit."

Varda was one of the original, acclaimed French New Wave directors; her 1962 *Cléo from 5 to 7* was discussed in company with Truffaut, Godard, Resnais. However, Varda's movies in recent years have played to smaller and smaller audiences in the USA, and to diminished critical interest.

Les Créatures (1966), her star package of Catherine Deneuve and Michel Piccoli, barely had a theatrical run. *Lions Love* (1969), an LA-set underground movie, managed a tiny cult reputation. It's Varda's most "far-out," Warholian reverie on sexual relationships: the Garbo-like Viva writhing in bed between the two male stars of *Hair*. As for *Daguerreotypes* (1975): Varda's documentary appreciation for Rue Daguerre, the Paris street where she resides, has yet to pick up an American distributor.

Varda is adamant that she's been the same all along, that *One Sings* departs from earlier films more in method than in ideology; it's the latest incarnation of her struggles, since age eighteen, with women's issues. She is a long-time abortion activist in France. (The most famous Gallic feminist demonstration—the trial at Bobigny in which the rapist of a young girl denounced his victim for having an abortion—is re-created in *One Sings*.) Women's films? "Look, I've done them since 1958," Varda lectures me. "*L'Opera Mouffe* was a short film about the contradictions of pregnancy. I was pregnant at the time, told I should feel good, like a bird. But I looked around on the street where I filmed, and I saw people expecting babies who were poor, sick, and full of despair."

Varda also talks of *Cléo*, her real-time drama about a beautiful singer who thinks she has cancer. "It's about a passive woman who becomes an active woman. She takes off her wig and begins to look at people. Sometimes a woman needs a shock as big as death." And, yes, the artist's prerogative is to contradict themself. Suddenly, it's Varda who takes to task the wife in *Le Bonheur* for standing by while her husband adopts a lover. "That woman wants to be an angel. Nobody is an angel. She should have said to him, 'Go to hell! I want to be alone with you.'"

Varda evolved her theories about feminist art while making nonfeminist leftist films. For *Salut les Cubains!* (1963), she took six thousand photo stills in Cuba and animated them into a work that "makes a point about socialism and cha-cha-cha, that you don't have to be heavy when you stand for socialism, or feminism either. Feminism can be fun." *Far from Vietnam* (1967) confirmed Varda's theory by negative example. Varda and various French director-intellectuals (Godard, Chris Marker, Jacques Demy, etc.) combined for a heavy-handed, didactic anti-war tome "which didn't help anyone. We weren't simple enough. We were on a cultural artistic intellectual chic Left Bank trip. Do you think we managed to get peasants and workers to think about Vietnam, 'Wow, that's just like the Algerian war'?"

Most important for her feminist education was Varda's journey to Oakland, California, to cover the Huey Newton trial for her *Black Panthers: A Report* (1968). "The Black Panthers were the first to say, 'We want to make the rules, the theory.' And that's what made me aware of the woman situation. A lot of good men had been thinking for us. Marx did. Engels did. These people did beautifully. Yet maybe we need to get through Marx, for Marx doesn't give the keys and answers for us women." If women must independently find their images, what of feminist-friendly men? "If men want to join, leave the door open. They can listen," Varda says.

By this time, deep in our interview, animosity has seemed to slip away. Varda volunteers her strategy for *One Sings*. "Make it clear, simple, not too complicated. If I put myself on the screen—very natural and feminist—maybe I'd get ten people in the audience. Instead, I put two nice young females on the screen, and not too much of my own leftist conscience. By not being too radical but truly feminist, my film has been seen by 350,000 people in France. It's better if they all got half the message than to have five thousand people seeing a courageous 16mm film."

I note: "You say you aren't so radical, but your films are much more radical than many by people who say they are radical." Varda shrugs, but she looks complimented. And the interview is over.

One Sings, the Other Doesn't:
An Interview with Agnès Varda

Ruth McCormick / 1978

From *Cineaste* 3, no. 3 (1978). Reprinted by permission.

"I feel bad that there is not more understanding in the women's movement. As feminists, we have to be tolerant, with each other and even with men." —Agnès Varda

Agnès Varda's name has always been associated with both the women's struggle and politics. In her twenty years as a film director, she has dealt with subjects as diverse as a pretty young woman who discovers her strength and humanity only after learning she may be dying (*Cléo from 5 to 7*, 1961), the Cuban Revolution (*Salut, les Cubains*, 1963), the possibility that one person's happiness may necessarily cause another's suffering (*Le Bonheur*, 1965), the creative process (*Les Créatures*, 1966), U.S. imperialism in Vietnam (*Far from Vietnam*, 1967), the black struggle in this country (*Black Panthers*, 1968), the culture industry, the youth movement, and the assassination of Robert Kennedy (*Lions Love*, 1969), the Greek struggle against the Junta (*Nausicaa*, 1970), the day-to-day lives of seemingly ordinary people on one street (*Daguerréotypes*, 1975), and the views different women hold about work, love, marriage, and the family (*Women's Answers*, 1975).

Throughout the work of this militant and dynamic director runs a strain of humanism and insistent optimism that perhaps comes out most fully in her latest film, *One Sings, the Other Doesn't*. Cheered by some feminists for its warmth and positive depiction of the friendship of two very different women over a fifteen-year period, and attacked by others for its avoidance of militant politics, the film has been very successful in France, and promises to gain a wide and friendly audience in the U.S. Ms. Varda was interviewed by *Cineaste* editor, Ruth McCormick, while the director was in New York recently for the opening of her film at the New York Film Festival.

Ruth McCormick: Many feminists, especially radical feminists, have found fault with *One Sings, the Other Doesn't*. They say your characters are too male-related, that you're too kind to the men. Others think the film is too positive, not critical enough, too much like a fairy tale.

Agnès Varda: Perhaps people want too much. But I understand what you're saying. We have the same radical feminists in France who say to me, "You don't hate men enough!" Of course, we need the radicals, they are important, but I don't agree that a feminist film must put men down, or show that it's because of *them* that we're down-trodden It's the institutions that are the problem. Even if the institutions in society are made by men, the men are often merely carrying on the ideology they've been taught down through the centuries of civilization when they were the leaders.

RM: Right! And men have very often been taught by their own mothers and female teachers that this is how it should be.

AV: I feel bad that there is not more understanding in the women's movement. As feminists, we have to be tolerant, with each other and even with men. I think our movement needs different kinds of women; there shouldn't just be one line, one way. That would be again what we have been settling for all along.

RM: Would I be correct in saying that you've tried to make a popular women's film, one that all women could relate to, not just conscious feminists?

AV: Yes. In politics, or as feminists, there are different ways in which we can work. If you want to make a feminist film, you can work outside the system, in the underground, and you can make a very radical statement, but even if your message is very good, you will reach perhaps five thousand people. You will never reach the mass of women.

RM: I'm thinking of people like Marguerite Duras and Chantal Akermann, and you're probably right. Have you done well with *One Sings*?

AV: By working in the system, in normal cinema distribution, you are no longer underground. In France, our film has already been seen by 350,000 people, and the rights have already been sold in many other countries, so I would say that if the meaning of the film and its feminist point of view is even half or two-thirds as strong as that of a more radical film, at least we've gotten a lot of people *thinking*, and not in the wrong direction. I don't believe we have compromised to get a larger audience or more money, because I could have made an easier film, with big stars. I wanted to make an honest film, and even to get this film distributed I've had to fight a lot!

RM: I can imagine that distributors would have been a little afraid of *One Sings*. After all, it's not exactly a formula film.
AV: I fought because I wanted thousands and thousands of people to be able, for once, to see a film about the world of women. Women in the sun, as Molly Haskell says. I like that! That's where women should be—not always off in the shadows. Pomme and Suzanne are not cop-out women, they're not stupid! Perhaps they're not radical, they don't burn their bras, they are not political in the sense that they don't want to break up the world around them just because of their own feelings. As I said, there are many kinds of women, and we should speak to all of them. Some women don't want to throw their men out. Some women still want children and a home.

RM: Perhaps most still do!
AV: And it's very important not to put those women down or say, "You're stupid, get out of your kitchens, get rid of all that!" Do we really want an all-women society? If there are women who feel that they have to live away from men to find their identity for a period, even for their whole lives, who may in fact be lesbians, that's fine with me. I'm tolerant with them and they should be tolerant of me. I know these women, I've worked with them, I respect them, but I do not feel obliged to follow their rules. Each woman should be able to find her own way. If we just go into a new system of rules, like Communism or Leninism, then we are just following again the same rules, as we have been doing for centuries.

RM: The point of a revolutionary society would be to really break away from all the old rules and regulations, then?
AV: Yes. That's my first statement. And I don't want anybody to take my film, or my position, and pit me against other women and say, "At last we've found a nice feminist who still loves us and thinks the system's OK."

RM: The opposition likes to divide and conquer. They'll always try to use any artist who doesn't use the official rhetoric against the women's movement, the radical movement or whatever.

AV: I absolutely refuse to allow myself to be used that way. It's very important to set it straight that I'm not using the movement against itself. That would be disgusting. I hope I'm very clear.

RM: How did you get the idea for the film?

AV: Now, my film is a feminist film, but it's a *film*. I'm dealing with images, images of women, and I conceive of the film as a painting with a background and foreground. In the foreground are the figures of the two women, while the background is a very special and specific documentary about the laws and institutions regarding women's rights in France between 1962 and 1976. In 1962, as you know, abortion was very difficult, it was illegal, though if you had money you could go to Switzerland. Otherwise it was very dangerous. A man could not recognize a child if he and the mother were not married. After a lot of struggles, in which I worked—the abortion manifesto, demonstrations, trials—finally in 1972, a girl was acquitted of criminal charges after having an abortion and now some laws have been changed. Abortion is now possible, the pill is available, and so forth.

RM: In that sense, it's a historical film.

AV: It's our specific French situation, where even planned parenthood groups have fought the opposition of the Catholic Church and become very open. I show this in the film. I wanted to show that if some people begin to say, "If you don't like it, change it!" and women begin to talk and fight together, things can change. The story of the evolution of our laws and institutions is the background of the film. In the foreground are these two women. Again, I didn't want to be rhetorical. I thought that two figures with different temperaments, different backgrounds, would help to show that there are different ways of getting yourself together, of finding your own identity. My concern is with tolerance, so if radical women don't like the film, fine, but please don't take it the wrong way! They have a right to their way, too.

RM: You place a great deal of emphasis on motherhood, and this may bother some feminists. Pomme, the character with whom the radical feminists would most likely identify, insists on having a baby for herself when she decides to leave Darius. It's very civilized of her to let him have the child they already have, but why is a baby so important to her? There are women who have been made to feel guilty and selfish if they don't want children. Of course, you do try to answer that question in the film, when a woman watching the group's pregnancy skit objects that they seem to be insisting that women have to be the Blessed Virgin.

AV: That's why I put that sequence in. The woman is right, and they tell her so, that she shouldn't feel guilty, but if you do have kids, or you want them, let's enjoy it!

RM: In other words, women should feel good about their bodies when they're pregnant. It's not being fat, or ugly, or sick. You're trying to say that if you want a child, pregnancy is a beautiful thing in itself. A pregnant woman shouldn't have to be the Blessed Virgin.

AV: Right! If I enjoy pregnancy as a sexual event it's my life, my body! Many anti-feminist women don't. If you choose to have children, pregnancy is a natural event, you should enjoy it. I'm not recommending the way the Church tells me to enjoy it, as a duty, or to strengthen the state, or the family. It's never talked about, but most women actually enjoy sex more when they're pregnant, for reasons we don't really understand. I suppose that has to do with many things. But should I deny it? Would that make me a better feminist? A woman should let herself feel good being fat and full of baby, that's her privilege. A model figure isn't everything, and if that's what you want, you can go back to it later.

Let's not push women toward motherhood, let's re-invent it! But let's fight for abortion and good contraception so that we have the choice. That's most important. That's where women should get together. In the film, when Pomme goes to Amsterdam for her abortion, with so many different kinds of women I've tried to picture this.

RM: Simone de Beauvoir tells us in her autobiography that there was a point where she decided deliberately not to have children, that it would be too great a commitment to exist with her other commitments. I and quite a few other women I know appreciate this point of view. It is not that we don't love children, but that perhaps, since society is set up the way it is, without a great deal of money motherhood is such a commitment, especially without an understanding man, that it is impossible to be a good mother and an active, creative person outside the home at the same time.

AV: As Simone says, "You are not born a woman, you become a woman."

We are not slaves of our biology any more. We've fought for that. Does anyone ask if a man is a real man if he doesn't have children? Einstein didn't have children. Lenin. Maurice Chevalier. We don't question their manhood. The same should be true of women. We are all human beings.

RM: The other thing people object to in your film, women and men both, is that you make the two women's success in finding themselves, making something of their lives, a bit too easy. How does an oppressed woman like Suzanne become an independent feminist organizer? Pomme, who's a little better off, but not rich, seems to have no trouble supporting herself as a feminist singer. Perhaps you make women's lives and problems look simpler than they actually are.

AV: Ninety-nine percent of the films you see are so much *against* women, that when women come to me a say, "you don't give them hell," I have to say, "Look, for once you have a film where women are shown without guilt, without shame, without dependency, without stupidity, fighting against laws and institutions, getting value and putting value into women's ventures. Don't you think you are already getting quite a lot?"

RM: Certainly.

AV: Then why come to me and say, "What about women's unemployment? What about lesbians? What about women not looking good? What about old age?" A film is not a basket to put everything into. It is a piece of entertainment, of communication, and if you want communication with many men and women, you have to find a fluid way to communicate. I have tried to show women moving from the shadow into the light.

RM: The film certainly is full of light.

AV: I tried to show that. The film goes from dark, contrast, shadows, black and white images in the photos of women in the gallery, through fluidity to clarity. The last sequence is light, sunny, but is not a happy ending.

RM: Would you call it an ambiguous ending?

AV: Not at all! It's just that everyone is allowed to have a little peace for two weeks near a lake with friends. It doesn't mean that the struggle is over, that they won't get back to the family planning, the show, the demonstrations, their roles, their hopes. This is an aesthetic problem. It's like in music, like in a fugue, with its theme and countertheme, ending in a coda—one sings, the other doesn't—you get the feeling that it's not really finished, but you are allowed a certain peaceful feeling.

I don't agree when they say I've made a stupid, happy ending. Pomme is alone, without a husband. She has to support her daughter. Two of the other singers are alone, one has a man. Suzanne has a man now, but she still has her responsibilities. Her daughter is just beginning to be a woman. This is not stupid happiness, the struggle goes on! As an artist, whatever that means, I deal with images, I deal with words, I deal with dreams. If I'm utopian, that's my way! I don't agree that you should be pessimistic, or say that things are going badly. Let's fight, but let's dream, too. We need that! I think women need to know that life can be better. It could be good!.

RM: Well, there hasn't been a revolution, but I'd agree that even if we don't have a just society, things are better for women, for blacks, for the Third World even, than they were in 1962.
AV: Yes, of course, you are old enough to see that. Now I've been fighting for twenty-five years! Some of the kids speaking up now weren't even born when I began fighting for contraception. There were only a few of us, and everyone was against it—the right-wing, the Church, even the left-wing was against it, because they needed people to have children to vote for the left! We were left-wing women, but we had to fight the Communist Party which didn't want their deputy to vote for contraception!

RM: I guess they were catering to the Catholic vote, too. Not wanting to turn anyone off.
AV: At that time, I still fought as a strictly political activist. Later, I began to see that I should fight in the cultural field. Reading Simone de Beauvoir and others, talking to women, I began to understand. They would give you literary masterpieces like Henry Miller, but nobody ever said at that time how he put women down, treated them like doormats. What literary critic ever brought that up? Look at Orson Welles, whom we all love as a filmmaker, who was such a misogynist! Twenty years ago, who talked about that? They said, "What beautiful films!" but who ever noticed how badly he treated his women characters?

RM: You began making films about women very early. I'm thinking of *Cléo from 5 to 7*. There have been a number of films about men facing death, but evidently a woman's life is so unimportant that aside from

Dark Victory and *No Sad Songs for Me*, which in any case defined the dying women as chiefly worried about the men they loved, there have been no films about a woman having to re-assess her life.

AV: Yes, because of her fear of death, Cléo discovers that she has been a doll, an object, so she gets out of her fancy clothes, takes off her wig, puts on a plain dress, and goes out to look at people. She no longer cares about being looked at, she wants to relate to people, to become a person. That was in 1961, when no one was thinking about the roots of a woman's feelings. In 1958, when I was pregnant, I made a short called *L'Opera Mouffe*, about a woman's feelings during pregnancy. It's a very strong film.

RM: There have been a few good films by men about women, but I think women have to re-think how we want to talk about ourselves.

AV: Yes. I've been around, and I hear these feminist men say, "Not bad for a woman." This is condescension, paternalism, like "Not bad for a black man." We, blacks and women, have only recently been decolonized, and we must find our own way. We have to decide what kinds of images we like about ourselves. We should not be ready to go along with the anxiety of so many male artists who try to put their problems on women's backs, like Modigliani, Giacometti, or especially Bergman.

RM: I was just thinking of him.

AV: And, of course, we love him. But he puts his anxiety, as a man, on our backs. A man is entitled to bring his fear, his guilt, his suffering to his art, but as a woman artist, I wouldn't want to project my anxiety onto men. We must make a break, create our own images. I don't want to be competitive. I don't want the power of a man! I don't even feel sorry I don't make more money. I make quite enough! More than people who have to work in a factory, and unlike them, I like what I do. I find it disgusting that some directors get so much money, and actors even more.

RM: The best-known actors and directors are all multi-millionaires! But of course, you know, most of them are more businessmen than they are artists.

AV: Let them be, it's their game. I'm not in the game. The rules of the game have been made by people I don't trust. It's the game of competition, that's what women must understand. I'm not playing any kind of men's game, like I'm stronger than you, brighter than you, richer than you. I don't care. I'm strong. I'm bright in my way. I have a different scale of values, so if the critics like my film, perhaps they've found something in the film. Perhaps something new.

RM: What about Darius, Pomme's husband? He seems fine, and we understand why she loves him while they're in Europe, but, when they're in Iran, he reverts to being a real Moslem patriarch. And making him Iranian would have seemed to make it opportune to comment on the political situation there, which you don't really do.
AV: When Darius is in France, away from home, he has an open mind.

RM: He even picks a feminist to fall in love with!
AV: Yes, and he goes to demonstrations, supports the women, but when he gets back to the Iranian family, he has to play the role. Look, I don't like the character that much, but this is his environment, and there is almost no way to get out of it in such a country. I was trying to show how people change according to where they are and with whom they are. I mean, at first Pomme was in the trap, the blackmail of love, and love can be even more beautiful in a beautiful setting, like the Arabian Nights. Think of all the sexual imagery in the architecture, like breasts and phalluses, and you begin to feel what Pomme was feeling.

RM: When she first gets to Iran, it's unreal, dreamlike. Later, when she begins to wake up, we see the veiled women, the poverty.
AV: It is what you call a trip. When you come down it's no longer a trip. Pomme has been out of her world, in love. But her world is not cooking ratatouille for an Iranian man! Pomme had to get out of that mess! At that point, I first wanted to make it more political, make the point that she's also leaving because Iran is a disgusting place, a police state. But let's face it, in almost every country it's disgusting. You can't go to Chile, to Lebanon. For years you couldn't go to Spain or Portugal. I am half Greek, and for twenty years I wouldn't go there. I found that the image of the hidden veiled women made sense for me because as Pomme becomes more and more enlightened sexually, she finds herself surrounded by real women who have no sexual freedom at all. So I make the point that there is something twisted in the contrast between her speaking about her body and her freedom, and these unfree women who are forced to deny their bodies.

This is a political point. I didn't feel I needed to make a polemic against the police state in Iran. Feminism is political insofar as it is dealing with institutions and power, and showing how women don't need these institutions, don't want that kind of power. The spirit of the family, love and communication, is not bad—I enjoy living with a man and children, having dinner together, laughing together, protecting one another—but it is the *institution* of marriage, of the family, which the state uses to keep us down. The women sing a song in the film which quotes Engels, that in the familly, the man is the bourgeois and the woman the proletariat. That's true, and we have to fight it.

RM: Orchid, the singing group in the film—do they really go around to small towns singing about Engels and women's liberation?
AV: Yes. I did the lyrics to the songs in the film, but their repertory is very good, a way of singing that has nothing to do with classical love songs. Phillips is putting out the original soundtrack of the film, and the songs are more political because they're not broken up as they are in the film.

RM: Are they well-received out in the country? Was your film? I guess that in France the small towns are strongholds of conservatism.
AV: Yes, they make friends and do well. And my film has done very well in France, in the small towns where they usually only get classical American films and big star vehicles. It's done very well in the countryside. But even there, I found a radical woman in the audience who told me, "I don't like your film because you deal too much with men," and a man who said, "I don't like your film because you don't pay enough attention to men." So it happens. Both sides. The men feel betrayed because even though they're not all that bad in the film, we really don't see that much of them. But that's the story. In a woman's life, in the long run, men are not *that* important!

Agnès Varda

Philippe Carcasonne and Jacques Fieschi / 1981

From *Cinématographe*, March–April 1981. Reprinted by permission. Translated by T. Jefferson Kline.

Far from Beverly Hills, far from all the bustle of Hollywood, Agnès Varda has moved into a house in Venice, a beach town near Los Angeles, formerly built on a series of canals. "The ocean is nowhere," says the film director, who's fascinated by the popular art of a neglected community: the Chicanos.

Carcasonne & Fieschi: Why did you decide to settle here?
Agnès Varda: Oh I haven't really "settled" here . . . I'm here but I don't feel as though I've moved in. I just sort of ended up here a bit by chance, to do a project (which I wrote) for ENI (a French Integrated Energy company). I was asked to develop a scenario based on a news item from Los Angeles. I wrote it in '79 and I think that we're supposed to shoot it this year unless they cancel. Before that I used to come pretty often, like all French directors, to present my films, *Cléo, Le Bonheur* . . . In '67 Jacques Demy absolutely wanted to make a film in Hollywood (it's true that things were pretty tough in France in '67). So that's how we got here. He shot *Model Shop* and I just sort of hung out and began writing a bit. At first I wasn't so excited to be here. But then I made a short film on a Greek uncle of mine who lived near San Francisco (*Uncle Yanco*); and after that, a documentary on the Black Panthers . . . The film was supposed to be broadcast on TV on a French show called *Five Headlines* but at the last minute it was censored: it was October '68 and we weren't supposed to "reawaken the students' anger." Meanwhile, I had written a scenario for Columbia, *Peace and Love.* They didn't allow me to do a final cut and I got really angry, but I ended up doing *Lions Love*, which I really enjoyed. So here I am ten years later doing the project I mentioned, *Maria and the Naked Man*, based on a news item that I found very important: a guy

went out naked one morning and a cop shot him, alone and without witnesses. It was difficult to invoke any kind of legitimate defense. I got to meet the woman who lived with him and one thing led to another and I wrote the scenario about her and the consequences of this near-assassination. And in 1980 I made a documentary on the murals here. It's really a portrait of Los Angeles, especially in what these paintings reveal about the problems of the Mexicans, whom the media absolutely never mention. The Black question has been pretty much resolved, but not the Chicanos' situation. The Black mayor, Tom Bradley, has only been in East Los Angeles Chicano neighborhoods once. They don't even have representation; an Irishman is the congressman for East L.A.; and the Mexicans from Mexico detest them. So they express all that in their murals with lots of violence and lots of fantasy as well. My film is called *Mur Murs*; you know the phrase (Victor Hugo's I think) "The wall enmuring Paris is making Paris murmur." That's the situation here, right?

C&F: So how did you come across these murals?

AV: I do a lot of walking. I like being on the move. I know a lot of French people here who know only four restaurants, ten houses, and who go from party to party. But Los Angeles is an incredibly varied city; I don't think there's a more varied city anywhere. There are entire neighborhoods that even Americans don't know, down there, after the downtown area, the entire east part of town. People are afraid: "What?! You go there *alone*!" as if I was going to the land of the Zulus. But you know Venice, where I live, is more dangerous than East L.A. . . . Los Angeles is without a doubt an edgy city: on the edge of despair and on the cutting edge of a lot of research too. Research in many different disciplines, in science, in cinema, in drugs . . . it's a town of excess. There are enormous numbers of people who go West, who get here and realize that they can't go any farther; it's sort of the end of the world for America. I chose Venice because of the ocean; the ocean is nowhere, you're not forced to adapt (at least you've got that advantage on the enemy . . .) and I feel very stable here. And I can't say that I'm suffering from not being in France because I'm not really in America either. I'm out here on a beach. I really like not feeling established geographically, economically, or socially.

C&F: What kind of connections do you have with the film world in Hollywood?

AV: I know everyone, but I practically don't see anyone. I really don't like it that aside from a few directors (Casavetes, Cimino, despite his politics)

I find the American cinema a pretty sorry affair. I mention Cimino be-cause, leaving aside the question of his enormous talent, he's made a film that really expresses how America thinks, much more so than any of the "radical-chic leftie films" that you see here; in this sense *Deer Hunter* is infinitely more honest than *Coming Home*. It seems to me particularly hypocritical for Americans to be criticizing the imperialist politics of Cimino. And then too, I find it interesting to what extent this film shows how the silent majority, the stupid rightwing majority was affected and even a bit destroyed by the Vietnam War. This touches me much more deeply than Coppola's lyricism. But I'm not quite sure why I'm talking about all that since to tell the truth I've never really been attracted to Hollywood films. Jacques Demy always dreamed of making a film here (which is why we're here) since he adored the American cinema. Me, I'm like everyone else; I like a good musical comedy, and I enjoy the Holly-wood blockbusters as well. But I can't really say I take the bait. I'm here but I could be anywhere else. But at the same time there's something that fascinates me here. I walk around going from one place to another. Sometimes I go to fund-raising parties—those cocktails where they col-lect money for films. "I'll give two thousand dollars . . ." "and I'll give five thousand dollars . . ." There are all these representatives from the studios who are playing at being benefactors; that's how Barbara Kopple ended up partially funding *Harlan County USA* (which is a beautiful film by the way). You have to see how all these incredibly rich and powerful people throw crumbs at the left-wing cinema while munching on petites-fours in a mansion in Beverly Hills. They get up and set high-stakes bids: "Hey, if you can manage five thousand dollars, I'll match it!" They all manage to clear their conscience, it's a beautiful thing to watch. But Hollywood cinema remains profoundly conservative, profoundly stupid, and often painful. About one out of every ten films is okay, meaning a little bit bet-ter than the average.

C&F: What do people think of you and your work?
AV: As someone who makes little European films which are "so charm-ing, so true, and so inexpensive." In any case they are unable to distin-guish between Lelouche's *Cousin Cousine* and me. Godard's *A Man and a Woman*, Demy's *The Umbrellas of Cherbourg*, Malle's *Murmurs of the Heart*, and my film *Le Bonheur* are all the same for them—charming little films. They really like me though; I know some people in the establishment who are mad about *Le Bonheur*, who organize dinners in my honor and

want to introduce me to all their friends. But when you get right down to it, the French really don't matter: the fascination with the New Wave is ancient history. There's Malle who won't quit and who has made it here to some extent, but he's the only one. At the moment when it comes to "cultural film" the Germans seem to have the wind in their sails.

C&F: Is it your sense that the Americans' lack of interest in foreign culture is increasing?

AV: It's always been the same. They look on us like some little underdeveloped countries. What's new is that the French who have tried to work here have become particularly unpopular in the last few years. No one seems able to get a foot in the door. *Model Shop* was a complete flop here despite the fact that Jacques didn't lack for financial backing. His real American film, though, more engaging than any of the American musicals in my opinion, was *Les Demoiselles de Rochefort*. We suffer from an ongoing misunderstanding: they can't imagine how anyone could see their country the way Demy does in *Model Shop* from a critical perspective. When Americans have emotional problems they go right to a psychoanalyst. They love under the imperative of efficiency: results are everything. If you're shooting a scene costing ten thousand dollars it has to look like it was made for twelve thousand dollars. People who don't work that way simply don't count; no one listens to them. The underground cinema is completely underground. Between Hollywood and experimental film there is a kind of dead zone. Well, now that I've said all that, I have to admit I like it. Hollywood lets me get some rest from the heavy, pontificating culture of good taste in Paris. I feel revived here. In France we don't have much of a choice either: we have to line up for small government handouts or for money from producers. You either have to present something eminently highbrow or else *My Ass Is on the Potty*. Here, I feel very relaxed being on the margins if I do say so. I have my little guaranteed bit of prestige when I go into the city and I've been allowed to make two films with no restrictions of any kind, with practically no money and in the same conditions and with the same pleasure with which I made *Daguerreotypes*. In addition to all the things I'm learning here, I've had the chance to spend some time getting to know East Los Angeles; time which, I don't know, I wouldn't appreciate so much in Aubervilliers. No doubt because travelling awakens our perceptions. In Paris, I get lazy, always moving in the same circles, and also the whole rigamarol of production gets to me over there.

C&F: So, how are things working out here in terms of production?

AV: It's very hands-on. We manage with very few people to do production, administration, camera and sound work, editing, and final copy. There are so many excellent non-union technicians around here who are doing things they've never seen, like hands-on shooting without lighting that produces very high-quality results with very complicated lighting techniques. The cameramen of my last two films were not Americans: for *Mur Murs* I had Bernard Auroux and Nurith Aviv for *Documenteur*, a story we shot right after that. What surprises people around here is that in a single film we manage to combine very rudimentary means along with very sophisticated techniques. The other day we were shooting here on the balcony and I met a cameraman (who lives upstairs) who told me: "Watching you shooting so simply with just two lights like that, I thought it was a porn film!" Around here two lamps necessarily means porn . . . As for the American technicians, I always warn them quite frankly: "Look, we're making a French film, so the prices will be French as well, take it or leave it . . ." Because the problem of the unions here is very tough; they make the rules. For *Model Shop*, Jacques ended up with a team of eighty people; so, he ditched them in a parking lot and went off and made his film with the people he needed, less that fifteen. As for them, the don't give a damn as long as they're paid; they hang out in their trailers playing cards . . . So I don't personally have a Hollywood problem . . .

C&F: What's left of the world and characters described in *Lions Love*?

AV: Oh almost nothing. Most of them have recycled themselves and the rest, those who continue to believe, are being picked off by small arms fire, like the naked man that I was telling you about. Idealism is passé as they say here. Americans have such a healthy way of adapting to things . . . One day it's "Peace and Love" and the next it's pollution, quitting smoking, the day after it's jogging, so everyone starts running until five or six die of heart attacks. They're constantly changing their address and changing their lives and habits as well. Ultimately that's okay. People are less stuck in their ways here; they have no roots. A sister in Ohio, a brother in Boston. They change jobs, move three thousand miles away for a couple of years. The majority of people I know in France have always lived in the same town; they settle in and never move. Americans are not very curious by nature, but their life-style forces them to be somewhat curious anyway. They experience a social mix in their daily lives, a kind of natural democracy. At least this is true of young people here; when they get older it's not so true anymore.

C&F: Are you planning to stay here, return to France or keep traveling?
AV: "There are always voyages to be made," they used to say. I came here by chance and I've been able to work. I wanted to make a film on the murals and I made it. I wanted to make another and I made that one too.

C&F: Can you tell us a bit about this other film, *Documenteur?*
AV: It's the shadow of the previous one, the shadow of *Mur Murs*. It's an idea I've had for a long time: to do a series of films on the same subject, the way painters do sketches, drawings of watercolors. *Documenteur* is the story of the narratrix listening to the voice in *Mur Murs*, the story of a woman who is not very settled, this place being nowhere. And I've planned a third version, a "normal" film, psychological, with a scenario and all. I've always tried to make a cinema . . . of what exactly? We used to say "art and experimentation" but I no longer believe much in art, or in experimentation . . . so a cinema of what? Cinema without senility? Does such a thing exist? I wouldn't like to just drivel on, you know. I still think there are things to explore, a "ciné*mature*" (I haven't found the equivalent of "ciné*criture*" [cinema-writing]), something that would be cinema and words: images as words, each with its own meaning, without being linked through syntax, a story or a reasoning process, like in poetry, where you use words as words rather than sentences which organize these words. But to do that I needed to have some tranquility, some solitude, to get away from the French cultural buzz. I'm not very comfortable in France; I'm not intellectual enough for the intellectuals and I'm too smart for the idiots. I always feel betwixt and between: *L'Une Chante*, for example, wasn't feminist enough for the feminists and too feminist for the others. So if I couldn't do what I wanted to here, where else could I?

Interview with Agnès Varda

Françoise Aude and Jean-Pierre Jeancolas / 1982

From *Positif*, April 1982. Reprinted by permission. Translated by T. Jefferson Kline.

Aude & Jeancolas: Ever since *La Pointe Courte*, you seem to have had the will or desire to produce your own films yourself.

Agnès Varda: Is it a matter of will or desire? No, it's a necessity. I become a producer when "they" don't want to produce my work or when the project looks like it's going to be difficult; after all, who would ever want to produce, find funding for, or work to complete a film such as *Mur Murs*, a film about walls in Los Angeles? And *Documenteur*, a film about words, exile, and pain? These are by nature difficult projects. So, I take myself by the hand and I produce my own work. I'm reminded of a fortune cookie I once had in a Chinese restaurant whose message was, "If you look for a helping hand, you will find it at the end of your own arm." That's why I produce, so as to not give up on my projects.

When I was making *Le Pointe Courte*, in 1954, who would have had confidence in me? I also paid for *Opéra Mouffe* myself. Afterward I had some producers, such as Georges de Beauregard for *Cléo de 5 à 7*, Mag Bodard for *Le Bonheur* and *Les Créatures*. It was like a dream; all I had to do was direct. With Max Raab, who co-produced *Lions Love*, things didn't go quite so well; he found the money and I managed it . . . That was in 1969. Since then, I've never again had any producer, male or female, except myself. But I don't want to do that anymore. Producing my own films is too tiring. Too much energy is wasted that could be better spent on the films. What's more, the producer has a terrible role. You end up being the terrible boss . . . Not always, but still . . . I exhausted myself producing *Daguerréotypes* and *L'Une Chante, l'Autre Pas*, *Mur Murs*, and *Documenteur*, not to mention *Lady Oscar*, which I produced for Jacques and on behalf of the Japanese. Enough of that. I'm not producing any more. Might as well give up making films altogether.

A&J: Is that true? You'd quit?

AV: I don't know. But I need help. I want to be paid to do what I do best, which is to write and direct. I tend to hide the fact that I'm out of work by becoming both the employer and (unpaid) employee on the set. After ten, twelve years of such badly disguised unemployment, I've had enough! I'm not saying that I haven't been able to make films, etc. . . . What I'm saying is that all this energy devoted to producing my work has veiled the fact that no one has expressed confidence in my work in the normal way this is expressed in the economy of French cinema. If experimental film must be made in such difficult conditions, we'll end up losing this "cultural gadget" that has had such success in other countries. It's funny, I think back to Cléo, beautiful Cléo who said, "Everyone wants me, but no one loves me." As a filmmaker, I could say "Everyone one loves me, but no one wants me"!

I don't mind doing the usual acrobatics to help the production, to figure out how to make fifteen extras look like there are twenty, but I no longer want to look for the money to pay the fifteen extras, and the money to pay the technicians that will film the fifteen extras, and to find the money to pay the accountant who will make the pay stubs for the fifteen extras and the fifteen technicians, and to find the bus that will transport the thirty people to the set, and finally to try to make these fifteen extras seem to be twenty or twenty-five. *That's* no longer creative acrobatics. That's three-eight time! A hat dance!

I remember when I was filming *L'Une Chante*, I was running between two shots to a telephone booth under a plane tree and calling the CNC to find out whether the advance on the expenses would be approved and paid . . . And, at that, lucky to have even been promised the advance, this "dowry" without which I couldn't imagine ever presenting my films to the great ballroom of the cinema.

Things started off well enough for *Mur Murs*. The Ministry of Culture advanced a bit of money; Antenne 2 and Klais Hellwig as well . . . But the film went from a short subject to a feature-length film without any increase in funding. It was up to me to make up the difference.

As for *Documenteur*, a feature-length film, it was a whole other story. I could only find a small grant from the CNC and the film made almost no money. So I ended up with some debts. Not for the technicians; pay wasn't delayed or cut; everyone got paid. I still had to reimburse all the monies loaned by the film industry and other organizations, but I've been able to pay them off in installments.

The film industry . . . You know that in Los Angeles people ask "Do you work in the industry?" as if it goes without saying that the industry is the film industry. *I* always respond, "Not exactly, I am artist filmmaker." I'm trying to recover the term artist and artisan for those who, in the Seventh Art, don't exactly make major motion pictures, but films, films that are also part of cinema. "I make films, not deals."

I can't stand hearing businessmen say, "Cinema is action, cinema is fear, etc. . . ." They usually add, "And it's not the intellectual theories of some miserable elitists that . . ." What pretentiousness to define what cinema is . . . How can you not understand that cinema includes all films of all kinds? I'm only repeating truths that we all know, but we can never repeat them enough. It's because of this nonsense that I don't make "normal" films with normal producers.

I dream of working with someone like Marcel Berbert who does everything for Truffaut. In exchange, François has him appear in all his films. Berbert cameos, just as discrete as Hitchcock's cameos in his own films. I'd be happy to include cameos in all my films for a serious and faithful producer-manager!

A&J: At this point in your career, where do you find yourself?
AV: Out of gas. Not out of inspiration, but out of courage. And yet I have the impression of having done some good work recently, of having made progress. Not especially with *Mur Murs* which was made rather classically . . . Classic in my own sense, documented and personal. I took the time to really listen to people, to reflect on things, to have fun. Look, I'm not talking about what others consider "good work." There are tons of film artists these days who make okay films in lots of different ways. For me "good work" means something else. It's when the imagination takes clichés and stereotypes and reinvents them. It's when the mind really lets go, when associations are free to take over. It's when I start writing in purely cinematographic terms. Cine-writing, can we say that? New relationships between images and sounds allow us to unmask images and sounds that were previously suppressed, or hidden in us . . . There you have it—making movies with all that plus emotion, that's what I call "good work."

And I had the impression of moving forward with my work while making *Documenteur*. I have always imagined my life as a work in progress, without much concern for building a career. There are some films that I make, and I *like* to make them, but my work is not moving forward much as other films where work is progressing.

A&J: If anything, an unmade film can lead to exciting work?

AV: Of course! I've written several scripts still as yet unfilmed, or that I will not film. *La Mélangite* in 1960, and *Marie and the Naked Man* in 1980. I hope to make the former, with Theresa Russel, whom I find wonderful. She was in *Bad Timing* by Nicholas Roeg, and France in *Enquête sur une Passion*. And with Simone Signoret, whose talent and voice I really love. I still have to find an American who can play the naked man killed by a cop . . . The film may yet be made . . . in any case, it's not an abandoned project.

A&J: And *Christmas Carol?*

AV: I filmed ten minutes of it in 1966 or 1967, with Gérard Depardieu making his debut . . . That would have been a film about youth before 1968, but I didn't get an advance from the CIC and the distributor gave up on it, and so did I and headed to the US. You need to know when to let go.

I remember that I went to see Prévert with Jacques. He said something to us that made a huge impression on me: for every one of his screenplays that was selected, paid for, and filmed, he had at least two works, complete with dialogue and finished, that nobody wanted . . . When you think about how much time it takes to write a script! It took me five months to write *Maria and the Naked Man*. I coauthored it with an American screenwriter and we started from thirty pages that I had written on my own. I needed help in writing everything in English. In creative English . . . We would work all day long, every day, Saturday morning as well. We were paid. It was good.

On the other hand, I also like to film as soon as the idea comes to me, especially documentaries. That was the case for *Daguerréotypes* or *Oncle Yanco*. A shock, an emotion, a structure, and we film. I like that as well. As for *Yanco*, I met Yanco, this marvelous man, one Thursday and we filmed Saturday, Sunday, and Monday. It was a wrap! During the whole thing I was emotionally engaged and happy to be filming. We shot the film while I was in the throes of imagination.

A&J: This leads us to your connection to *le temps* (weather and/or time). Can you tell us about it?

AV: I'm tempted to say, of course, I prefer cloudy weather for shooting in color and sunny weather for living . . . But since your question can also involve the other meaning of *temps*, time that is forever ticking away, I like to feel in life as though we don't really feel the passage of time. Time is fluid. What I find astonishing is that kids grow up and trees get taller. The other day Godard dropped by our place on the rue Daguerre to see Rosalie who has been constructing some huge angel's wings made with real feathers to be used in his film *Passion*. When I saw Godard and Rosalie I laughed. Godard and I met in that same house twenty years ago when Rosalie was three and was always underfoot.

I find it difficult to capture in film that time when we didn't feel we were so different from who we are now, even though twenty years have passed. In film, in order to be credible we have to mark the passage of time, using makeup etc. . . . In our heart of hearts we don't feel that we are aging. We don't live in front of mirors, we don't perceive our reality from outside. We know this but we are only rarely aware of it. The aspect of time that fascinates me in the cinema is the time of the film itself the time of filming, the stuff of time itself, its sudden density. I worked on this in *Cléo*: when time takes on a sudden density or when it begins to flow freely again. As though time resembled the circulation of blood. Or as in *Documenteur* when time is emptied of substance and becomes pure space: the beach, or a corridor between two buildings in a labyrinth.

In Nancy recently I saw a very interesting experiment. It was done by Windy Clarke, the daughter of Shirley. She had a small fairground cabin installed in the main tent of the Theater Festival there to make and exhibit her "Love-tapes." About five years ago she began making films of group therapy sessions. The participants filmed themselves and each other with video screens placed around the room so they could see their work. Then they described themselves and each other. It was, in a word, heavy. But then she went to work and discovered a formula: She asked each of the participants to speak for three minutes about love. She has already collected about seven hundred minutes of such witnessing. There are video screens mounted around this cabin on which are displayed the entire seven hundred minutes of these "Love-Tapes" in both French and English. If anyone wants to try it they go in the cabin. She explains to them how the video works, has them choose a framework, has them choose background music, and leaves them alone. The person locks the door, and makes a film, facing the camera. Three minutes. The camera shuts off after three minutes. Windy comes back in and replays the tape. If the person accepts to have it saved, Windy will add it to the collection. Otherwise she erases it.

These Love-Tapes are fascinating, they reveal everything about the people who make them and about those who watch them. And about the time of filming. I was struck, for example, by one woman about fifty to sixty years old, hair in a bun, glasses, a bit grandmotherly. She loved everything: flowers, life, her work, her colleagues . . . It was really sweet and I was astonished by so much love for life in a person whose flame seemed to burn so weakly. Then in the fortieth second she repeated "I like flowers and life" and then suddenly "my children and also my husband" and then stopped talking; then she said, "Oh three minutes is too long." So during the last two minutes she said only from time to time, "I wouldn't have guessed three minutes could be so long" or variations of this . . . "It's long, it's so long to spend three minutes talking about love." It was incredible to watch. I had the feeling I was actually touching the very fabric of time in which this woman was stuck, and it was also the fabric of the present time in which I was watching and listening to this "Love-Tape."

In *Documenteur* I tried something new which was to introduce a space-time of silence between moments of great emotion, to allow the audience the time to get there or to hear in themselves the aftershocks of the emotions displayed, the echo of the words, forgotten memories. It's as though I wanted to use their own lived time in the film's time. I propose emotion-filled moments, then images onto which these emotions can be transferred and then a silence in which the two can reverberate.

A&J: So it's sort of stockpiling of emotion?

AV: Yes, a stockpiling and a manipulation of possible emotions in the movement between one shot and the next. A slippage of emotion. This vocabulary fascinates me: the words and the images that these words elicit. The word-images are signs or signals to us but not always in the ways we expect. In *Documenteur* I shot a love scene (realistic, concrete, love-making) between Emilie and her lover. It's the illustration but also the sign of amorous voluptuousness bodied out in each others' arms. In another scene shot by Nurith Aviv, we watched a woman one night in a Laundromat with her back to us caressing her hair. She's absentmindedly weaving childlike braids in her greasy hair. It's a troubling image, of impossible voluptuousness yet evident sensuality. When I showed this film with Sabine Mamou—who also plays Emilie—I noticed this gesture that Sabine, as actress, does while making love. She would raise her elbows above her head. I remember how happy I was when I realized I could juxtapose the shots of the woman in the Laundromat with these elbows raised in the act of love. In this way I could effect this slippage between the images of a vocabulary that represents love and, in the next shot, pure voluptuousness becoming the sign of desire.

A&J: This sort of unhitching of the given and the sign was already visible in *Opéra Mouffe*.

AV: Yes, that's true. But I've rarely done it until now. In *Opéra Mouffe*, yes, and a bit in *Cléo*, when Dorothée poses nude and with the baby in the incubator.

A&J: And the two nudes? You wanted to separate them one from the other in time, as if to signify their separation. And yet these two bodies belong together . . .

AV: That's a nice idea. I hadn't thought of it that way. These two bodies, you only see them together in the love scene, doubtless an association of memory rather than one produced by an anecdotal or erotic progression. On the other hand the shots of the naked man sleeping alone, and those of the naked Emilie by herself for an entire afternoon are signs not of desire but a time absent of voluptuousness. Just the time of the body alone.

A&J: But these two shots are voluptuous as well because there is a feeling of absence.

AV: Yes . . . that empty feeling . . . Absence has a very powerful presence. The representation of desire in the cinema is a difficult thing. I'm not talking about desire and its signs when desire is fulfilled. I'm talking about desire that can't be described, of that unspeakable tension which is unrepresentable except through an emptiness which has a form. Like Henry Moore's sculptures where the empty form is as powerful if not more powerful than the full form. In pottery we also have to think about emptiness as a form: there emptiness has a form that the pot surrounds.

A&J: *Documenteur*, is it a film about a child's desire to have a father or a film on voluptuousness?

AV: All of that undoubtedly. The child misses his father and desires his mother. In the mother's case it's a confusion of fullness and emptiness where words become a kind of painful eroticism, words which are substituted for desire. In the second part the child's words, as minimal and right as they are, replace the mother's words. The words that express her desire express her desire in general, everyone's desire. For example,

"I don't want to sleep alone," or "There's never been any love without you." When he says, "I want to see daddy"—anecdotal words—I end up with the child-subject, the subject is dispersed. And in the third part, it's others. All those men and women who express confusion, people not identified in the scenario (however slight it may be) but who become the identity of the film: a waitress closing her café, an addict sleeping on a bench, and the woman on all fours in the sand who was crying while scooping sand with one hand. Nurith Aviv told me afterwards that she thought it had something to do with a voodoo ritual . . . I didn't know; I was just very moved that this woman in such pain would come and be in my film.

A&J: The other scene where two people seem to be holding a wake for a dead person seems even more ritualistic.
AV: It's a scene I saw one day but couldn't understand what was going on. So I reconstituted it with a woman lying as if dead with a Bible on her stomach and the two men kneeling beside her.

A&J: *Documenteur* seems to move away from your taste for the opposition between light and dark, optimism and pessimism.
AV: Within the film, yes. The film is all shadow. But when we look at the two films together, *Mur Murs* and *Documenteur,* we move from sun to shadow, from outside to inside etc. . . . It's the two films together that express this taste for contradiction.

A&J: This opposition hasn't always been as rigorous or bivalent. For me, *Opéra Mouffe* is 90 percent anguish and 10 percent hope.
AV: Yes, perhaps. It's true that the two films have points in common, including Delerue's music. And that they're in color, stamped with very strong personal feelings. They were also both quite difficult for me to make; it's as though I tried not to make them. *Documenteur* was really hard for me to write. I kept putting off the date to begin filming, and then, when everything was decided, the day before we started the shoot I succeeded in losing all my identification cards in two entirely different locations along with the only copy of the manuscript of the scenario that I hadn't gotten around to Xeroxing. Sabine managed to find the scenario. Without her patience and Nurith's as well, without their insistence on bringing this project to fruition in spite of me, I probably wouldn't have started or finished the film.

And then I kept getting hung up on various obstacles. I absolutely insisted on renting an apartment where I used to live and the owner wouldn't have it. I insisted, I waited, and we lost a lot of time. And when I finally gave up on the place three days before the start of the shoot, I discovered half an hour later the series of poor houses from the thirties whose interiors are a true labyrinth. For Emilie and Martin we couldn't have done better than this weirdly calm and disquieting setting. It was ten times better than the apartment I'd made such a fuss about. So that's the work I was talking about: masking and unmasking, obsession and reality, surrealism, magic, the desire to film the unfilmable.

A&J: Why the word "*menteur*" ("liar") in *Documenteur*? There doesn't seem to be anything in this film that's a lie.
AV: On the contrary. The whole film is set against "*cinéma vérité*." It's "cinema-dreams-fables"—the truthful lie as Aragon would say. It's not me. And then everything I say now—that my films have escaped from my control and others can see them—is like an afterword. I speak about the films, I paraphrase, I dream about them, I try to understand them, I talk about the plans for the film and its construction, I discuss details. When I was working on them, I was part of the organic reality of the film. For *Mur Murs* this meant working with Sabine Mamou for six months of editing, playing with images and words, watching them, listening to them. Waiting for the images to clarify and to emit other messages. Only then could I start to write something else and only then could we come back and edit some more. As for *Documenteur* there was all this "truthful lying" in the voices, faces, and bodies. Who is speaking? In whose name? We'd really get confused when Sabine would bring up on the screen images of Sabine and I would say, "So you . . . or rather she . . ." and we'd laugh at our own labyrinths where reality, the virtual image, the real image, or the imaginary images all ended up resembling each other.

A&J: We'd like to end with a history question . . . How do you situate yourself today vis à vis the New Wave?
AV: To paraphrase Renaud's song, I feel like a whole group of kids all by myself . . . But I was never a member of a group. Pioneer, as they say, before the New Wave, I was entirely self-taught, not part of the film culture. I *was* in the wave of the New Wave. Thanks to Godard, Jacques made *Lola* produced by Georges de Beauregard. Thanks to Jacques, I made *Cléo*. The baton was passed in that way with some common tendencies, like making low-budget films with characters walking through the streets of Paris. From this perspective we can see that Rivette never got old when

we watch *Le Pont du Nord*! But I'd never really belonged to a group so there was a tendency to forget me and exclude me. I wasn't included in the Musidora book about women, *Paroles, Elles Tournent* in 1976. And again last year in 1980 there were two special issues of *Cahiers du Cinéma* devoted to French cinema. I wasn't mentioned even in passing, nor was a single one of my films. God knows there were a lot of people mentioned, and very interesting people, different people, French film-makers of all stripes, men, women, people from Auvergne. But not me. Was it because I was in the U.S.? Louis Malle was also over there. Was it misogyny? Surely not. Catherine Breillat, Marguerite Duras, and others were included. Was it the omission of anyone less than five feet tall? No, Chantal Akerman was in there. I was just plain forgotten. I wasn't con- tacted, never got a questionnaire to fill out and yet all my mail was for- warded to Los Angeles. That really hurt. If *Cahiers du Cinéma* which had conducted several long interviews with me over the years was excluding me, it really felt like an exile.

But it's not a matter of chance or an oversight. I happened to be work- ing on a film that talks about this, about separation. It's about the lack of shelter, the lack of warmth of one's former situation or group, the lack of a shoulder to lean your head on. Now I'm here with my two films (it's strange how little we've talked about *Mur Murs* in this interview). I've come back and everyone is seeing my films and talks to me and asks me questions. There's lots of warmth in this welcome. Maybe I do exist in French cinema, maybe I don't get much heat or shelter, but at least I'm inside and not outside now.

Interview with Agnès Varda

Françoise Wera / 1985

From *Ciné-Bulles* 5, no. 3 (1985). Reprinted by permission. Translated by T. Jefferson Kline.

"I'm not behind the camera, I'm IN it!"

At the time it was said of her that she was one of the most innovative directors of the New Wave. Thirty years and twenty-five films later, Agnès Varda continues an unusual career and a very personal methodology that won her the Lion d'Or at Venice last year for her latest film, *The Vagabond* (*Sans Toit ni Loi*). In this remarkable work she traces with almost cold calculation an intense and emotional portrait of a young woman whose enigmatic look and solitude will continue to haunt the memory of those who cross paths with her.

Françoise Wera: *The Vagabond* is your twentieth film, and you have the unusual distinction of having made quite a number of shorts.

Agnès Varda: Yes, that's about the right number. Between each full-length film I make a number of shorts. Unlike many filmmakers for whom shorts are a kind of spring-board to get to feature-length films, I frequently make short films—a label I insist on to distinguish my work from summer apparel. You can portray or express emotions, discoveries, and imagined moments in a very short amount of time. These films help me progress in my work: it's a kind of knitting together of my perceptions with those of my future audiences. It's also like playing scales: I exercise my eye, my ear, and all that!

Take *Ulysses* for example. I refilmed a photograph I'd taken in 1954 in which you could see the sea, a naked child sitting on a stony beach next to a dead goat, and a naked man standing looking out at the sea. Starting from this image, I set out to find its models and attempted as well to rediscover the moment this photo was taken. What interested me was not only to question my memory and time, but to question the image itself, the representation of memory, to question the relationship between memory and representation. And that is what the cinema is really all about: a re-examination of time, movement and especially the image. By digging around in this image, finding the people who'd served as its models (now twenty-eight years older!), learning about the day and representations of the day I'd taken it—for example what had been on TV that day, what was in the news that day—by reintroducing movement into the image I'd fixed, it was the cinema I rediscovered and re-examined. Out of my faulty memory of that day there emerged this image, which was a photograph that somehow resisted all my attempts to analyze it and all my research on it.

Every one of my short films marks a stage of my development, for example the little commissioned film I did called *The So-Called Caryatids*, for which I had to go back to the 1860s and the death of Baudelaire. Through a combination of references, memories and free-associations, each film engages me in the exploration of topics which seem to me to be rarely treated in the cinema. They always want us to tell stories with action and psychological drama but there are other very interesting directions we can take in time, space, and memory. Emotions, recollections, surprises.

FW: You made some films in the States, including *Mur Murs* and *Documenteur*. Is this latter film a bit autobiographical?

AV: Well, yes and no. I think my films are all autobiographical. *Ulysses* is completely: there are even photos showing me and this child, Ulysses, and in a certain way you might even say *The Vagabond* is autobiographical. But not to the first degree . . . To come back to *Documenteur*, what creates the uncertainty about this question of autobiography is that the child, Martin, is played by our son Mathieu Demy, and of course since it's the story of a woman living alone with her child in Los Angeles, that could be about me as well since I was living there with Mathieu. But I think more to the point, the film is full of emotions which are very powerfully autobiographical. But then so is *The Vagabond*, you see? Of course I'm not eighteen years old wandering around Provence with a backpack any more than I'm an eighty-five-year-old lady. But there's something of me in all of these characters. Like the one played by Macha Méril, since I'm very worried by the idea that all these plane-trees are dying and that they can't seem to find a remedy for the mushroom that's plaguing them.

FW: How did you construct the scenario for *The Vagabond*?

AV: Once I'd decided on the subject, I went to scout out the terrain, if I may put it that way. I picked up hitchhikers, I hung out at the train station, I went into some of the homeless shelters at night, etc. One day I picked up a girl hitchhiking and she was so extraordinary a character that I began to realize how much more interesting it is to see a girl hitchhiking than a guy. That's when I decided that my main character would be a girl. It presupposes more physical courage, more endurance, more guts, a greater capacity to say "up yours!" to people, and that kind of thing.

The film was also born of my wandering around in search of my characters. I made trips to meet people and talk with them. For example, because I like shepherds, I wandered among the flocks. So when I met this ex-professor working as a shepherd, his stories about his life suggested a character much more interesting than just a simple shepherd. So right there I asked if he'd play the part and I wrote a text for him. Because that's how I work with my characters: if he'd written the text by himself, I'd have had the impression of stealing what he is to insert him in my film. Instead, I define my characters as *fictional* by the texts that I write. In every case, the film takes what people have sketched or suggested but not directly expressed.

So the work had this ambiguity to it, I must say, between meeting people who seemed the best representatives of the category I was looking for, and then, from the conversations I'd have with them, take some of what they'd said and then write the text that they'd have to play. I kept their environment, their way of expressing themselves and moving. I found this play between fiction and documentary really interesting.

FW: So even though you gave yourself the liberty of using what happened as it played out, everything got written down?
AV: Yes, everything is carefully composed. Every line in *The Vagabond* is written. They were all written at the last minute, sometimes at four in the morning, sometimes on the side of a car, but all of the non-professionals were reciting written texts. It's truly a fiction film that I nourished with the lives of real people: the way of gathering the material is documentary but the work on the scenario and the shooting is manipulation, i.e., fiction.

One of the characteristics of the scenario is to have invented a character (Mona) whom I don't entirely control. I myself chose the character but don't totally know—and won't ever completely understand. And the film is like this relationship, this gulf that can't be crossed. Even the film's witnesses who approach her, then distance themselves a bit from her, seek her out, hunt her down, judge her severely but are nonetheless very nice people . . . all of them end up having contradictory views of her and ultimately come up against her refusal to communicate with them.

This way of working is entirely contrary to what I'd done before, in *Cléo from 5 to 7* for example. I knew everything about Cléo; I'd written reams about her before and during the shooting; Corinne read them, and I worked closely with all the actors. I said, "In order to play this moment in Cléo's life, you have to fill it up, animate it"—I use that word because the word "soul" (*âme*) is in there somehow, I'm not sure how—to animate who Cléo is, what she's lived, her age, her youth, her relationships, her references when she says something. All that can help an actor. But in *The Vagabond*, I began with a character whom I caught on the fly, as she was passing by. And when we were shooting, with all those tracking shots, I tried to keep my own distance from her. I avoided the Bergman-esque use of extreme close-ups which plumb the face and the soul.

Maybe that's the thing I'm proudest of: to have figured out before beginning to shoot that the film would be nomadic and that my position as *auteur* had to be like that of the witnesses who watch Mona go by. And maybe that's why we've been able to pass on to the film's audiences and critics their own roles as Mona's witnesses. It's not just a film they're watching, it's Mona.

FW: Actually that's what I liked too. Through the reactions of the witnesses and the way you show them, this girl remains enigmatic, like a character who passes by and upsets the order of things, who enters the life of these people and remains engraved in everyone's memory.

AV: Because she's only passing through. And for me, in my own scenario, she just kept on going too. Claude-Jean Philippe, a very good French critic, reminded me of Stendhal's famous phrase, "The novel is a mirror travelling along a road." (The original is: "The novel is a mirror that one carries along a road.") The same applies to the character in a novel. Every work of art is a voyage, the work and the characters in it. There's no doubt that you felt this mirror-effect, the prism-effect. When anything passes by it becomes an image and this image makes us fantasize and reflect. Which brings us back to the beginning of this discussion: *Ulysses* is a reflection on the image and on the effect of this image on me and on others, including the children. Or to another series of films each of which was two minutes long which was called *One Minute Per Image*, in which different people talked about images they hadn't made. This work of examining what we feel, our way of looking, our feelings about the way others look at us, other emotions, other choices, this chain-reaction, has been the theme of several of my films and has now led me to *The Vagabond*.

FW: Mona was interpreted in the most extraordinary way by Sandrine Bonnaire. Was she your choice from the beginning?
AV: Yes. I believe she is the only one among our young actresses capable of playing this role with the vehemence that it required along with this little hard place in her that can't be touched. Sandrine is blonde, quite pretty, very gracious in her manner, and yet she has this hard place in her that I felt would enable her to play Mona: inaccessible and proud.

FW: How did you work with your actors? Do you do a lot of rehearsing before beginning to shoot?
AV: None before the shooting begins. I don't work on psychology before and/or after the filming. But at the moment of each take, we try out different things. Let's take, for example, a shot as simple as the one where Mona is crossing a field alone. We might have said, "Let's do a tracking shot," and that would be that. But no, we discussed the exact moment she should touch the shoulder straps of her backpack, or laugh to herself. I'd seen girls doing that—suddenly laughing to themselves for no apparent reason—or walking along smoking, against all the rules of scouting! We had to get at the illogicality or lack of practical sense of these people who must after all have some in order to survive. So, with Sandrine we looked for behavior that would portray her ability to survive on the road without suggesting she had the organizational ability to plan an ascent of the Himalayas. The story of her shoes which are so impractical, you might almost say the story of the death of her shoes, the fact that her sleeping bag is so essential that she won't be able to survive after it burns. It's the practical side of things we talked about, those realistic, functional gestures. I think actors must be shown in an ensemble of factors that are at least as narratively relevant as language and psychology.

FW: How do you like working with non-professional actors?
AV: I love it—and I love them! Even after all these years of working in film, I realize how difficult it is to invent a character, to surround her with everything that will make her entirely believable. Or else you have to have lots of money, like the Americans, who manage to do remarkable

things, for example Meryl Streep in *Silkwood*. You get the feeling that it takes lots of time and money to get things so right. I too take a lot of time, when I'm scouting the terrain, when I'm alone, when it doesn't cost anything, just walking around meeting people, observing things. Taking the time to choose the right people. Then I can use their surroundings, their costumes, their hair styles, their hands, their nails, dirty or clean, the tools they use, their way of speaking, etc. When I get to the point of writing a text that resembles what they might say, I can take advantage of all the rest—the power of their realism—simply because they're situated in a place they know, using their own things, opening a drawer which is their own drawer.

Take the vine cropper, for example, he's seated at a table just as he does every day, and he picks up a bottle of olive oil just the way he does all the time. He doesn't have to try out gestures, the way the professional actors, like Macha or Sandrine have to do. I have to rehearse every gesture with them to find just the right moment, the justification for each movement, sometimes without explaining why. Sandrine found I was very demanding, a bit maniacal, and it's true because Mona had to be real and she *is* completely.

FW: Kobayashi said that actors are only one element of a film; important but not any more so than the other elements. What's your reaction?

AV: I was greatly helped by Patrick Blossier. It's his first feature-length film although he'd done lots of other things including his documentary, *Around the Wall*, and he'd worked in a lot of challenging situations. He understood immediately that we had to make an "in your face" film, a raw film, not a cutsie film. And I was very grateful because he produced lighting that corresponded exactly to what I wanted. When we were in poorer areas, he managed lighting that suggested weak sunlight or a poor light bulb hanging naked from the ceiling. Or conversely, for example in the apartment of the rich old lady, full of knick-knacks, he manages very rich, even voluptuous lighting that illuminates all of these different objects. It's really great!

And I'm very demanding. I used to say, "No we can't shoot now, the sun's too strong. We'll come back at seven p.m." In the winter when the sun sets early we'd shoot at five or six in the evening to capture that dirty light at the end of the day; we often used that dirty end-of-the-day light which is the time you find yourself walking alone and feel so intensely your solitude. And even if Mona decided to be alone, to live alone, to say 'I don't give a damn,' it's impossible that she wouldn't feel this depressing ambiance. Patrick was very attuned to all that, to what I wanted, so he managed to capture this light magnificently.

As for framing, I'm always concerned with framing. Because I can't help believing that how people are placed, and at what distance is very important. I've been know to redo a scene that I'd shot at a distance of five feet in order to film it one foot closer. No need to tell you that the TV people don't worry about things like that. I film with the exactitude that I believe necessary to the work.

FW: Which part of the filmmaking process do you like best, shooting, editing, or writing?
AV: All of it. I've even begun using the term *cinécriture* (cinewriting). *Cinécriture* isn't the scenario, it's the ensemble of exploratory walks, the choices, the inspiration, the words one writes, the shooting, the editing: the film is the product of all of these different moments. I spend nine hours a day on the editing because that's when the film comes together and the clarity of the film's emotions is calculated, worked over, manipulated, and corrected right down to the last moment.

And I didn't even mention the sound that is so important. The sound engineer, who had worked on *Paris, Texas*, another nomadic film, did remarkable work for us. Because I'd asked him things like getting not only the sound of Mona's footsteps, but even the noise of her jeans rubbing, because these are noises you hear when you're alone, the sound of a zipper getting stuck, the particular resonance of a rock hitting a tent spike, different sounds according to the texture of the fields. I wanted to hear all of that because that's what will help us be with Mona, live with her. You need very skilled technicians to produce films like that, so that they don't seem fabricated but ring true.

As soon as you begin a film, and the idea begins to germinate, you enter into what I'd call a state of grace in your active relationship to chance. I can say that it's really chance and I that make the film together. You have no idea of the relationship I have with things that happen to come my way. Sometimes my team would nearly die laughing; I might say, "I need such and such" and the thing would be there. It was incredible! You know artists used to talk about inspiration and the muse. The muse! That's amusing! But it's not your muse, it's your relationships with the creative forces that makes things appear when you need them. Those are the mysteries of my passion for the cinema. This grace, this violence, I know what it is: it is to be inhabited by your film, it's so impressive, a bit unbelievable. It's happened fifty times on the set that things or people or chance encounters generated ideas we could use right on the spot.

For example, the police chief when we were shooting Mona's death. Someone told me I should meet him since he might lend us cops, police wagons. I let myself be talked into this meeting even though I don't like cops much. So while we're having a conversation in front of a nearby café, he explains that for some time they've stopped covering dead bodies with a blanket, but instead slide them into a plastic sack with a zipper. At that moment I could see the connection with Mona's sleeping bag. And this most compelling image of the film, this little frozen body that they put into a little snow bag of white plastic with a zipper that reminds us of the zipper on her sweatshirt and this sack that looks like the sleeping bag she was sleeping in. All that, all the emotion of this scene came from a police chief explaining his m.o.

Or, for example, the last insult to Mona's body—we haven't discussed this, but one of the major themes of the film is dirt and our intolerance of dirt. Mona emerges from the sea and gets dirtier and dirtier as the film goes on until she falls into a dark ditch, burned, dirty, and stained with wine dregs. I grew up in this region around Sête about twenty miles from this village where they do this ugly business, where, for three hours you have the right to throw wine dregs on people. The film takes place in a wintry landscape of grape vines where alcohol and drunkenness are a constant. But, would you believe, I'd forgotten all about this stupid celebration. And by chance some one showed me some photos of the event. Of course, it was one of the major themes I was working on! This girl who's afraid of nothing, gets scared only when these people attack her with her own medium: filth.

So you have to work with free association and dreaminess, let yourself go with memories, chance encounters, objects. I try to achieve a balance between the rigorous discipline I've learned in thirty years of making films and these many unforeseen moments and the vibrations of chance. If the film feels current, it's not because it portrays a young kid on the fringes, but because I work with what's happening at the very moment I'm shooting. The most current thing about my work is me on the day I'm shooting. Some people might call that taking risks without a safety net but that's what makes this work exciting and I believe that this powerful excitement can be felt in my film.

Agnès Varda: A Conversation

Barbara Quart / 1986

From *Film Quarterly* 40, no. 2 (Winter 1986–87). Reprinted by permission.

Agnès Varda has been making films for over three decades now, starting out at a time when less than a handful of women were directing. Varda's longevity as a serious filmmaker, her capacity for survival, is in itself moving, as other august figures have come and gone, their trajectories played out by death or burn-out in one form or another. It is not hard to remember how dazzling *Cléo from 5 to 7* was when it first appeared in 1962, or *Le Bonheur* for that matter in 1965. Varda has come in for her share of criticism but her place in film history is safe. Forerunner of the New Wave, she continues to work and grow, each new film a bold new direction, even though each is a massive enterprise that she must get off the ground, taking on the same miserable struggle for finances however known and respected she is, however glowing the critical reception of such a film as her strong latest one, *Vagabond*, her best film yet (and a commercial success in France).

Varda turns this time to the story of Mona, a young woman vagrant—not an easy subject though a brave one, and in Varda's hands of such interest from start to end that one needn't ask why the film won top honors at the Venice Film Festival. Through flash-backs and documentary-style commentary by those who encounter Mona in her wanderings, *Vagabond* creates the journey that led its central character to a miserable death in a ditch. However, Varda eschews psychological explanations and does not see Mona as a victim, but rather as someone who says no to everything so totally as to look like independence itself. Mona's is an intriguing presence (with an extraordinary performance by Sandrine Bonnaire) that one never gets bored watching, unpredictable, touching in both its tough resourcefulness and its vulnerability. The film's title in French, *Sans toit ni loi (Without a Roof or a Law)*, alludes first to the pitiful condition of living outdoors in an unbearably cold winter, but alludes

126

second to caring for nothing and nobody—a freedom so total that it is the same as total loneliness, as one of the film's characters says, and can only lead to self-destruction.

The film raises philosophical issues as naturally as it creates ravishing images of great though austere beauty. It also creates through Mona a kind of prism through which to look at a wide range of characters, allowing Varda an unusual, and always multi-layered, perspective on "normality." In speaking with Varda, as in watching the film, one is stuck by her refusal to take sides, and by the complexity she creates by laying different attitudes and perceptions side by side—while maintaining full control of the material. The film brings together what Agnès Varda can do best and shows her to be as skillful and intriguing a director as ever.

Vagabond's opening in New York seemed a fine occasion upon which to talk with Varda, to ask her to reflect about her work, about film and art generally, about the differences between the European film scene and our own, about feminism, as well as about the making of *Vagabond*. Habituated as we are to a film industry that is all compromise, for which the box office is almost always the central concern, to hear a director speak out of a larger vision of filmmaking, a vision she has struggled for all these years, in film after film, is an important reminder of what the art of film is all about.

Varda began our talk by asking where my "head is at," so she would know how to gear her remarks. I told her I am interested in women directors. The interview was conducted in English.

Agnès Varda: I have not seen a woman director in America that I could speak to as I can speak to European women directors—to von Trotta, to Chantal Akerman. They do what they can but I never spoke with an American woman director who had thought about what is the cinematic writing, and where are the goals of what I call in French *cinécriture*, which means cinematic writing. Specifically that. Not illustrating a screenplay, not adapting a novel, not getting the gags of a good play, not any of this. I have fought so much since I started, since *La Pointe Courte*, for something that comes from emotion, from visual emotion, sound emotion, feeling, and finding a shape for that, and a shape which has to do with cinema and nothing else. That conversation I almost never have had here. Either the talk goes to subjects, like women subjects; or screenplay, the story. Is it a good story or a bad story, it's a *wonderful* story—always that. And then what?

Barbara Quart: Do you think, the problem is the industry here?

AV: I think it's the industry. And also the way people are taught at school makes them believe that a good story is a strong film, a strong screenplay is a good film. What the cinema has to deal with is the way of narrating, and not the story. That's what makes Murnau big and Orson Welles and Bresson and Godard and whoever you take, that we respect, Cassavetes. It is the way that they decide to tell a story or a non-story. So that makes it vey difficult sometimes here. It is perhaps confusing that when I did *One Sings, the Other Doesn't* as a feminist story, I had to go more through the story and follow the story, even though the narration was up and down. But most of my films—if we get that one slightly out of the way because it was somewhat differently made—are very very thin stories. My work is how I use it. If you tell the story of *Citizen Kane* it is not much of a story. An old rich mogul man is dead. He said a word we don't understand. We don't discover so much, just some pieces of his life and finally it is just a sled. Is that a story? It is not much. So what makes *Citizen Kane* so interesting is the way he told us about the man—intriguing us about what people think about him. And what is good about Murnau is the way the tension grows, but no story almost.

BQ: I don't know if directors can survive that way here with that mentality. The few directors here who think that way have had trouble surviving. You were talking about visual imagination. *Vagabond* was so beautiful to watch along with the whole sense of an exploration.

AV: I agree with the word "exploration." I didn't make it as a beautiful film to watch.

BQ: It doesn't feel decorative-beautiful, it seems totally integrated, but the images you make are incredible to look at.

AV: They are strong, they are more strong than beautiful. Especially that subject which is dying from the cold, has to deal with being outside and homeless, and the landscapes—which I know because it is the area where I was raised—the landscapes of that part of France in winter are great, they are strong, they are hostile. Just to watch the remainings of the vines, the black things which stay there—the vine stock. They make the wine and then they cut the vine (what we see in the film), and this dark mini-tree remains—like a bonsai. And these little pieces of dark black in a huge landscape make the landscape very strong—I love it.

BQ: Not just the landscape, a window with people and goats, even what you do with a wall.

AV: There are goats all over the world, there are shepherds all over the world.

BQ: But what you do with them.

AV: This has to go somewhere. The technical and frames are only the means to go through what has to be felt. And it deals with strong feelings. And that's why I put her dead at the beginning of the film—we discover her dead. We're not telling the story of that girl so people will think, "Maybe they'll save her." It's clear that she died. Alone in a ditch, frozen, which is an awful death. And the way she looks—she's a mess— she's the colors of the ditch almost, like the color of a gun. The way the story is told is not to be pitiful, not for understanding, that is not what it's about. It's about what it is to be so much in the "no" situation—she says no all the time—and I don't know why she ended up on the road and saying no. But I like to see how her "no" opposed to the society gets reactions in such different ways according to who is meeting her. So by trying to capture more or less, less rather than more, who she was and what was in her mind, since we go through other people's reactions, we discover more about them than about her.

BQ: I like the openness of it and the contradictions, but it doesn't feel confused, it feels totally in control, but open and rich.

AV: And rich because there is no way to say, "This is good, this is bad, this is mean, this is nice." So obviously we got to the point where that *structure* or *portrait* is more important than knowing did she have a lover, did she escape from a jail, or who knows?

BQ: You didn't want to deal with her as pathological.

AV: No, not even with psychology. Not even with social-psychology.

BQ: Why?

AV: Because I'm interested in now and here.

BQ: Do you see her as making a philosophical choice?

AV: Certainly not. She doesn't look to have a philosophical head to me. The shepherd made that kind of choice, but that was in '68 or in the seventies.

BQ: Was he really who he says he was—did you find someone who lived that life?

AV: Yes. But I made his lines for him, because he didn't want to speak for himself. Like he would have refused to make a documentary. When I made it clear that it was a fictional film, then he said, "Well, if you write my lines then I'm acting—then I'm being paid, and I'm acting."

BQ: Do you see the film as about the late sixties, what has happened to the sixites mentality, as Flora Lewis wrote about the film in the *New York Times*?

AV: Certainly not. Anyway, I found that article very confused.

BQ: You have talked about having a new experience with feminism in the early seventies.

AV: What do you mean, "a new experience"? I've been a feminist since I was nineteen years old, fighting for serious rights, for the same wages, for contraception. I started early, early, really.

BQ: I'm surprised because I had the sense that you had a change of vision in the early seventies and through the seventies.

AV: No, what happened was that there was a huge number of feminist women around and sometimes they used me, sometimes they pushed me away, sometimes they manipulated my work so it would be feminist or not. Some radical feminists hated my work, some feminists loved it—I was like a ping-pong ball. But in terms of real-life simple things, and not theoretical—because I never was, never read anything about feminists—all these people, they knew about Babel and Engels, which I came to know very late. But I was naturally involved in fighting whatever was prejudicial to women. So we started in France—I'm speaking about '48, '49, '50—going with other groups to the government, making petitions, I was there, helping women with that, and trusting women and working with them, giving them confidence and pushing them to be technicians—way ahead of others.

BQ: How did you have the courage to do it yourself?

AV: There is no courage there, I really believe it is natural. I had no reason to believe that my brothers were better. They were okay, but I didn't see anything that I didn't have which could make me do less than what they could do. Well, I hated war, it was clear that I wouldn't use weapons. I hated violence right away, I found it stupid mostly. And I hated a certain kind of stupidity which is related to power, showing the power, showing the strength. And using violence against other people disgusts me. But not only against women, against other people, against Africans, against Vietnamese, against whatever. The Algerian War was a great drama. But I was mostly an artist, let's put it that way. I was very much involved with taking pictures, using my eyes like mad, discovering things, but not just traveling like a tourist, I never was that.

BQ: Were you conscious of yourself as alone among filmmakers as a woman?

AV: I was not a filmmaker even to start with but a photographer. And when I started my first film I was alone for sure as a woman, but I didn't see myself as a woman, a courageous woman, I saw myself as a courageous artist, a filmmaker, because nobody was making films at my age at the time—men or women. The young New Wave came later. So when I did my first feature-length film in '54, at that time nobody young was making films. Orson Welles maybe had done that here. But in France at the time you had to be third assistant, then second assistant, then first assistant for years, and then you would have a chance to direct after age forty-five. That was more or less the way it was done. Some people started earlier, some artists like Jean Gremillon, but it was not in the hands of youth—writing a film and doing it like this. What I started was, not so much to be young, but deciding that a film should follow inspiration and not, again, the story, the screenplay. My first film was a very strange construction. Since you teach literature, you know about *Wild Palms*, Faulkner?

BQ: Yes.

AV: This is the book that made me think a lot about what narration is because I was so impressed that the two stories in *Wild Palms* never meet. One story is about two men escaping from a penitentiary in a flood, the other is about a couple with a difficult love story. It moves back and forth.

BQ: *Vagabond* does that, doesn't it? Move back and forth.

AV: No, no, I'm sorry. *Vagabond* is really constructed about different people looking at Mona—like building together an impossible portrait of Mona. This is not back and forth. *Wild Palms* is very precisely one chapter about the escape, one about the couple. So in my first film, one chapter—if I call that a chapter—was a couple discussing their love, a kind of failed love after five years; and then there was a village trying to get themselves together as a union—fishermen—in a very neorealistic way. So you went from the village to the couple and they would never meet. And this was very daring. This came from Faulkner because I noticed—not that I liked the book so much, this is not the point—I was trying to notice the effect of that narration on me. And how it works is that you get nervous, because you want to go to the second story. So I read it once like it is, first chapter A, then B, A, B. Then I got so nervous I read all the As together, jumping a chapter to get the story. Then I read the other one, all the Bs. Then I understood I was stupid. Then I went back to read it the way it is, which includes disturbance, it includes being frustrated from the narration.

BQ: Because so many of your films are no longer available here, the film that is very familiar to me because I saw it recently is *Les Créatures*, and you do interesting things with narration there too.

AV: This is what cinema is all about. Images, sound, whatever, are what we use to construct a way which is cinema, which is supposed to produce effects, not only in our eyes and ears, but in our "mental" movie theater in which image and sound already are there. There is a kind of on-going movie all the time, in which the movie that we see comes in and mixes, and the perception of all these images and sound proposed to us in a typical film narration piles up in a our memory with other images, other associations of images, other films, but other mental images we have, they pre-exist. So a new image in a film titillates or excites another mental image already there or emotions that we have so when you propose something to watch and hear, it goes, it works. It's like we have sleeping emotions in us all the time, half-sleeping, so one specific image or the combination of one image and sound, or the way of putting things together, like two images one after another, what we call montage, editing—these things ring a bell. These half-asleep feelings just wake up because of that—that is what it is about. This is not to make a film and say, "Okay, let's get a deal, let's tell the story, let's have a good actress, good-bye, not bad," and we go home and we eat. What I am dealing with is the effects, the perception, and the subsidiary effects of my work as proposals, as an open field, so that you can get there things you always wanted to feel and maybe didn't know how to express, imagine, watch, observe, whatever. This is so far away from the strong screenplay, the beautiful movie, etc., that sometimes I don't know what I should discuss. You understand, this is really fighting for that "Seventh Art" which is making films.

BQ: That's why your work has a dimension that none of these other people's do. There's a largeness of vision about your work.

AV: It is a question of our minds. What culture deals with is not that we have to learn to see all the Italian painting, all the Spanish painting, this is piling up information about culture. But what culture means is that we are able to associate real things, nature, paintings we have seen, music we have heard, a book we have read, a film we saw, with our real life, our emotional life, which means a lot.

BQ: To get back to women, I found the relationship between the tree expert in the film and Mona quite moving.

AV: Well, I have mixed feelings about it. It is written as mixed feelings. It is nice and also very different, one character is like a WASP and she has knowledge and she's a teacher and she's also a tree scientist and she's clean and she has a bathroom and she has friends and she has nail polish and she's got a car, okay. And the other one is homeless and dirty, knows nothing, and stupid, and stubborn and all that. She picks her up like this, out of nothing. What I like about the teacher, she has one quality that I gave her, which is just to be natural. She naturally suffers from the stink, she naturally overcomes it, because in a way she naturally speaks with that young outlaw runaway. She's the only one relating naturally, asking natural questions, whatever is the answer. Proposing food, but to eat it together.

BQ: That's a fine intimacy that you create.

AV: I wouldn't call it intimacy. What is intimacy? The other one doesn't even say, "Are you okay? Are you in good health? Do you have kids? You work?" The young one never asks a question, she's not interested in anything. I would say that the other one, because of her academic background, is sort of used to ask questions and to try to find where the mind of the other one is. It's almost professional.

BQ: You think so? It's more human to me.

AV: It is human, but she's also got the culture to ask the questions, and the right ones. But she's totally humanized. I like the way she buys these little cookies, and they eat them together and she says let's have coffee. She knows she won't take the girl home, so she buys her food, she gives her money, and she says bye-bye. That's what I call natural, she already has the situation in hand. She won't adopt the girl. What would you say, would you take her home?

BQ: Did you ever have a similar experience in your own life?

AV: I had a thousand experiences of that kind—with men and women I picked up on the road, and took home also. Sometimes I'd take them home, sometimes I didn't. I just follow what is there at the time. I don't have any kind of rule about that.

BQ: Why were you drawn to that?

AV: I always picked up people. I remember once in California I picked up a man—I was with my daughter at the time, she was about eleven—and he said. "Do you mind if I lie down in the back of the car?" I said, "Lie down, sleep." Then we arrived where we were going, and I said, "We are arriving, so we'll drop you off," and he said, "No, I'd rather stay here." We said, "We have to go and we can't leave you in the car." And he said, "Well, I don't want to go, I feel so good in your car, I want to sleep here." And I thought, what are we going to do, this huge man, one of those vagrants, and I didn't know what to do, he looked strong and maybe he was sick. I started to be afraid he was an addict on drugs or something. You can be in a situation when you can no longer make it nice and cool. I always did that. I've always been interested in people who have nothing because whatever you do they'll take it—this I found out very easily. You give them money, they'll take it, you give them food, they'll take it, you give them board, they'll take it. They don't ask you, they don't speak to you, they don't want you, they don't like you—they just need.

BQ: It's so interesting to me that you see them with all their flaws, that you're willing to be generous though you see them for what they are.

AV: I don't do it so they love me. They won't. They don't need my love or to love me. Recently we found one on the road when we were making the film already and she stayed with us, with the crew. We gave her board and food for a little while. She would ask for grass or money or food, but she never asked anybody something that you would relate to, not me or another. She got whatever she could out of us, out of me—and then she went.

BQ: Did you mean the maid who feels envious of the girl to be silly? The woman who keeps talking as if she envies Mona's freedom and her lover.

AV: Innocent—but innocent in a stupid way, stupid with her lover, stupid even with her boss. By seeing Mona with her boss, with the old lady, we understand that she could have anther relationship. Nobody obliges her to play the maid that much. We find out that Mona wears the same housecoat and ends up sitting on the couch and enjoying herself drinking and laughing. Why shouldn't Yolanda do that and say, "You're so alone, let's have a drink and play cards." I guess the old lady would love that.

BQ: You have such strong sympathy for the working person but you see her limits very strongly and clearly. I'd also like to ask, is there anything that binds your women together or even your films together? I mean, there are certain women directors, like von Trotta, who are obsessional—they go back and back over the same themes, the same kind of characters.
AV: Terrorists, you mean?

BQ: Sisters, two women together, obsessively. I try to think about your women characters and they seem so different from one another.
AV: Well, they have one thing in common too—women and men characters. I'm interested in contradiction—the inner contradiction—which makes everybody three persons at the same time, everybody is able to be so different from one moment to another. Even *Cléo from 5 to 7*, there was a contradiction between the objective time, which is 5:05, 5:10, 5:15, and what I call subjective time—that we feel so different when we have a good time, it lasts so little, and when we wait for something, it's endless. So that different and subjective way of perceiving the time made the film a very contradictory film. What I always had was two subjects in one, like *One Sings, the Other Doesn't*. In the first film I spoke about, the village and the couple are two entities you can't put together, collective life and private life. You can understand a union problem, and you can understand your own private life, but it's so difficult to perceive your private life in the middle of the union problem. And my two films about Los Angeles, *Mur Murs* and *Documenteur*—one is about Los Angeles, a portrait of the city through what is shown in the street, palm trees and sun and all these murals and everybody expressing themselves. And then the second film, which is like the shadow of the first one, which is what you don't see in Los Angeles, the nowhere city inside the city. And that was again my contradictory perceptions of the same city. A flamboyant place, and a totally dark end of the end of the end of the West scene. These two films were supposed to go together. So I would say the cinematic ability to perceive the contradictions at the same time has been the main element in my work. With Mona, I would say it's our society's contradictions that come out very clearly. We have all these social ideas that we should have night shelters, Salvation Army, welfare, charity, to help out other people, but

we don't know what to do when people don't want to be helped. There is a contradiction in our indifference and caring at the same time. So to get back to that woman, she seems to carry that very naturally, the ability of being naturally involved, slightly generous but with the exact limit of our society, which is not more than that little bit. And coming back to her house, to her job, to her bathroom, she gets away quite okay, some money, some food, bye-bye. But later on she has a guilty feeling that she should, she could, have done more. To tell the truth, I don't know what more she could have done. I don't think she was ready to adopt that vagrant—who, by the way, would not have been pleased to be adopted. So sometimes a film pushes us toward the wall where we have to face the limits of our vague understanding, vague generosity, and vague not understanding what it's all about. So I ended up structuring the film in the shape of an impossible portrait.

BQ: You've never been interested in putting a woman like yourself in one of your films?
AV: What is a woman like myself?

BQ: I don't know but not the wife in *Les Créatures* unless it's part of yourself, some domestic part of yourself.
AV: Well, look, I can see myself as a contradiction. I'm a grandmother but I'm also a very young director, in the meaning that I really fight for the same struggle that I have always been fighting, which is cinematic independence, cinematic vision, which is related to keeping a very alive mind about making film.

BQ: I'm astonished by how you keep breaking new ground.
AV: That's what I'm saying because I'm getting old also.

BQ: You seem to have amazing energy. That must be how you do it.
AV: Well, I'm losing my energy, little by little. I'll be dead soon. But the way I see my work is that I respect that work. Not in the meaning that I praise my work, but in the meaning that this is the work which is worth fighting for so much, being out of money, out of power, out of consideration, out for a while because people don't want me. They don't want me to make these films. They don't give me the money, even though they respect my finished work.

BQ: *One Sings* must have turned that around.
AV: This one is making a big amount of money in France. We have

reached a million people already. But what it does is more important than how much money it makes and if we will reimburse—which it will—because I borrowed, I took risks like nobody takes here.

BQ: Did you? Did you have to? Because I would think that *One Sings* would have done very well in the box office.
AV: It did. But with each film I have to fight like a tiger. They don't want me.

BQ: With everything you've done? With the size of your achievement?
AV: Oh, I'm a perfect cultural gadget, they have me in all libraries and cinémathèques. I'll be unforgotten. But they don't want me to make films.

BQ: Why? France the great film center?
AV: But still they do films to make money. Very few people are involved in creating that pile of pieces of films as you do paintings. I make shorts sometimes just to keep alive in my own research. You know, you saw *Ulysses*, who would give money for that? There is no market for shorts, very strange.

BQ: There seem to be many younger women directors in France now, people starting out, but they seem quite commercial.
AV: Oh, it's everywhere in the world, young men and young women, most of them look for money and fame. They make deals and become part of this stream of commercial films and it's fine if it fits them. If they like that, fine. We need products anyway. We know we cannot feed the need with only these research films or special films.

BQ: With art, you mean?
AV: But my last film, *Vagabond*—I was amazed that I did it with no compromising at all with my way of working. And so many people were touched and intrigued by the film. The film questions people, but not with guilt. I don't judge so it's not saying you should see the film, because shame on you, you don't give money to your neighbor. Nothing to do with that. I make it clear that not only nobody's perfect, but nobody's totally bad and nobody's totally good, nobody's generous really, nobody's mean really. They all do their own way. The shepherd gives her a whole lot, and he gives her a piece of land if she wants to raise potatoes, but then he's the worst judge of all because he wants to be marginal but in *his* way. He doesn't accept other people. He's the one who condemns her.

BQ: You feel harshly toward him?

AV: Yes, because he says errancy is wrong. How does he know what's good and bad? He just knows about his goats and his wife. So the film is really about tolerance also. How with tolerance you can accept other ways of existing which are so difficult to tolerate, difficult for me, difficult for everybody. And the film is made in such a way that it's more interesting because it's a woman. Because the same case could be a man in a way. But by making it a woman we add a lot of questions there—a different kind of solitude, but also a woman alone is a sexual prey, and for half the people a woman is alone because she didn't find the right man. So the film shows that she's not looking for a man, even though when she has them she can drop them like this, even in a bitchy way—as with the man she is with in the castle, and she leaves him hurt. She's mean, she's selfish. The Tunisian gives her an ability to work on something, he's not judging that she's lazy, she doesn't do a thing at home. He seems to accept her as she is. But then you see he's the victim of a group. He can't even hold his own opinion. So all these contradictions that I see all the time are what make me be touched—not only her dying from the cold, and a lonely frozen death is an awful one—but also all these contradictions that we can't stand and I can't stand. And I try to give a shape to it, not to make people cry but to give a shape to it that looks like a film.

Interview with Varda on *The Vagabond*

Jean Decock / 1988

From *French Review* 61, no. 3 (February 1988). Reprinted by permission.

In a Provence emptied yesterday of all of its tourists, Mona, the hitchhiker, ends her life of wandering or mistakes, frozen to death. "You feel solitude to the hilt in winter."

Maybe there's no such thing as generosity, there's only the right way to ask. Mona's way is as proud as that of the Tarahumara Indians who, according to Artaud, begged only in profile. In any case, imperious, indifferent, and sarcastic, Mona doesn't beg: "Got a fag?" People give or don't give according to their mood, the weather, the looks, age, or sex of the Other—we've all experienced the discomfort of this point-blank approach.

Neither documentary nor propaganda, Varda's film translates an existential malaise that will be with us for a long time. But it's also a rare pleasure: a bath of humanity with a warmth of intense feelings and a cinematic richness that has been re-baptized *The Vagabond* for its American release. The film is a masterpiece of editing, a kaleidoscope of long and short sequences. But like Levi-Strauss's notion of *bricolage* (puttering), the film allows us to perceive deeper structures at work. This is the secret of a film that looks entirely improvised (and is) but that nevertheless reveals the complete mastery of its director and puts her talent on display.

Behind the opening credits we see a landscape of vineyards punctuated by two small pines atop a hill—is the music we hear an early Italian composition or the transfiguring music of Joanna Bruzdowicz's quartet?—and we feel as the camera tracks slowly forward that we are approaching something like a Golgotha.

Next we see the film's prologue: a short, brutal, and disquieting sequence that focuses on a dead body in a ditch, a suggestion of incomprehensible violence: a young homeless woman frozen to death. A so-called natural death.

Over images of bird tracks in the sand, we hear the voice of Varda begin the film seeming to bring this body back to life out of a glacial ocean, naked and already desirable. We alternate between Mona's wanderings and the immobility of others, the summerfolk, a sedentary lot (more often than not sitting in front of a TV). The witnesses of her last days, staring into Varda's camera, tell how they met her, how she disappeared, how her absence haunted them, how much they regret not talking to her. Some of them saw her two or three times; they recall these encounters in mini-flashbacks.

Some of them talk too much: the truck driver, the mechanic, the slum pimp, the manager's wife. They exude a kind of run-of-the-mill sexism and racism, mistrust, judgmentality and bad faith. Some of them are more reserved: the agricultural worker, the Tunisian, the blood donor, the girl at the restaurant, the calendar woman, all communicate worry, admiration, a desire for freedom long ago crushed by parents or husband. Short summaries punctuated by a fade to black like eyelids closing. Some are more caring like David the wandering Jew who shares the warmth of his body and his provision of grass. Some are more calculating like the shepherd-philosopher with his theories on freedom, solitude, and return to the earth—if it only weren't for his stay-at-home wife, as mute as his sheep.

Mona refuses what they have to offer. She questions our and their lifestyles, charity, raison-d'être, marriages. The best among them are those who are most shaken by their encounter with her. Inclinations, mutual attractions, coincidences: Varda plays out these games of the road and of chance by developing two very funny and moving episodes that crisscross repeatedly leading up to a meeting in the Nîmes Train station. Yolande Moreau plays a good Belgian woman with her guy, Paulo, and Marthe Jarnais is the marvelous Aunt Lydie. Varda demonstrates great care in portraying this warm and caring friendship between women of such disparate ages that ends in carefree laughter. And then there's Macha Meril who skillfully plays a botany professor who is on a mission to save the plane trees and is accompanied by her young assistant, a seductive vulture who wants to get rid of Yolande and evict Aunt Lydie to take over her coveted apartment.

We end up loving them all, rich and poor, young and old, immigrants and well-intentioned intellectuals—just because of the way Varda lovingly portrays them. And yet it's in opposition to all of them that Mona has chosen her path of liberty and absolute solitude in her proud insistence on being an outsider right to the bitter end. "Every appeal to freedom is a direct message to each one of us," gushes the shepherd who holds a Masters degree in philosophy!

Who is Mona? Simone Bergeron, who holds a general studies degree— the diploma earned by all the secretaries and bureaucrats that she has disdained, has neither home nor family. That's all we will learn about her. The film's title, *Sans Toit ni Loi*, is a play on the old saw *"ni foi, ni loi"* (neither faith nor law) which suggests that homelessness leads inevitably to immorality. Mona will never possess much more than a plastic bag until she is shrouded in one in the morgue. She loves kids, empty houses, rock music, puns. The SPCA? She has "already given" and as for plane trees she couldn't care less. She feels neither solidarity nor compassion. Maybe a bit lazy or just uncaring. Just wants to survive. She's an enigma that remains unfathomable. But what's the question? Rebel without a cause without motivation, absent of desire.

Mona is thirst, hunger, cold, and fear, to be sure, but what we focus on are her poor dirty hands with worn down fingernails holding onto a cigarette or a sandwich but rarely a job. She personifies the need for water, bread, and warmth. She's the broken heel on Sartre's *Roads to Freedom*. Instead of the universe of doors and windows, wood or glass shutters, open or closed or broken, she has chosen the outdoors, the pale sun, the long march. And so the film breathes through its fifteen lyrical tracking shots, carried along by a discrete and serene sound track that assures us Mona is happy in her solitude. Mona's delight in walking corresponds exactly to Varda's delight in filming.

Who is Varda? Rather than Nathalie Sarraute, it's Colette she reminds me of with her love of life which touches with its grace people, animals, plants, and things, in the sun, in the rain, and in the wind. Varda makes us feel reality with all five senses. Her film is filled with animals and a few children, everywhere there are dogs to pat, goats, horses, chickens. It's filled with the green of trees and a blue that so dominates that it becomes a blue film. The love of the photographer for post cards, for the old family albums, for the texture of things in shots empty of people, for the taste of food. She has communicated her pleasure in language to Mona and to Macha, but she also respects the occasional deep silences of the mechanic, the incredibly moving Tunisian.

Towards the end, the film tips over into ugliness. Is it the city, its train station, its homeless people? Is it the multiplication of the homeless into gangs? Is it drugs, drink, and pornography? Just too much dirt? And then the final terror and aggression in this wine-producing village where tree-like men pursue their victims and douse them with wine dregs. Mona is shouting and can't understand this playful ritual that excludes and annihilates her. Exhausted, covered with mud, she heads back to her "radish hut," the last station of the cross. She stumbles, falls, and sobs hopelessly as she waits for death.

How do we recognize a masterpiece? In the pleasure of filming, in a camera whose joy overcomes the sadness of its subject. In the desire to look again and again when you know that the riches of your subject are inexhaustible.

Jean Decock: You began the film after Mona's death. Why?

Agnès Varda: For two reasons. The first is the false lead of a whodunit. There's a body, the police arrive, and the case is wrapped up when they discover she has no ID papers, but I also use this to show that the witnesses who are questioned during the film don't know that she's dead. It's just the opposite of a whodunit where you'd have the police saying things like, "Okay, we've got a murder here. Any chance you can explain how it happens that you've got three buttons missing on your right sleeve?" Here the idea is that the film follows an "anti-cop" type of investigation on the death of a girl who's passed through the area, without ever saying that she's dead.

JD: But the film's viewer knows this.

AV: Yes, the viewer knows that they don't know she's dead. But the second and, for me, more important reason is that the dice are not loaded. The cards are all on the table, and I don't want to make a film where they'll say, "Oh, maybe they can save her! Oh, maybe she will find David again and he'll get her out of there!" But it's what you might call a "cold case" or a "winter's tale"—someone freezes to death.

JD: As for me, I might say, "Pity the dead Mona!" since it seems like her death fits some kind of determinism: her freedom seems to drive her towards death.

AV: Pity? I hadn't thought of it that way, though it's a nice idea. She isn't a very engaging character and, we can see that she dies for lack of human connections, so we might well feel the kind of pity that should somehow accompany the exasperation she elicits at times. She is sometimes a real pain and yet because we know that she's paid dearly for her freedom and her rebellion, we can't help feeling moved by her case. So, yes, I hadn't thought of that before, but it's quite true.

The good thing about *Vagabond* is that it has a powerful subject. A girl whose motivations remain obscure, wanders around the roads of Provence in the cold, and, after a number of tough situations and some bad luck, freezes to death. I can give you the plot in three lines, so it must be a good story line.

JD: So here's a literary question for you. Why did you dedicate the film to Nathalie Sarraute?
AV: I read her work, I like her and I've admired her for the last thirty years. If there's a writer who touches me through her desire to produce the kind of work that she's chosen to write, it's her. I'm touched by the subtle connotations of her novels more than by *The Age of Suspicion*. In *The Planetarium* there's a nephew who has his eyes on his aunt's apartment. In my film it could have been a grandson, but I made it a nephew because of Sarraute.

JD: Perhaps we may see shades of her work in the chance encounters, the vibrations, and the influence of this girl in the structure of the film.
AV: Yes, *Tropisms*. And although I would never dare to say "just as in Nathalie Sarraute's work" because my admiration for her wouldn't allow me to suggest that I've done the equivalent of what she has, still, as in my film, at various times in her works we can see the point of view we have toward certain of her characters get very problematic. For example in *Martereau* this terrific guy becomes a thief . . . And then we think, no he's not a thief, he's a great guy, so our opinion of him constantly changes.

If we think of Mona in purely cinematic terms, we situate her in the center, acting as a mirror of other characters. As these characters talk about her and become witnesses they are introduced into the film as visual parentheses using a technique of fade in/fade out that I modified. Instead of a fade to black, I did a kind of half-fade in/fade out where they emerge from shadows so that their image is there but gets gradually more visible. Their testimony tells us as much about the witnesses as it does about Mona and makes a kind of two-step mirroring effect. We get a sense of them first, but then they mirror back an image of Mona. Her image changes, gets gradually both more defined and paradoxically more blurry.

JD: And the structure of the flashbacks?

AV: In that case I what I wanted was, within the very rigorous framework I'd created, to be completely free. There were testimonies that preceded the action: the mechanic says, "Thirty francs to wash the car and your hands." So right away she washes the car. And then there are the testimonies that come after the action so that they contribute to a kind of summation of the case since the action has already taken place. In the case of the mechanic it's a bit of both—before and after. I worked a lot on these testimonies, what each one said: one talking about freedom, another about saying no, a third about filth. There was a very precise framework for the actors who weren't always chosen before the shooting began. So there was room for improvisation and last-minute additions even though the testimonies had been prepared in advance. For Yolande, Mona is, if you will, a fantasy of love. I really enjoyed the thought that Mona could represent a fantasy of tenderness for a girl who has a guy but nevertheless feels lonely. So you see, it's a bit complicated at times, but it's fun to be complicated when people are always oversimplifying things and it's precisely such simplifications that leave Mona so totally isolated, whatever one may have said or thought about her. In short, the film is constructed out of false leads—most notably her relationship with the hippie, David with whom she is squatting in the chateau and who reappears at the train station. We say, maybe he's going to find her, but when he arrives at the chateau he doesn't see her. Lots of people miss their connections with her. So ultimately it's just bad luck.

JD: I'd like to talk about *cinécriture*, your conception of film writing and the use of tracking shots, shot counter-shots which is a pretty technical subject . . .

AV: . . . because my work is completely technical, because what we do happens at a very practical and technical level rather than at some ideological, theoretical, or metaphoric level, which is what interviewers usually ask about. As for *cinécriture*, as I've said elsewhere, when you write a musical score, someone else can play it, it's a sign. When an architect draws up a detailed floor plan, anyone can build his house. But for me, there's no way I could write a scenario that someone else could shoot, since the scenario doesn't represent the writing of the film; it doesn't indicate the lighting, or the choice of lens or the speed of a tracking shot or the timing of the actor's lines or their expressions. Of course their behavior can be described but you can't measure the length of silences—whether they're two seconds or seven—you can't anticipate the weather you'll be filming in, and any changes in dialogue or behavior necessitated as a consequence. No writing-of-cinema exists per se. And for lack of it I now refuse to write my scenarios. I write down everything on two pages and use this as a challenge. I do this because of so many disappointments, where well-written scenarios got turned down for various bureaucratic reasons and because of the fact that you can buy scenarios. I seemed to have spent my life getting turned down by everyone. When I reached the milestone of thirty years of filmmaking last year I decided that I was completely free to do what I wanted. I no longer want to pretend I'm writing scenarios for submission to others. From now on its: I'll make it or I won't. From now on I'm going to make films on my own terms.

JD: Tracking shots: you start in front of Mona, you catch up to her, you pass her . . .
AV: Tracking shots are connected to Mona's walking, she's only one piece of a landscape that is still there. She's rarely there at the start of the tracking shot, and rarely there at the end. For example, there's the countryside, then she appears, she's walking, and then she disappears and we continue on and then throw in a detail of her actions where she is, to indicate that THIS just keeps going.

JD: At the end of the tracking shots there's clearly a punctuation mark.
AV: Each of these tracking shots ends with something we see in the next one. The first tracking shot begins at the beach: there's a white streak on the road and music, the music starts up so that the film begins on a musical note and we're off, rolling along sixty meters of rails, then the narrator's voice begins. She's walking, she gets a ride on a truck, which we don't see, we only hear the noise of the engine, she disappears from the frame and we stop on a *road sign*. Then there's a little bit of film and a second tracking shot: on the second *road sign* we read: "Go Slow: School Zone" and she reappears in the frame, buys a loaf of bread and we stop at *a tree*. Third tracking show, we begin in *the woods*, etc. In another she's walking through a large ochre field with crows, she walks along, puts down her backpack and we pick up a *farm machine*. Quite a bit later in the next tracking shot there's another *farm machine*, a black wall, all blackened from the burn off which anticipates the charred ditch in which we find her dead body, then she exits the frame and we continue on past a tire hung on a fence post.

I like it when people ask me about details like this, which doesn't happen too often. I'm not as smart a theoretician as I'd like to be. I'd already finished shooting half of the film when I realized that this series of tracking shots of Mona walking were exactly what was missing. I thought, "It's funny, even when she's dead she'll still be walking, even when she stops she's still walking." At night I dream a lot about the film. She's walking—but we don't feel it enough, so I have to make her walking *the* walk. I began this series of tracking shots to express this sense of discontinuity/continuity. I did them with these links that can be found from one to the next. There's a very beautiful one in the village with the fountain: she comes out of the bar, passes the gas pump, leaves in a car, and we end up with a shot of a phone booth and an old woman on a bench and it's the nephew and his aunt. And in the very last tracking shot where she's dragging herself toward death there's the other structure: the music in this scene begins with the musical theme from the very first tracking shot. The tracking shots reproduce uninterruptedly the music of the entire film that we've heard during the opening credits. The death scene is entirely silent since the scene is too emotional to be accompanied by music.

The danger was to make an unstructured film. Naturally I only discovered it while shooting and that's what slowed us down since these tracking shots took an extra two weeks. On the other hand, the testimonies were all planned. I had thought that building the character through these third-party reports would be enough but they weren't. So the idea of the tracking shots put us two and a half weeks behind schedule, cost a lot of money, and put the film in the red, which is just the way things are in the cinema. I could never have enjoyed such creative freedom if I'd been working for a studio like Gaumont.

JD: And establishing shots?
AV: I don't embroider much on this technique. Let's be clear. When there is a conversation, a dialog, the somewhat classical vocabulary of the cinema is a shot-counter-shot. It's a bit like saying a sentence must contain a verb. What is, however, different in my film is that there are very few close-ups. Everywhere there are faces and so there are some medium close-ups: when Mona is eating sardines, when she's crying, when she's hitchhiking in a sleeping bag and, panicked, gets close to the window. There are only about four or five in the film which is extremely rare. And in the first shot when she's picked up by the truck driver, her first words are, "There's me." She's defined by her first sentence. She exists, her grace, her fatigue, her poverty, her rebellion . . .

JD: To come back to the construction of the film, everyone is wonderful with her! Whatever their social level, they seem to be possessed of a kind of goodness . . .

AV: I'm the one who likes *them*, not the reverse. They're not wonderful with her, they're not nice at all. I'm not the least bit cynical; I'm not even capable of cynicism with really awful people. I just can't show them in a bad light. I try to tell myself, "Hey there must be some good in them! They can't be all bad!" Which is true.

JD: Towards the end of the film in the Nîmes train station, there's a more somber tone with the drugs and all.

AV: Yes. I wanted to show that the town is in some respects dirtier than the countryside: with all the gangs in town it's worse than the vagabonds on the road. And then she links up with this guy who's not particularly moving. My idea was that the last testimony kills her. When all you can say about a woman is that she has a nice ass, then you've effectively annihilated her. What's awful is what he says about her, that's what's awful. The last time anyone mentions her, it destroys her.

JD: The violence when David gets beat up, for the rape scene in the woods, you go offscreen.

AV: Did you see this tracking shot in the woods? Sixty meters, four hours of set-up! Don't you see how beautiful that is? We escape into the woods. How does he rape her? You understood it was a rape scene.

JD: She won't ever talk about it.

AV: Now *that's* an interesting subject. She doesn't react. Doesn't say anything. In fact, all the violence is in the film, all the eroticism can be found in the very fact that men see a girl all by herself and think, "I'm going to have her." Here it's suggested, you can feel it. Showing the rape doesn't interest me. I have an ethical system that tells me what to show and what not to show. In any clinical description of violence, of rape, even of war and even when they say it's meant to condemn violence there's always some degree of pleasure and some pleasure shared with the audience. That's not something I can condone under any circumstances. I don't want to do it, that's my choice. What I, Agnès, think (and I'm not sure this is so for my character—I can't, I don't want to speak for Mona), is that there's not a whole lot more violence in a rape in the woods than there is in the way everyone treats her, making her sleep under a porch in ten below weather, from the moment they reject her and she rejects them. I'm not sure that the connotation of being raped is the same for me as it is for others. I'm obviously not saying it's okay. The mechanic in the tent, I'm not sure that she is so willing there either. She doesn't talk about it. The entire scene is shot in silence. That's a challenge I set myself since I have a tendency to make very talky films. Here I tried to be less verbal and keep what I like the most: the Tunisian who smells her scarf and who kisses her. There's a spoken testimony at the beginning—mine, spoken without images and there's the silent testimony at the end—his. I am a kind of echo: I announce that I met her, but you don't see me. You see him but he can't say anything.

JD: Here's another technical question: did you chose Fuji film deliberately?

AV: Deliberately . . . I've used Fuji in several films already. It produces less contrast but we use a Kodak bath for developing it. The film was shot cold, and there's a shot were Mona goes to buy some bread, and in one of my long tracking shots, she goes back into the bakery and while she's there I noticed that they also sell waffle cakes. I suddenly had a flashback to my childhood and I thought of Little Red Riding Hood (there's a lot of that in the film). So I had a little girl dressed in red come out of the bakery with a waffle cake in her hand and her red dress the perfect red of my memories. Even the color of reality in the film is controlled shot by shot, and when there's red in a scene we'll repaint it. There was an orange bench at the train station that we painted grey (and we got bawled out for it by the director of the station). A film is controlled second by second. Technically there's a choice to be made every second. We try things out. I made my recent films in Fuji negatives but I don't like the Fuji prints. I've tried different things like making Kodak prints with Fuji film that brings out the contrast better, and by dressing up the colors in my sets.

JD: Here's a very American question—about the financing of your film.

AV: The money came from the Minister of Culture who gave us a grant based on a two-page proposal without going through all the bureaucratic channels that usually turn me down—boards named by the minister that refuse my applications. This had happened the previous year. It's not as though I'm a *persona not grata culturala*. I'm just a marginal figure and that upsets them. In this case the minister said "yes" and Antenne 2 said "yes" just like that, based on two pages. Based on these two grants that made up about a third of the film's total budget (actually a bit more), we were able to get started, with the rest made up of borrowed money and calculated risks. In the meantime we found some people who were interested in the project. No established director would make a film with only half the budget in hand. *Ciné-Tamesis* is the company I've started. Since it's my production I'm responsible for the risks . . .

JD: What's your secret, your philosophy of filming?

AV: Well there are certain advantages that come with age. I also possess, I hope (if this is the way to describe it), the privilege of having something in me that no one can touch, which no one can destroy. Even here at the Venice Film Festival where everyone is pretty tense, I went swimming in the sea this morning at eight a.m. There was nobody on the beach, not a single other bather. I'm not interested in taking vacations. What my years have brought me is this tranquility about what I have to do. Of course I get very excited and goal-oriented when I'm working on a film.

That's the opposite, no doubt, of people who get really worked up in life. I am a bit "speedy" as they say for everything that's work related. I tend to wear out the people on my team with the extreme speed at which I do things and also by my demands on them. I get up at five a.m. to write my dialogs. I get to the set an hour before anyone else to check things out. I may have last minute ideas and want to set them in motion right away. I made incredible demands without any doubts about whether they'll work. You know I love what you're doing here, but who on earth will read it?

Agnès Varda:
Playing with Tarot Cards

Jean Darrigol / 1994

From *Mensuel du cinéma*, May 1994. Reprinted by permission. Translated by
T. Jefferson Kline.

On the day we met, there were sessions for photos, a TV shoot with the
crew from Paris-Premiere, the final touches to the editing before the happening for Varda at the Cinémathèque, *L'Univers de Jacques Demy* and
The 100 and 1 Nights . . . so why not a fantasy Tarot reading—for each card
a symbolic meaning, a discussion of love—just to hear Varda reading?

Agnès Varda: It's like the beginning of *Cléo* . . . The cards. So here goes.
In general I always choose the card with my left hand, but whatever. I'll
take three cards. The little one that's stuck there. Let's pull one from the
other side . . . that one which seems to want so much to be chosen. Six.
We've got a reading here.

THE LOVER: Of course it's Cupid and his arrow. There's a woman; she's
very severe. She seems to be the mother of the young man holding him
back with her hand on his shoulder. A sort of preventer of love.

JD: This card also seems to be linked to the idea of choice. In 1965 you
chose *L'Opéra Mouffe* which you'd shot in 1958 with its street and its lovers, as your favorite film.[1]
AV: In '65 I really liked *Cléo from 5 to 7* but it seemed to me that *L'Opéra
Mouffe*, a silent film with Delerue's beautiful music, was more instinctive,
almost primitive. Those faces passing in the street speak so eloquently.
And I was the pregnant woman who was looking at them. A look that I
call the subjective documentary. The subjectivity of a pregnant woman.

A look that says, "They were all newborns before becoming old people, bums, blind men. How did people look at them when they were babies? How can one get pregnant when one feels situated between the hope of having a baby—this little bit of tender flesh that we will kiss—and the reality of these former babies? I was incredibly moved since I was doing the filming in the Rue Mouffetard, which relayed back to me all these images of my own feelings. But a lot of time has passed. Today, *Sans Toit ni Loi* has become my favorite film, linking up so beautifully what I wanted to do, what I managed to do, a season that I loved, a narrative, the perfect settings, real characters, and a great actress in Sandrine Bonnaire, whose presence and intensity are magnificent.

THE FOOL or THE MAST: A greasy pole, a flag pole, maybe it's the stick of the wandering minstrel. A minstrel with bells on his head and a little sack on the end of his stick like the vagabonds or pilgrims.

JD: This card inspires madness, genius, adventure. You often talk about the Noirmoutier Mill with a view of the ocean, where you lived with Jacques Demy. Do you like the excesses of Don Quixote?
AV: When I was a photographer I did a photo-essay on the idea of Don Quixote and the places that belong to his legend.[2] This character who battles wind-mills . . . I like battles which lead to something, a book, a poem, or a film; or in politics, battles that lead to a change in the law, some improvement in life, a response, lives saved . . .

THE POPE: Here's a card that's not upside down. It's the Pope! It reminds me of a song I wrote for *One Sings, the Other Doesn't* and the feminist struggles. It goes something like this: "It's not papa, the Pope, or the King, the Judge or the Legislator who are *my* masters!" The Pope rules the Church, the Legislators write the laws of the land, my papa, my husband, or sometimes my brother may rule the home. But women needed to be liberated from those kinds of lawmen. The Pope continues to believe that one shouldn't practice contraception, and refuses to see the reality of the galloping spread of AIDS. Our new conception of sexuality, whether liberated or not, is more a matter of conscience and less a directive from the papacy. Instead of kissing the ground when the Pope arrives, we should be kissing each other . . .

JD: It's a card linked to conciliation . . .
AV: Oh no! Not THE POPE!

JD: There's a kind of optimism and energy in you, as if you had made peace with this period and had moved ahead.[3]

AV: *Le Bonheur* is strange, *Documenteur* is sad, *Sans Toit ni Loi* pessimistic but I try to keep somewhere in these films—even in the darkest of them—a feeling of energy. That's different from pessimism or optimism. Inside these films, the mental activity and the pleasure of filming come together to create an energy that ends up replacing the feelings of happiness or sadness. Vital energy . . .

THE CHARIOT: A blue horse, a red horse: they are the two magic domains of *Peau d'âne* that Jacques Demy created in 1970. In Marais's domain everything is blue, the little servants, the horses. In the Prince's domain, where Jacques Perrin gallops through the forest, everything is red: horses, doublet, even his room. It's only in Jacques' work that I've seen anything like it.

JD: This card is linked to progress, to forward movement, toward the "docu-dream," your magical side.

AV: I'd say, rather, the unreal that finds expression in the real; the fantastic; a certain surrealism in daily life which ultimately evokes the magic of the chance encounter, the collage of life. But it's less magical for me than surreal.

LA MAISON DIEU (HOUSE OF GOD): This is a card that evokes the Middle Ages. There's the tower with its acrobats. The man walking on his hands seems very clever and his movements are quite beautiful.

JD: Romanesque art, religious art seemed to have been very important to you when you were making *O Saison, O Chateaux*, the film that was commissioned after *La Pointe Courte*.

AV: Commissioned films are always precisely linked to a particular subject, a set length, and, ultimately, a pedagogical intent. So the film takes as its reference point the painters of the Middle Ages who were invariably asked to do a limited set of iconic religious subjects, for example, The Annunciation. And so, with the modesty of one who was responding to such a request yet painting according to their particular talent and/or religious feeling, they succeeding in giving each painting their personal stamp. The "Crucifixion" of Van der Weyden, and that of Robert Campin are not alike at all and yet they're telling the same story. It's not so much the subject that counts the most, but rather how, with what violence or what personal feelings they conveyed the subject. That's why, when I look at a Crucifixion, I think every bit as much about the man who painted this subject as about the subject itself. That's why in my book[4] I talked about commissioned films and about the commissioned paintings, The Annunciations and the Angels.

JD: So much of daily life was captured in their paintings. And these are subjects we find in your work as well . . .

AV: The various trades, the works and days. There is a certain humility that goes with painting or recounting what one knows. And with looking at our neighbors. When I made *Daguerréotypes* I was interested in studying their trades and, in *Sans Toit ni Loi* in looking at different types of agricultural work: vine pruners, highway workers, masons working on winter building sites.

JD: Your book is made in this same artisanal tradition.

AV: This is the way I've always worked, in this house I've lived in so long. This is my book, these are my choices, but with Bernard Bastide, the documentarist and author of the filmography, with Claudine Paquot, editor of *Cahiers du Cinéma*, Eric Patrix, the set designer, and my friend Annette Raynaud, part of the work was collective. Claudine, for example, aware of my interest in making a chronological study, produced a study of all my awkwardness and all my shyness in the beginning. She told me, "Let yourself go, the writing will take care of itself." I understood, it was as if I'd hesitated and stumbled before jumping into things. When you make a book on forty years of work in film, you have to lean way back and be careful not to fall. "Agnès and The Others," would be a better title (than *Varda par Agnès*). This book has a very organic feel to it, a rhythm, a life of its own. There are images of films mixed with hundreds of images of life that served as "proofs" or amusing accompaniments. For example, in the section entitled "G as in Godard" we put in a drawing from an ad for Nicolas Wines "G like glug glug!" showing a guy holding eight bottles in his hands.

THE WORLD: This card displays a small nude dancing or jumping in the center of a vegetal oval containing what look like sheaves of wheat. So . . . well there are lots of things I like about this image. It reminds me of a poster the Surrealists made for their Manifesto, that I put in *Varda par Agnès* (p. 31). Surrealism is connected to my adolescence. The poster is a collage with a nude woman standing alone surrounded by ID photos of about twenty men with their eyes closed, Soupault, Aragon, Desnos, Eluard, Jacob, Crevel . . . and the text says, "I don't see the woman hidden in the forest."

JD: In *Sans Toit ni Loi* we see Mona walking for the first time in an image of beginnings, a mythological image. The spirit of the sea bathes your films, you who are half-Greek.

AV: Yes, it's a mythological image, it's Venus emerging from the sea, a woman standing in nature—what they used to call "landscape with figure." Mona is alone, she's walking, she's hitchhiking and the first word she says to the truck driver, who has commented "Not a lot of people at this time of year," is "There's me." She has a burning desire to be herself. Her self-affirmation consists of saying no. Like the Tarot card, Mona has a kind of beginning-of- the-world quality, she emerges naked from the water. The idea was that, every day, she would become dirtier until finally, in the local Festival of Pailhasses (Day of Ashes), the crazies cover her with wine dregs until she falls, filthy and alone, into a ditch. It's true, though, the beauty of the sea.

JD: The card is also linked to cosmic worlds, foreignness. You are one of those people who, happily, are curious about what lies beyond.

AV: That's the reason I have no nostalgia, no regrets—well, maybe *some* regrets, but that's all. If I make films it's to communicate, to share so people can receive what's in the film—not the message, there's no message. In *Lions Love* I have one of my characters say, "There are no messages, only mistakes."

JD: From *Créatures* to *Daguerréotypes* as well as in the project that was cancelled, *Simak*, there's a persistence of the kind of imagination we see in science fiction.

AV: *Simak* was subtitled "The Outer Courtyard." A guy in an ordinary house with a door that opens on to another world. I think we are mediators between what we know but don't always know how to say, and the form that this takes in films where you rediscover things you know but don't know how to express . . . But we have to be careful in creating other worlds without thinking it through. You can't procreate just anything at all!

JD: Let's end with the trailer for your coming attractions.

AV: We're doing the final editing of *L'Univers de Jacques Demy*. It will be a feature-length documentary, somewhat didactic in nature but not very objective, very well documented on all of Demy's films, features and shorts. It will be a kind of reference work where you can learn more about Jacques Demy. I've had to push back the date when we'll be doing the mixing and final touches. *100 + 1 Nuits* is a fiction film, a fantasy, an amusing film about the cinema that I love and that the public loves as well. I should hurry up and finish writing it!

Notes

1. In *Les Cahiers du Cinéma*, April 1965.

2. "Si Dulcinée m'était contée," *Marie-France*, no. 18 (September 1957).

3. See *Visuelles*, no. 2 (1980).

4. *Varda par Agnès* (Paris: Cahiers du Cinéma, 1994).

Agnès Varda:
A Very Worthy Young Woman

Mario Cloutier / 1995

From *Séquences*, no. 177 (March/April 1995). Reprinted by permission. Translated by T. Jefferson Kline.

Agnès Varda has been making films for forty years. This woman who has been nicknamed The Grandmother of the New Wave has made seventeen feature-length films and as many short subjects. Experimental, documentary, and fiction films . . . She's tried everything with intelligence and a conspiratorial smile. It's with this same approach that she's set out themes of death, memory, and the cinema in her latest film *The Hundred and One Nights*.

Mario Cloutier: After two documentaries of Jacques Demy and two fiction films focusing on Jane Birkin, it's somewhat surprising to see you arrive here in Montreal with lighter fare.

Agnès Varda: Yes, you're right. I wanted to make a more entertaining film, I prefer the word "entertaining" to "comedy." I wanted my audience to be entertained by a story of an old man, and to entertain myself as well while making the film. This film thumbs its nose at all the embalmers of the cinema. I wanted to celebrate the cinema by making a real film and not just doing another homage film. I agree with Buñuel, who said that commemorative gestures are dangerous.

MC: Certain French critics haven't really understood what you were trying to do in this film. How was the film generally received in France?

AV: French film criticism is very pretentious and "cinephilic." I find this funny because they're pretty serious and I'm much less so than they are. And when I make an entertaining film, you have to accept it for what it is. We don't expect a light-hearted dance with pirouettes to be an existential treatise. At the very beginning of the film we see a servant leaping as if she were a circus acrobat, another is spinning plates, and the majordomo is disguised as Arlequin. It isn't serious and shouldn't be taken as such. On the other hand I don't expect this kind of humor to appeal to everyone.

MC: These critics have taken you to task for having forgotten certain cinematic genres in this film full of winks to the audience.

AV: When you're having a party you don't invite everyone in the phone book. Their response strikes me as exactly the same problem. This is a cinematic party to which I invited certain films, certain stars, certain composers to join the main characters, Simon Cinema, his Italian friend Marcello Mastroianni, his servant Henri Garcin, and from the other side of the footlights a bunch of kids who represent the second century of the cinema and a real desire to make films. Because that still exists, you see . . .

MC: What's more the cinema they're creating isn't very original. It's genre film, pastiches.

AV: Like they themselves say, it's practicing scales. But that's what they're taught at school, to create the atmosphere of a thriller, à la Antonioni or à la Tarantino. I think that's normal. They copied the New Wave, Wenders, and the others. That doesn't mean these young filmmakers lack personality, but simply that they're twenty years old. They're still so close to childhood.

MC: Like all old guys, Simon Cinema and Mister Cinema regress to childhood. Can we really say he's happy, that he's alive and well at age one hundred?

AV: You don't have to see the film as restricted only to the cinematic metaphor. What you see in the film is the description of an old man. Old men are happy when they have visitors, distractions, friends. At night when they can't sleep, they're a little sad. And even if he cries sometimes, Simon Cinema is happy in his old age, and pretty rich. There are old guys a lot worse off than he is. Simon's losing his memory and mistakes Gerard Depardieu for Gerard Philipe. But he doesn't want to die, that's for sure.

MC: We should take it as the fear that cinema is a dying art?

AV: I didn't go that far into the symbolism of the thing. What we know is that the main character is a mythomaniac. He accuses Mastroianni of having robbed him and dreams of walking up the grand staircase at Cannes. I find him to be a pretty normal old man. He has as many fantasies as a woman has pairs of shoes. He's a happy mythomaniac. But he's a bit stingy. Cinema is about money. I wanted to keep the story at a superficial level while at the same time exploring questions of death, memory, the false and the true, money. Deneuve and De Niro as a couple . . .

MC: To poke fun at certain critics we could say, "That's not very serious, Madame Varda!"
AV: There you go! But you know there are some French people who got it and said, "What a fantasy, what fun!" Someone wrote and told me that my film "really stuck it to all the gravediggers of fun, to all the snobs and cynics. This film will be golden in a few years." The inspiration and master of my film is Buñuel and his short film, *L'Age d'or* (*The Golden Age*). I created this funny monument in this film with an eye that looks inward and a camera that films our inner life. The next day we destroy the monument. When people in a museum start shouting when they see people screwing in the mud I think it's time to say that life and emotion are more important than monuments.

MC: Your film reminds me of the old short by René Clair, *Entr'acte* . . .
AV: Yes, both films share the goal of entertaining without having to answer to Madame Logic. And, remember, the French are Cartesians . . . Luckily I have my Greek side. My father was Greek. I think cultural mixes produce very interesting results. Because the Greeks aren't a very funny bunch either . . . My family moved around a lot when I was a kid, and that gave me a sense of freedom . . . I have no roots.

MC: Neither roof nor law, as the title of your film says . . .
AV: If you like. But on second thought, not really. The portrait of this girl was impossible to do, told by a hundred thousand people . . . And I still can't claim to have completely portrayed this character. Despite being the author of the film, I confess I don't feel like the demigod of the character. As I have said, "I invented the Mona person but I don't claim to know everything about her." It's like Godard's expression, "Two or three things I know about her." And the film's spectator is another witness with her own interpretation. And in *The One Hundred and One Nights* I have the same approach. Of course the film represents my statement about the cinema, but there's also the modesty of realizing that each spectator makes her own film. I just let myself go thinking about

Buñuel, about a few films and about two characters, and old man and a kid. I had fun with it.

MC: On the other hand it must have been difficult to get all these stars together for the film?

AV: Yes, we had to figure out how to shoot the film according to each actor's schedule. Think of it! One minute they're free, the next they aren't. We had to get them by plane, helicopter, the Concorde. Ooh la la! It was also very tough choosing excerpts from eight to ten seconds long from films and film scores. We had an entire team devoted to getting the rights for these sequences. The editing was also very hard. I wanted the film to be a ball of fire and to speed along like in a clip. In a sense it was a kind of two hour long clip on the cinema.

MC: It's also fun to go back and see the bits we missed, right?

AV: The cinema doesn't want to die, so it has to rediscover different survival techniques. I'm more worried about the *cinema d'auteurs*; the movie industry is doing fine. The song in the film expresses it pretty well: "The cinema is fine. The cinema is not! The cinema makes me dream a lot!" The *cinema d'auteur* is having a bad time of it. Now we're in the reign of industrial film production with bunches of screen writers and publicity agents who guarantee good production values. Thank god there are still a few *auteurs* left, a few in each country who have things to say and an original way of expressing them. But they're in danger of becoming extinct because the public seems less and less responsive to their work. The movie-going generation of today goes to see films for very different reasons than the generation who went to see Chabrol, Truffaut, or Varda. Reputation is no longer a gauge of success.

MC: Are the young *auteurs* turning more and more towards video for its immediate accessibility?

AV: In France, it's true we're beginning to see some very good videographers. But there's new energy in the cinema as well among a number of young women. That's encouraging. It remains to be seen whether either group can find a language that can reach the larger public. At least they're supported by grants from the government and by the critics. Even if they carry less weight than they used to . . . But I'm discovering lots of positive energy from the younger generation to help me make this new film. And that's what's worth holding onto. *The Hundred and One Nights* will be an entertaining film.

The Grandmother of the New Wave

Carol Allen / 1996

From *Talking Pictures*, www.talkingpix.co.uk, January 6, 2011. Reprinted by permission.

Carol Allen: Tell me about the films being shown in this retrospective.
Agnès Varda: Some are very old including *La Pointe Courte*, my first film, made in '54 which was how I became the grandmother of the New Wave. For years this film was never subtitled in English because it's more a cinematic piece, I would say, than a film for general release. But now it has been subtitled by the ministry of foreign affairs' *bureau de cinema*. Others in this retrospective are better known, like *Cléo from 5 to 7* or *Sans Toit ni Loi*, called *Vagabond* here I think, *Jacquot de Nantes*, and *One Sings, the Other Doesn't*. There is also a film I made in the States.

One of the last films I made, well three years ago, was about the shooting of the *Young Girls of Rochefort* by Jacques Demy. It's called *Young Girls Turned 25*, that's the one I introduced Monday. I guess if Jacques were alive I would not have done these films about him, his work. Things happen the way they have to happen, I guess. I made a documentary about him, all his films called *L'Univers de Jacques Demy—The World of Jacques Demy*.

CA: I want to ask you about *The Umbrellas of Cherbourg* particularly because this is going to be carried when the film opens in London, but *Jacquot de Nantes*, I thought, was a documentary, because I'm afraid I never saw it, and I was passing the French Institute just now and it says "starring" so was it fictionalized?
AV: It's a fiction—I would like you to see it—it's the story of a boy between eight years old and eighteen years old in the time of the war in France in the forties in a garage in Nantes, and he's so excited about making shows. He does puppets and then he starts alone to begin working in

cinema and in his attic he fights like a tiger to do a little piece of film so that he would convince his mother to be able to go to a cinema school in Paris. Obviously this is the real story of Jacques Demy but it's a fiction, as if you would say *I Shot Andy Warhol* is not a documentary, that's a fiction. So you can have different levels of fiction. This one is strongly related to the real Jacques and he appears in the film in a way to say, yes this is true, this is my story, and it has also little pieces of his future film. It was cast with three children growing up, because it couldn't be the same doing eight and eighteen and a fake mother and a fake father. It's a fiction film, but largely it is dealing directly with Jacques' memories that he allowed me to use and I wrote the dialogue, I wrote the scenes. Maybe I push or I was beyond or after what he would have done himself but he gave me the right to make a fiction, but I know I tried as much as I could to be like—I was like digging in my own memory as if I were him so I made a very bizarre "mediumique" approach to what I had in mind even though he was alive when I did it, he was coming on the shooting, he did see most of it.

CA: *L'Univers de Jacques Demy* and the film about the *Young Girls of Rochefort* twenty-five years on, they are documentaries though are they?
AV: Absolutely. My project was very clearly when I started *Jacquot de Nantes* to make a fiction about a boy who wants to become a filmmaker and then to make a documentary about the adult who made these films, but Jacques passed away just at the end of *Jacquot de Nantes*. So I had to make the documentary with pieces I found in diverse places—an interview he gave on television, and I had interviews with everybody—Catherine Deneuve, Jeanne Moreau, actors and actresses who'd worked with him and Anouk Aimee, everybody, Piccoli, so these people spoke about him intercut with pieces of himself. The real typical documentary about a filmmaker. So for me it's like a diptych—he's a child, it's a fiction, he dreams about making movies, he's adult, it's a documentary, he has made movies, so that was the project.

Now the one about *Young Girls of Rochefort* came in between—it twists a little my first idea but you have to follow what's happening, you cannot make a clarification like they do in the industry. Some of us are artists still.

CA: How long were you married, Agnès?
AV: Thirty-two years, no we didn't marry right away. We were together thirty-two years, we were married twenty-eight and fighting and loving.

CA: Over thirty years is a long time to know somebody and live with somebody. When you were making these films about your husband, were there any surprises? Did you find out things about him that you didn't know?

AV: Yes, when he wrote himself his childhood memories, even though he had told about it, he said by writing, it's like a pump you know, by writing other names other stories came out. But this I got from him on the paper. In writing, I discover myself. My point was to make a film about the filmmaker so in the documentary, everybody tells something. Sometimes in the interview, the person surprised me by saying something like, you are so manic about the world, but I knew it, I wasn't surprised.

CA: You knew he could be manic?

AV: Well he was manic about his own lines. Jeanne Moreau says, "I couldn't change a comma, I had to say the exact speed he wanted," and other people say things like this but . . . I think it's fair just to show the work, the evolution of the work from the first documentary he made, when he didn't want so much to make documentaries but he started like this, then going to his own world of idealizing—do you read from French? Because the thing about *Umbrellas of Cherbourg* that I restore and I can explain that—I don't like to—you can imagine, I can do the work but I cannot speak for Jacques, I would hate that and I think it's—that's it, I'm a filmmaker, I can speak about my own films, I can speak about the films, the documentaries I made about his but it's my cinema, I'm still speaking about my work.

About his work, especially *Umbrellas of Cherbourg*, at the time it came out in Paris, Cine Tamaris did a little Cekadidemy—it's phonetic, it means "what Jacques Demy said" but it's like children's jokes when they learn to speak. And this is what he said himself about the film: "I'd rather idealize the real, if not why go to the movies?" And he said: "*Les Parapluies* is a film against war, against absence, against whatever we hate which destroys happiness." The interviewer said, "You've given Catherine Deneuve the face of innocence and youth," and Jacques replied: "Catherine is innocence and youth." "What would you have done if you had not done cinema?" and he says, "I would have been a painter or musician." I don't think they are contradictory. "What did you do before making cinema?" "Cinema." He explained how it started and he said very nice words, he said, I would say it's a film "enchanté" like we say "en couleurs," but it doesn't translate very well . . .

CA: "Enchanté" is "enchanting" and it's also "sung" . . .

AV: Like you say "en couleurs," in color. So in singing and in colors. But it makes a joke with words in French. [Later in the article] he says how he worked with Michel Legrand and he says how he found Cherbourg, in case somebody reads French, and this is when he came to Cannes. He's asked: "What kind of pleasure did you get by making *Parapluies*? Answer: "An extreme pleasure, refined. Not bestial at all!" Question: "Your wife Agnès Varda is famous. She has been selected at Cannes"—because I had been with *Cléo* before. "In her talent what touches you?" Answer: "Poetry. It's bizarre." Question: "Whom would you most like to meet at the festival?" Answer: "The little Dorleac sisters, that is Catherine Deneuve and Francoise Dorleac." With whom he later worked. He was already wishing to do it.

CA: Could I ask you about this restoration of *Les Parapluies*?

AV: I will tell you. *Les Parapluies* is made following the movements of the heart. It's the little pieces of an existence, a life in which memory is the music. It's very interesting the way they use the music. You have to listen to that music with your ear as if it were a dream but you have to look at the film with your eye stuck on the glass of reality. It's very interesting because he really pushes it.

And this is a page of his handwriting. The way the script was written before it was totally like a normal script—it's now written like an opera, under the music. It's really a script. About the restoration, I would like to do it.

CA: As I understand it, it was something you and your husband wanted to do for a long time.

AV: He wanted to do it but the producer was not ready to because it cost a big amount of money. It cost about £80,000, that kind of money, so she was not ready to do it because she thought it was not worth it. But she still had done something very important, that Jacques asked her to pay at the time, 1964. The film was shot with a color negative and he knew that colors fade, so he did ask her to copy the negative on two positive prints, black and white.

CA: Two not three?

AV: Three. One positive print just getting the reds, one just getting the blues, one getting the greens. This is not a technicolor process but it's the same kind of process. It's like when you print in paper you have three layers printing—the machine goes for red, the machine goes for yellow—you know. So because he saved in black and white the value of the colors, but the producer didn't want to afford it. When the producer realized Jacques was right and he got back and made an arrangement with her to get the material back in the family, then we did the restoration.

CA: Where had these prints gone in the time between? Were they easy to find?

AV: They were, thank God—French cinema has a national archive and Jacques had insisted they would be kept there. So while there was a lot of paper to organize, Jacques wanted to do it but he couldn't technically do it, he didn't start to do it but that was the project. Then I was busy taking care of him more than usual, plus finishing *Jacquot de Nantes*. So as it was finished I started the renovation. And it consists of putting back these three positive prints black and white like a very thick black and white print—it has to be very well adjusted. Then you refilm it in color. You end up with a brand new negative which is exactly the same as in '64, just as colorful.

CA: Once you've got hold of those three prints, that doesn't sound like it's going to be too horribly complicated—I'm sure there's more to it than that . . .

AV: We had to redo the sound, find the three stripes, mix, and ask Michel Legrand to come and re-mix. At that point we did it in Dolby Stereo even though it was not shot in Dolby Stereo so it's kind of poor last cousin in the family of Dolby Stereo, but because with real stereo you have sound coming from everywhere, the car comes here, goes out there, what we did with a kind of semi-stereo. It gives a sound some roundness. Instead of coming out of one speaker it comes out three places in front. It gives a little something to the sound—it's not a real Dolby but it still is better and we had to redo the negative optical—the timing—because you get a new negative but it's not timed. Well, it took me four months, in and out, four months.

CA: So when you were grading the print, you had to remember what the colors had looked like before?

AV: Yes, that's why I did it because the director of photography was retired in the South of France. I asked him to come and he didn't want to and there was nobody—Jacques and me and knowing the decorator, the one who would have remembered colors, I could have brought him to the lab but he had a heart attack, a stroke that year so couldn't move— well, I remembered vividly and I could do it. So I did it day after day. It was like an embroidery, you say, "oh, I'll never finish this, I still have this to do, and the background and the little grey," but when it's finished and it's beautiful, you say "wow!" and you forget the time, you know.

CA: How long did it take in all?

AV: In and out four months.

CA: Because it started so long ago, or you had the idea so long ago, I was visualizing it took years.

AV: No, no. Four months of my work is not nothing. The research of the things, that was before, this is not work like going to the lab, but it is work: we called, we wrote, we made papers, we found the money. First I went to Technicolor London to have explanation and went to Technicolor Rome to have explanation. I did my best to understand what I could of the problem. Then the machine came, then we had to try different stock to get the best and the longest lasting color. Look, we came through it, it's done. Now the film is beautiful. Have you seen the screening yet or no? You will see it because the restoration has brought back what Jacques wanted. It's not colorization, it's not adapting, correcting, or making it shorter or wider, it's the exact film he shot, but that's the way he shot it, that's the way the colors were on the set.

CA: And it's been seen in France and in the United States?

AV: It came out in Paris in the same theatre where he had opened in '64, which was touching. It was incredible, like time had forgotten to exist. It stayed a long time in France and it went to all the cities in France, then it was shown beautifully on TV twice with all the restored video elements, including digitalization, which holds better the contrast and the colors frame by frame. The restoration of the elements for TV and video cassette are just as important. They made a beautiful evening at Canal Plus with my documentary *L'Univers de Jacques Demy*. Then they showed *La Baie des Anges*, then they showed *Les Parapluies*, and then they had a pre-opening at the Museum of Modern Art in New York after which it opened in a cinema, and showed for fourteen weeks. Now it's going to sixty theatres throughout the U.S., and the American press said that for the first time they understood the film. They'd thought it was just sentimental, but now they see there is a violence in the fact that the bourgeoisie acts like this. The bourgeoise mother is ruining her daughter's life but on the other hand Algerian war has broken their happiness.

CA: A very similar thing I think happened in the U.K. when it first opened in the sixties. A lot of critics just dismissed it as sentimental.
AV: I hate people who say, it means this or that. You take whatever you wish. In the film if you see it now, for some reason maybe because the color, I think the vivid color helps you to see the violence. That's my point. I don't know.

CA: Because it looked beautiful people didn't look beneath the surface?
AV: It looks beautiful, it's still very sad and sentimental but some issues appear clearer now. It's the story but it has Jacques' thoughts behind and you'll have to find out whatever you think it is.

CA: There is an anti-war element in it . . .
AV: You hear him sing, against war, against whatever breaks up in his life. It's like war breaks up and the mother breaks things up. It's about revolt but in a very sweet way, you know.

CA: There's something rather ironic and pragmatic about it. I often think if it was a Hollywood reunion they'd either have a reunion or the ending would be seen as a huge tragedy. As it is there's a far more European . . .
AV: I tell you the ending that I've seen now fifty or sixty times, is very enigmatic for me, very interesting. There are some little funny things, like the end when they meet again and the child of love is in the car. She brings the little girl and says, "Do you want to see her?" and he says, "No." But the little girl was Rosalie, our daughter (now she's grown up). And in the garage Nino's son is played by Michel Legrand's son, so we had our family there.

CA: Rosalie played Francoise?
AV: And Michel Legrand's son played the boy François. Besides the pleasure of renovating it, when I see the kids and think like this I have fun watching it. It's like yesterday I went to the French film festival in Edinburgh where I introduced *One Sings, the Other Doesn't* and spoke and had a wonderful debate about it. I don't know if you remember it. But it was a feminist film and at some point they are on the road, the woman singing, and they pick up a man with a child on the road hitchhiking and

the little boy playing the role is Mathieu Demy. Now the man who presented *One Sings* said to the audience, "You have to see the little boy; that was Mathieu Demy who came last year as an actor and presenter and presented another film at the film festival." That's so funny. He came with the film *The Hosier, A La Belle Etoile*, he was the leading actor, he was nineteen or twenty but it was funny the way the man said, "He came last year as an actor." Well, they grow up.

CA: *Umbrellas of Cherbourg* I always thought was the first all-sung musical film. Is that correct?
AV: In terms of musical film yes. There was an opera called *Le Medium* by Menotti, an avant-garde opera, that Menotti himself filmed some years before and that Jacques had seen, but it's different. It was a stage opera, difficult music, a lot of cacophony, you know, that the composer himself made a film out of it, but almost nobody saw the film because it was a very difficult piece. It was done like this so one cannot say *Parapluies* was the first. I'm told *Evita* is entirely sung. Is that true?

CA: It may well be. I can't remember whether there was dialogue in the stage version or not, but an awful lot of musicals now are entirely sung. As far as I can remember *Umbrellas* virtually broke the ground—they're not just singing about love, they're singing about car engines.
AV: When they say, "You want some gas, super, ordinaire?" "How old is this? Twenty?" or somebody comes in and they say, "No next door," all is sung. As I tell you, because the Menotti thing, it is a film but nobody saw it, it was like a memory of the opera. I saw it; it was totally sung. I saw it, Jacques saw it, I remember twice. Now as a film hoping for large audiences it was the first one and Jacques said, I want to do a popular opera—that was his word. Like an opera but popular like the cinema, not those incredible voices, incredible songs. He wanted to keep the singing and he discussed it with Michel Legrand to get as near as possible to the (spoken) voice—even though the melodies are beautiful—but like a conversation. He was right that after a while you get used to it. You don't think it's so odd to sing everything. After seven/eight minutes you just accept it as a way of thinking.

CA: Where did your husband's love of the musical come from?
AV: You have to see *Jacquot de Nantes* my dear, because when he was young he went to what we call the operetta. You know what operetta is, that kind of early musical, some very nice but some not too good and his

mother would take him to the theatre—sometimes to hear Offenbach, so in *Jacquot* I reconstructed an operetta that he goes and sees and is so happy since he loved operettas.

CA: How about the Hollywood musical? In *Young Girls* he imported Gene Kelly and George Chakiris from Hollywood.

AV: The more classical *Young Girls of Rochefort* is a classical musical *à l'americaine* but in a French setting, very classical architecture so it makes it very different. It doesn't look very Hollywood to me. But it has the shape, typically they speak, they sing, they speak, they sing. He wanted that. He imported Gene Kelly because he loved him, and he wanted a good dancer so he asked Chakiris.

CA: *Young Girls* has dialogue in it?

AV: You never saw that?

CA: No, in fact a lot of people are asking now if that could be restored.

AV: It is. I'm doing it. I'm fed up with restoration I must say. I'm tired of doing it, but I tell you sometimes when lost in the desert and you have a problem with your car, the only one to fix it is a mechanic. At some point, I'm the one able to do it so I do it.

CA: Why do you think *Umbrellas* in particular is well loved and remembered and regarded as so important?

AV: Many things. First it's a beautiful film. Then it won the Palme d'Or in Cannes, then it was nominated for the Oscars, five nominations, best music . . . I can't remember, and it's loved so this is it. It even happened that they did three stage musicals. I didn't like them but in Tokyo, in New York, and in Paris they did a stage version. Some four years after the film, late sixites and Tokyo was a little later, Paris in the seventies, but it doesn't for me have the magic of the film at all.

CA: So is that what makes the film so important, this particular magic?

AV: It's well done as a film, you know, the way Jacques handled the combination of movement, the camera and music and emotion and directing the actors and the beauty of the actors. Nobody is suffering from Catherine Deneuve being twenty!

CA: She doesn't seem to have changed much in thirty years. A little more about you . . .

AV: Along with this painful restoration I'm restoring *Le Bonheur*, because I'm in the process of restoration so I did one of mine because I also had the same producer (Mag Bodard), and she had done the same positive things. Jacques told her to do it at the time. Too bad she didn't do it for *Young Girls of Rochefort*, so it's much more difficult, I can't explain, too complicated.

CA: So you're in the process of restoring *Rochefort* and *Le Bonheur*?
AV: Which is almost finished. Before the end of the year I'll be finished with these technical things. I go to the lab every day, or almost every day and when my office calls in the morning to say, "Can you do Friday morning at the lab—and Monday afternoon—and Tuesday morning?" and its an hour and a half drive to go to that lab and back. Now I have music in my car and I even put in a telephone because I'm doing so much driving to do this, to go to that lab in the North of Paris. I will try to get back to myself in '97.

CA: You mentioned earlier you're known as the grandmother of the New Wave. Do you regard that as a compliment or an irritant?
AV: As a compliment! Better to be the first than the last. I was a pioneer and a pioneer is always somebody who looks for adventure and I've done a lot of cinematic adventures. I did a film in Hollywood called *Lions Love* and I made different films, more or less well-known because few people know them. I've been doing strange films and I still see myself as *"une tête chercheuse"*—a researcher, because in the industry they need to have people asking, "Could we do this?" trying not to repeat myself. I don't repeat myself but my ideas at the time became the ideas of what has been called the New Wave especially the idea of starting as a younger film-maker with less money, or do films in which most of the time someone's walking endlessly, this is the mark of the New Wave. I would say I am very lucky that my films haven't been forgotten. People speak about *Cléo from 5 to 7* all the time, forty-two years after it came out in '62.

CA: You didn't have an easy time raising money for your films?
AV: Always difficult, it still is now. My last film called *101 Nights* was se-lected at the Berlin film festival, and did OK. It's opening in Japan soon. I've have just come back from Japan promoting the opening but French cinema doesn't come to the U.K. Very little.

CA: Some does. *Le Bonheur* and *Cléo* did.

AV: But those came thirty years ago. At that time they did fine. So did *Vagabond* but this is already ten years ago. In the last five years not many French films have been distributed.

CA: Not compared to the amount made.

AV: And even British television is not so thrilled to buy French films now. The economic situation has changed a lot. I'm grateful to the Bureau du Cinema, the French minister, to have made this brand new print of six of my films in six copies of each, so my series is here, was at Edinburgh, it's going to India, it's going to many countries, to Mexico, the Cinemathèque of Hollywood; MOMA will show them, and it's nice to know they have a certain sense of culture.

CA: So your six nice new prints of those six films . . .

AV: Thirty-six, six times six, are going around the world, well printed, with a program which has been organized. It's nice because it's a way of saying even if I knew film is not right now playing it's an opportunity for people to see them, to discuss them, to not forget me which we'd rather know before we die than after.

CA: So this is an enterprise by the Bureau de Cinema of the Ministry of Foreign Affairs? So they put up the money for a nice set of prints of six of your films to do a world tour?

AV: That's what it is and I go, when I can. I can't do the *tour du monde*, but I'm invited everywhere, I could go to India, to Estonia, to Copenhagen, they asked me. I have to work, I'm not a salesperson. I came here because it was interesting to combine Edinburgh and Glasgow and here in the three cities they were shown and some people like my films. Otherwise a man and his wife said they like my films; they said they saw the whole series in Glasgow and the whole series in Edinburgh. It's not that far, a one hour drive, but because it was combined it was almost a drive every other day to get to see them twice.

CA: Do you think anybody's likely, now there are nice spanking new prints of your movies, to take them up for commercial release again?

AV: We hope so. There is demand now, it's coming back into fashion now. There is demand for a remake of *Cléo* for the second time. The first time, Madonna wanted to do a remake of *Cléo from 5 to 7*. I love that woman. Ten years ago she would have been perfect, but then she was upset because her mother died of cancer, and couldn't do it. Now there is someone else asking for the remake rights in America. I may re-release them. *Cléo* was re-released in France eight years ago, did very well. When I have fixed *Le Bonheur*—I don't know if it is the right time for *Le Bonheur*, I'm not sure, you have to think about the way audiences are oriented. Sometimes it's not the right time.

CA: I was thinking *Vagabond*, which was very successful . . .
AV: Successful—meaningful for the people, that's what made it successful. It also won the Golden Lion at Venice; this helps a little and Sandrine was exceptionally interesting also.

CA: And the documentary technique in the fictional film.
AV: Well it's a documentary texture; it makes it believable.

CA: That came nine years after your previous film and we had to wait another five/six years for *Jacquot*?
AV: But I've done films in between that you didn't see. I made *Jane B by Agnès V*, *Kung Fu Master*, then *Jacquot*, since *Jacquot* I made *Young Girls at 25*, *101 Nights* with an incredible cast—de Niro, Delon, Deneuve, all the "de," Depardieu, Gina Lollobrigida.

CA: A celebration of a hundred years of cinema?
AV: It was a fiction around all that. Since I do documentaries now everybody thinks I only do that. It was a fiction with very wonderful actors in it. The story is, Monsieur Cinema is one hundred years old, his name is M. Cinema and he's played by Michel Piccoli, and his memory's totally fucked up, so he hires a very young girl to help him work on his memory about cinema, then he has visitors, so those visitors, like when Depardieu comes to visit him and we have Alain Delon spend a little visit, and because his visitors are famous and he mixes up the whole thing it becomes a kind of comedy about memory. But this did not come to the U.K. We were not even invited to the London film festival.

CA: Do you have another film lined up?
AV: Not yet, but I will come back to myself in '97. I may have some inspiration, I may make another film.

CA: I heard you were having lunch with Jeremy Thomas.
AV: He co-produced *101 Nights*, that film and finally got out of the production because he was doing the Bertolucci film, but at the beginning

he was the co-producer and we remained friends, especially with one of his line producers there, whom I've known for many years. No, I'm not in business if this is what you mean. I don't have a deal signed or something. I always wait to be sure that my mind is oriented, my desire, my energy. I work from inspiration, I don't do deals, do business. I don't even make a career you know, I make films.

CA: You've just published your autobiography *Varda par Agnès*.
AV: It's about my life as a filmmaker but because I'm a woman and that is the way we live, it includes other things you know but I tell mostly how a film starts because I think this is the mystery. Why I do this film and not another and stories about the shooting and images—it's a huge book but I made it when I'd done forty years of filmmaking, in '94, having started my first feature in '54.

CA: Likely to be translated into English?
AV: I would like to. There was a little discussion in New York. So far no, I'd love somebody to do that, but will they print it? You know, money is always one of the problems, not to say the hugest one.

The Modest Gesture
of the Filmmaker: An Interview
with Agnès Varda

Melissa Anderson / 2001

From *Cineaste* 26, no. 4 (Fall 2001). Reprinted by permission.

Often hailed as the grandmother of the French New Wave, Agnès Varda has been making films for nearly fifty years. Her latest film, *The Gleaners and I* (*Les Glaneurs et la Glaneuse*)—awarded the Melies Prize for Best French Film of 2000 by the French Union of Film Critics—documents those who scavenge and salvage to survive in both rural and urban areas of France. Varda spent several months traveling through France to meet these present-day gleaners, using a digital camera to record her encounters. Varda's warm, wry voice-over narration is heard throughout *The Gleaners and I*, making the "I" of the film's title a vital, visible presence in the film. Varda captures—sometimes inadvertently—her own signs of aging, such as the graying of her hair and the age spots on her hands. Fittingly, she speaks of her role as filmmaker as one who gleans images and ideas. Fully realizing that her subjects have the power to instruct her on the subject of gleaning, Varda never condescends to or sentimentalizes her interviewees. The gleaners in the film—particularly François, a formidable young man who survives solely on what he finds in the garbage—are compelling individuals who speak candidly about their lives and economic situations. Varda's is a serendipitous path, one which leads her to film a man who rummages through the detritus left over in a Paris market; later Varda discovers that this man has been teaching literacy for six years and interviews him in his classroom.

Varda's observations during her travels in *The Gleaners and I*—a film that she has described as a "road documentary"—reveal the class disparities in France. Filming a group of school children who make art projects from recycled goods, she wonders, "How many of these children have ever shaken hands with a garbage collector?"

The Gleaners and I marked a return for Varda to the documentary format after her 1995 film, *One Hundred and One Nights*, which presents a rich assortment of film clips culled from cinema's one-hundred-year history and a host of cameo appearances by international stars and features Michel Piccoli and Varda's son, Mathieu Demy. Prior to that celebration of film's centenary, Varda, in the early nineties, commemorated the life and work of her husband, Jacques Demy, who died in 1990. *Jacquot* (1990) is a narrative film about Demy's childhood interspersed with footage of his films and brief interviews with Demy himself.

The documentary *The World of Jacques Demy* (1993) features interviews with both Demy and the collaborators on his films. *The Young Girls Turn 25*, also from 1993, revisits the French port town of Rochefort, where Demy filmed his 1967 musical *The Young Girls of Rochefort*, starring Françoise Dorleac and Catherine Deneuve. Like *The Gleaners and I*, *The Young Girls Turn 25* features Varda's own ruminations on memory loss, and the significance of place. Melissa Anderson spoke with Agnès Varda last October about *The Gleaners and I*, documentary filmmaking, and her films of the nineties.

Melissa Anderson: How did you become interested in filming the gleaners?
Agnès Varda: There were three things. The first one was noticing the motion of these people bending in the open market. The second one was a program on TV. The third reason—which pushed me to begin and continue this film—was the discovery of the digital camera. I picked the more sophisticated of the amateur models [the Sony DV CAMDSR 300]. I had the feeling that this is the camera that would bring me back to the early short films I made in 1957 and 1958. I felt free at that time. With the new digital camera, I felt I could film myself, get involved as a filmmaker. It ended up that I did film myself more, and it did involve me in the film. Later on, I felt that I was asking so much of these people to reveal themselves, to speak to me, to be honest with me, that I should reveal something of myself, too. I felt that although I'm not a gleaner—I'm not poor, I have enough to eat—there's another kind of gleaning, which is artistic gleaning. You pick ideas, you pick images, you pick emotions from other people, and then you make it into a film. Because I was also at a turn of age [Varda turned seventy in 1998], I thought it should be mentioned somehow. That's how I ended up changing my hair, and showing my

hands as a sign, as an exterior. It's like I always say: it's both objective and subjective—like the way I used time in *Cléo from 5 to 7* [1961]—and then inside that time we feel, we can *see* the time in a very subjective manner. For this film I thought the same way—I can show my hand, or my hair, but then it is my perception of my aging as a subjective thing. It's joyful and it shows in the film. I can feel very childish when I play with the trucks. I can use my hand, 1 can see things and I enjoy them, so, again, it's always very objective and subjective.

MA: How were you able to establish the rapport you have with both the rural and urban gleaners? There's very little sentimentality in the film, and that's usually a sign of the filmmaker's ability to establish trust with her subjects.

AV: As you know, there is a way of saying, "Oh, my God, these poor people." At the beginning, this sentiment led me to make the film. I felt bad for them. I could see an old woman bending with difficulty, and I remembered that image so strongly. I felt she's obliged to do it—if she could afford to buy without bending, she'd do it. There was a kind of . . . not sentimental, but pitiful feeling. When I slowly approached the gleaners, some of them didn't want me to speak to them, didn't want me to film. One person said, "You will ruin our business. If you tell everybody, they will come and pick the fruit." It was so interesting. Some people were not aggressive, but discussed the facts of the subject. I respected them. If somebody didn't want to be filmed, I wouldn't steal an image. Only in one scene in the market, and from very far, or from the back. I wanted to show that gesture, that humble gesture, of picking up things from the ground. In France, we have a saying: "*le geste auguste de semeur* [the majestic gesture of the sower]." That's why I spoke in the film about *le geste modeste de glaneur.*

MA: The cafe owner puts it very well when she says, "Stooping has not disappeared from our society."

AV: Yes, but it has totally changed, not only because the things that people glean are totally different—it's no longer some grain here and there—but gleaning today is also by chance. And it's no longer just women having that "modest gesture"; men also glean. So the social behavior has totally changed. I got very excited about discovering how the image of gleaning—the image which is in the painting of Millet—had changed. When I thought about the people in the street, I could see that was the same gesture of Millet. Yet Millet portrayed an era when gleaning was collective, in that women would be together, and enjoying it in a way. I could sense that the gleaning of today is totally different: it's men alone, there are tons of food, tons of waste, much more than before. And then I noticed the same thing in the streets and in the cities. I think that documentary means "real," that you have to meet these real people, and let them express what they feel about the subject. The more I met them, the more I could see I had nothing to make as a statement. *They* make the statement; they explain the subject better than anybody.

So it's not like having an idea about a subject and "let's illustrate it." It's meeting real people and discovering with them what they express about the subject, building the subject through real people. So it is a documentary, but the shape that I gave to it—including the original score and the editing—is really for me a narrative film. Not that documentary is "not good" and narrative film is "good." But I really work as a filmmaker, I would say, to give a specific shape to that subject. And so far it's worked, because whether people are cinephiles or not, they like the film. They like the people they meet in the film.

MA: How did you meet François, who so proudly announces that he has lived "one hundred percent from garbage" for the last ten years?
AV: I met him through one of my assistants on *One Hundred and One Nights*, whom I asked to help me on *The Gleaners*. His family has a country house near Aix-en-Provence. Our method for *The Gleaners* was to ask all the people we knew to talk to everyone—the peasants, the owners, the farmers, the fruit growers—about our film.

I said to my assistant, "Call everybody you know." By calling people in his parents' village, he was told there was a man in Aix-en-Provence. We looked for him, but didn't find him. So when my assistant told me François cleaned dishes in a pizzeria, he went into all the pizzerias, like an inquiry, almost like a detective, to get him.

He found him one day, and said, "We are looking for this . . . would you be willing to speak about that?" And François said, "Yes, as long as I can express my very strong ideas that waste is related to not knowing what to do with the waste, or badly handling the waste, and it's related to the oil catastrophes of the Erika boat." You may not have heard of it, but that incident ruined half the coast of France. François was the first one who made the connection. So we made an appointment to meet in a cafe. We're sitting in the cafe, and here he comes, with his boots, and we filmed that the way it really happened. He said, "I'll have a coffee," and we started to talk. I felt that we should do the interview walking. This is something you have to grab right away: what the movement of the person is, how the person reacts, how the person will best express him- or herself. François was in a walking mode, don't you think?

MA: Yes, he has a very defiant walk.

AV: Defiant and so vigorous. I said to the cameraman, "Why don't you just go with him?" That scene was made with a cameraman and a sound boom and my little camera. I'm asking him the questions. François really eats out of garbage. He says he never buys anything. Whatever he finds—including clothes—it's all in the street. He says he doesn't want to buy one thing because of the waste. I learned that he had studied economics at the university in Aix-en-Provence. So we spent all afternoon filming him. He's very opinionated. He spoke about what we call the Black Tide, which had happened two months before. I had been filming the Black Tide because I was shocked. I didn't think it had a connection with my subject, gleaning. I went to the ocean to see it—it was horrifying, all these black beaches. Thank God I had filmed that so I could, when he spoke about it, edit in my footage. What I learned—and I learn this always when making documentaries—is that people are surprising.

This is a man who has nothing. At the end of the day, the assistant said to him, "Well, we can give you some money." "Oh, I don't want money!" he said. He got very mad. But he said he'd like a book. The shooting is finished, so we go into a big bookshop. He rummages through the books about art. I'm wondering what kind of painting he would like, and I say, "Choose whatever you want." Know what he picks? He picked very refined, very sophisticated eighteenth-century drawings of rich people. He said to me, "I love that period." So I bought this big, expensive book depicting the times of rich people in castles and giving balls. I was amazed. What I'm saying is that a screenplay—and I am a screenplay writer when I make fiction films—often does not have the distinctive quality of imagination that real life has. I buy the book, and I tell him, "I'll let you know when the film is coming to the theater." So the film comes to Aix-en-Provence. I write to him and say, "Please be my guest; I would like you to be with me to speak to the audience and to answer some questions." I started the question-and-answer session, and somebody asks how we found the people. I tell the story of François and then I say, "Here he is." He comes up with his boots and he's very joyful and he gives the same speech. He tells a funny story that the best time for him is June because that's when the "stupid" students of Aix-en-Provence University go back to their families and they throw away whatever is in their fridge. He said,

"I can pick all kinds of good food; I have it in my own fridge for three months." It was very funny, his explaining the "high season" of gleaning in the street.

Then he started talking about another one of his favorite topics—expiration dates. He said, "You should not follow the rules; use your nose. I'll give you proof: I brought you gifts-cakes I found in the garbage." The audience laughed. He said, "Well, they were supposedly good until two days ago. I tasted them; they are perfect." Then he gave them to the audience and asked, "Tell me, are they good? See, I told you, they're good." Somebody asked him, "Do you like what has been done about you in this film?" He said, "It's OK, but it's too short." It proves that there was a real relationship. He admitted to being a participant in the film; I didn't steal him. The way he reacted to the audience was so nice and so interesting. He wanted to prove to them that he was right and that the film had a meaning—that we should talk about big waste. He was incredibly strong. What I'm saying is that this kind of film has two very important things for me: it really deals with the kind of relationship I wish to have with filming: editing, meeting people, giving the film shape, a specific shape, in which both the objective and subjective are present. The objective is the facts, society's facts, and the subjective is how I feel about that, or how I can make it funny or sad or poignant. Making a film like this is a way of living. It's not just a product. It has been organized and finished and delivered: what I had to do just to meet the people, what came before the film, and what happened with the film, with the people we met. Afterward I go with the film to festivals and to different cities. I also show the film to peasants, in villages and other places.

MA: What has their response been?
AV: They all love it, they really love it. They know it deals with something they know. What is difficult is that you have to be very vivacious when you shoot. You have to understand right away where the right place is, what the right move is.

MA: Did using a digital camera give you more freedom?
AV: The filmic decision has nothing to do with the camera. Since something will not happen again—you cannot make people repeat an action—you have to grab the feeling right away, and you decide to do it very slowly or still or running with them or, perhaps different things with the same person. With François, I knew I had to walk with him, capturing the movement of his very energetic, very angry way of strolling in

the streets. At one point he says, "With my boots I'm protected from the hostile world. I'm the *seigneur de la ville.*" [Both spellings *vile* and *ville* are given, leading to one of Varda's puns: I'm master of the city and the vile.] But these shots are done here and there, and you have to constrict the description of his character with strengths . . . and there is no pity, no reason to be pitiful of François.

In another case, let's say; how I found the man in the trailer park. What I did was, I drove along—anyplace—I saw a lot of trailers, I parked my car, and I asked for somebody who didn't exist. I asked for, say, "Philippe Garnier." I said, "I've been told that Phillipe Garnier lives here." "Philippe Garnier? I don't think so. Maybe you should ask the next trailer." I said, "Is there another place like this?" I went in like this, lying, in a way, but they started speaking to me. After a while somebody would say, "Would you like to sit?" I would say, "Yes, I wouldn't mind sitting with you for a while." I looked around, I saw they had no heating, no lights. Then I'd say I'm a documentarian and that I would be interested in speaking with them, and they'd say, "Well, why not?" Then I would come later and film. Being alone when you do location scouting is one thing, but people scouting is much better if you're alone. Sometimes I had my little camera, sometimes I didn't. Sometimes I said, "Do you mind if I take some shots?" When they asked what it's for, I said, "Some is for television, some is for me." I told the truth. Sometimes I had my tripod; sometimes I said, "I may come back with a crew." They were nice. I have a feeling that the people never thought I would betray them. They must have felt right away that I would share what they said, that I would really listen to them.

MA: Would you talk some more about this idea of filmmaking as artistic gleaning? You did a lot of "gleaning" for your film *One Hundred and One Nights*, a celebration of film's first century.

AV: My idea for that film was that a bad memory can become an unorganized gleaning. Simon Cinema [Michel Piccoli] picks things that he has in his mind, but are not well-organized. His "saving" of memory isn't too good, so he mixes things up. And I like the idea that he makes mistakes all the time in his memory. He allowed me to be free about the history of cinema and very free about what I picked. One film writer came up to me and said, "You are unfair! You didn't show Russian films." And I said, "So what? Do we have to show the history of cinema exactly as it was?"

MA: Did you have fun when you were choosing the film clips?

AV: I had a lot of fun. I love this film for two reasons. At the time, everyone was speaking about cinema very seriously, planning a big commemoration. I remembered a line of Bunuel's: "I hate commemorations. *Vive oubli* [forgetfulness]." I found that so beautiful. I have a bad memory, so I thought, what if you're very old, and even though you love film, you just pick this image and that image, and you mix up names and the titles of films? I thought it was an interesting way of approaching the desire for memory. Sometimes, even with a film I really love, I cannot tell the story precisely. Sometimes I cannot even tell what happened chronologically. But I'll have flashes of some things. Sometimes it looks almost like a still. What I know, what I can remember is the emotion I felt. I know I loved a film because I remember feeling good in the film or feeling odd when I came out, either in tears or touched or mad. So because of that bad memory, which leads to very subjective emotion, I thought we should work on that, on a man who's so old he grabs this and that. Using the star system, which I've been avoiding all my life, was a way of saying I can bring stars into this film, but just as visiting guests. So it was fun for me to have Delon or Belmondo or Depardieu—famous people. But nobody loved the film—it was a flop everywhere, even in France.

MA: Memory and the documentation of aging seem to be themes in your more recent work, especially in *Jacquot* and *The Young Girls Turn 25*.
AV: Right, but that happened only after Jacques died. I had always been very much into the present, which I'm now back to. I was not really interested in memory, but it started with *Ulysse*, which was made in '82. Then I made other films, such as *Kung-Fu Master* [1987], *Jane B. par Agnès V.* [1987] and then Jacques died. *Jacquot* was made in his memory. The experiment was very challenging. Can you go into someone else's memory? He had a very good memory; he could remember everything. So traveling in his memory was wonderful for me because it was difficult—I had to make it up.

MA: Were you traveling in both your memory and Demy's memory when you made *The Young Girls Turn 25*?
AV: Yes. Jacques' death brought back a lot of memories. He was my memory of where we'd been together. *The Young Girls Turn 25* and *Jacquot* were his memory, and I did *The World of Jacques Demy*, which is a documentary that is an "answer" to *Jacquot de Nantes*. A kid dreams of being a filmmaker [in *Jacquot*], and the documentary is about an adult filmmaker—people speak about his films. There are clips of other films in *Jacquot*, but

they are related to his youth. *The Young Girls Turn 25* came about because the city did something to commemorate the twenty-fifth anniversary of Demy's musical [*The Young Girls of Rochefort*], and I went to Rochefort for that. Now I'm really trying to get out of that. This film [*The Gleaners*] is not really about memory. I think *now* is so interesting: now as a society, my own life, situations I see, the rotten politics everywhere.

MA: Do you think your combination of the documentary esthetic within a narrative filtn—so present in *Vagabond* (1985)—has inspired contemporary French filmmakers such as Bruno Dumont (*La Vie de Jesus*, 1997, and *L'Humanité*, 1999), and the Dardenne brothers (*Rosetta*, 1999)?
AV: Some people come from documentary, like the Dardenne brothers. And when they started to make narrative films, like *La Promesse* [1996] or *Rosetta*, they really used a documentary technique to approach the subject, and made what I think are beautiful films. What I'm trying to do— what I've been trying to do all along—is to bridge the border of these two genres, documentary and fiction. In my first fiction film, *La Pointe Courte* [1954], I used the real people of the village, but I also had actors. In *Cléo from 5 to 7*, which is a fiction film, when Cléo [Corinne Marchand] is in the street and starts to look at other people, I had to have a texture of documentary so that we would believe what she sees in the street such as the man swallowing frogs. I've been trying all my life to put into fictional films the *texture* of documentary. Like in *Vagabond*, with the exception of Sandrine Bonnaire and a few others, all the other people are real workers, real people in the fields. But I asked them to say my words, so it still is written; it's not improvised at all. I asked them to do it, we rehearsed, but because they knew how to behave with their own tools in their own surroundings, they acted very much like people within a documentary.

Now, when it comes to documentaries, like *Daguerreotypes* [1975] or *Mur Murs* [1980], in *Mur Murs* there are some incredible, real people, but I made them so strong they are like fictional characters That's something in *The Gleaners*: you will never forget François, you will never forget the man who teaches. So they become fictional characters, in a way. In documentaries you have to be smart, to propose something, to set up something like François's walk. Then the subjects say something that a screenwriter would never invent; they almost become fictional characters. So I've always been working on the border. But I know when fiction is fiction, and documentary is documentary. It still is very precise. I didn't ask any of the people in *The Gleaners* to say anything specific. We never cheated because it wouldn't make sense. Although my narration and my presence in the film are elements we added, the film is also a reality.

MA: What are your current projects?

AV: To—slowly, slightly—get out of this film. I admire people who can say, "I'm doing this in 2001, this in 2002, and this in 2003." I cannot plan anything. I have to have the desire to make a film. Then it's a joy. You have to pick something you believe in. You have to believe it's worth it, and that it makes sense for you to do it. If I don't have that much passion, I won't work. I thought *The Gleaners* would be a very modest film that nobody would see. I was lucky that the people selecting for Cannes came to see it as a work in progress and they picked it. So we had to finish it. I would've been working on it longer—perhaps looking for more real people on the subject. You have to fill the audience with excitement about meeting different people, thinking about the subject, covering different aspects. I was lucky to meet so many different people. I really think of the audience a lot. I think they should not be bored with the subject.

Every time you make a film, you learn something. You approach other people, other people's work, some landscape you never noticed before. It's like giving sudden life to what you see and capturing the beauty in it.

The Gleaners and I by Agnès Varda

Julie Rigg / 2005

Printed by permission of the author and Australian Broadcasting Organization.

The Gleaners and I is a decidedly personal video documentary by Agnès Varda, a film ostensibly preoccupied with "rubbish." Agnès Varda takes us on a journey where we encounter those who live apart from other people—from people who eat out of dumpsters and "glean" provincial fields after harvest, to those who make art from tossed-away furniture and beyond. It's a brilliant and playful film and one which Julie Rigg declared she was "in love with" when she interviewed Agnès Varda.

Julie Rigg: Agnès Varda, I'm curious about this film. Did it begin as a film about yourself or a film about gleaners?

Agnès Varda: It's clearly about gleaners, it's clearly not only the intention because who cares about an intention, what is important is the film you see. And not only that, it's a very important subject, a social issue, which is, "who are those people who eat the leftovers, the leftovers of others?" Who is eating my leftovers, you know? And that was really concerning me, like it does to other people, and I thought instead of having a subject, a subject line and say could we find people to illustrate it? I totally had another attitude and thought how can I meet people who are the subject? So I don't have to explain and make any narration about that, find the right people who will be able to show themselves by their life. [With this film] I was saying "why will those people live and eat what we throw away, and can I meet them, can I speak to them?" And they are able to say when and what and how.

And so my concern was to be able to meet them which took a certain time, sometimes by chance, sometimes by one person telling another, or by going to the country, looking alone for people and going in these trailer [parks], speaking from one to another. So that was the subject and the project. The question was that, meanwhile, it was the year 2000 and everybody was saying "what's happening to cinema in the year 2000, what's happening to this and that in the year 2000?" And one day I thought, what's happening to Agnès in the year 2000, when I was doing that film about what's happening to the gleaners?

But it came to me that I'm ageing and I thought, "My God, I'm ageing, I'm still a gleaner, I'm still a filmmaker, I'm still enjoying what I do." I enjoy travelling, but I'm ageing. And that came like I say, like the gleaning ideas, images and emotions; it's like gleaning also first impressions. I allow myself to live in the film, to "let in" the film, because I thought by making a film like this I don't want to be separate from it, to live in another world than those who speak so honestly, so clearly about themselves, and speak about situations in which they could be ashamed or wish to hide or wish to say "don't bother with me."

I thought I have to be part of that, I should not back out of it. And it came naturally that I should be part of the film.

JR: I liked that because you don't stand apart from your subjects, and the subjects are also revealed as sensitive and they have dignity and intelligence and occasionally humor, and but there is an honesty also and there is poetry in there about the project of gleaning images.

AV: Well, all artists spend their lives going about, you know reading something, listening to a story, going in a café, artists they glean you know, you shade the big things and we take quotes . . . They are wonderful. We look, "pick" and then use things, too. But as filmmakers we do it in a different way when we do a fiction film, but we still glean things here and there. Now this is really deeper gleaning, you know facts. The gleaners, they glean potatoes, they glean foods, they glean furniture in the streets. So it became such an important subject and I wanted to cover it by asking questions . . . enquiring here and there. And I must say I was thrilled because I really had an incredible chance or luck, that I met so many incredible people. I think three or four of them are unforgettable.

I think sometimes a documentary brings people that are so unforgettable that they could act in a good fiction. I think two of them stand out as you know, beautiful, so I was lucky. And they are the flesh of the film.

JR: When a documentary does that, it's when a good documentary maker recognizes such people. And they're really people who have the capacity to bring forward the drama of their own lives and their own observations. So what's the responsibility of the documentary maker there?

AV: Well it's total . . . When you say responsibility as a documentary maker you mean in the film or in real life?

JR: I was thinking in the film, but I'm curious about both.

AV: Both. In the film well it's a choice anyway, a documentary is subjective and by editing what people say, you could make them look different. I spoke sometimes three hours with somebody and then they have five minutes in the film. You know there is editing. When I cut what they have to say . . . there is a choice. Anybody else could take the same words, the same images, and show something else of these people, these real people.

And I chose to pick what in them was, I would say, the best clear explanation of their own life and how they had a judgment . . . an opinion about the huge ways of our world. And that's interesting because one could say "these people are wonderful," well they could have been less. I wanted the best of them like when you love somebody, you don't want to show what is so-so, you choose the best when you speak about somebody you love, you won't start with what is bad, you start with what is good.

In *The Gleaners and I* I made that choice because I'm fed up with showing poor people speaking badly, behaving badly, or complaining or grumbling. And I thought what was wonderful was that they were able to speak without self pity, and among what they said I chose what showed the strengths of their own nature and character. And so it works because I really had admiration and tenderness for them. I wanted them to look very good and they do look good, and they need approbation, and people to like them. And I feel like I have been a person who has friends and wants other friends to meet them. I say, "I just have this friend who does this, and I want you to meet her, she's wonderful, I want you to meet her." Or "That man is great." I felt I was the one who said to every person in the audience, "Oh, I want you to meet this one and this one."

JR: So there's a sense in which the documentary maker embraces the subject as a friend?

AV: Oh, they are the subjects. I'm the person telling, being, filming, and not that courteous in a way. And I think part of the fluidity and the pleasure that the audience finds in this film comes from my liking them. My way of travelling and playing with my hands and the trucks and, you know, that's important.

JR: There are so many questions I want to ask you. You talk about playing with your hands (in shots from the film): you are there in the film playfully, but your own "Agnès in the year 2000" is also there. And there are some very brave shots in this film when you show us . . .
AV: What do you mean brave? I mean I have an attitude as a filmmaker, this is not a woman who will say "can you give me cream for my little hands because I never wear gloves. I go in the garden, I put my hands directly in the earth, I did that all my life. Now could I do something for my poor hands?" That has nothing to do with this, this is a filmmaker filming herself, and seeing a kind of beauty of the skin, because I think it has a shape, it has lines, it's just like a painter.

I'm not into fishing for compliments, I don't care. I get compliments anyway, and you know it's happened many times, after the screening when I come to speak with the audience I've seen people kissing my hands. And women, say things like "you're brave." And I say I'm not brave. I mean I enjoy the shape of things, and the shape of things including yourself, the wrinkles, the lines, the veins, this is the beauty, the same thing you look at on a tree and you see how you know an old tree has these incredible shapes. And you say "Ah, what a wonderful olive tree." Why couldn't you say "What a wonderful hand"? Do you understand that?

JR: Yes, I understand that and it's also a respect for the things that are not new and the people who are not new.
AV: Respect for life, the way it goes, and ageing is just a part of life. We have been so much in this civilization of being beautiful, being young, being seen, being this, being that, being rich, and consuming. And the film is totally on the other side. What is the left of consuming, but tenderness and peace with people. Some people don't even look at gleaners. They see them in the gutter and they turn their head, because they think they will be ashamed. But it's the one who looks who should be ashamed, because the other one, when [the gleaner] opens the garbage he can say, well stupid people who throw out everything.

JR: You know in Australia we have a word which I think we only use in this country and it's called "scrounging," it's a verb. To scrounge.

AV: "Scrounge," my God what a beautiful word! Because in America they say rummaging, picking.

JR: But it's great to represent us with the tradition of picking, as you do in your film.

AV: I've got to say something. In French we have the masculine and the feminine, so the title is *Les Glaneurs et la Glaneuse*, which doesn't translate in the English language because you don't have "la" you know, you don't have the feminine, the woman gleaner. So we had to translate it as "The Gleaners and I," which emphasizes in a way the "I." When in French, *glaneuse* is a very anonymous gleaner, an anonymous woman gleaner. That little nuance explains your first question. But it makes it more important than me.

Now I must say I have had an incredible reaction to this film, incredible letters, never in my life was I loved as a filmmaker like this. Can you believe this?

JR: Why, do you think?

AV: Oh I know, I know, little by little I find out. It's because it concerns everybody for different reasons, from their grandmother, their mother, the country, many people come from the country you see. But also now today this is not about the past, this is about today in the street, and they know they have seen these people, they know they have thought of it without thinking of it. It's like giving shape and words, but I like the shape of the film. Somebody will "lift" you know, they will resist the invasion of huge cinema, of the massive sound system, of . . .

JR: . . . of the society of waste.

AV: . . . and trademarks and all this. People, they are part of it but they don't like it. Most of them don't like it.

JR: The young man in your film who strides down the street in his big heavy Wellington boots, his rubber boots saying I need . . .

AV: He's incredibly bright you know.

JR: Yes, and he speaks for a lot of us I think.

AV: But you know, because the way he does it—he does it aggressively—and when he says, "Oh stupid people throw out everything," it's funny because he's mad. He says people are stupid. He said, "I'm the king of the city," like in gambling . . . It's difficult to translate, but it's like he gambled and gets everything on the table you know? Where he puts his arms and scoops up all the chips. Anyway, at the most, I thought, this little documentary would get two weeks in the theatre and on a television station that shows a lot of documentaries. I felt I needed to do it but nobody would be caring about it.

Now suddenly I'm in the French selection in Cannes—did you get the award list? I couldn't believe how many [awards] I got . . . I got so many awards with this film. The film went to seventy festivals and here in Paris, it is still playing! It has been on for forty-eight weeks or fifty weeks, more or less.

JR: Let me ask you about one of my favorite shots in the film. You bring home the empty clock face [Varda finds a clock with no hands on a pile of rubbish in a street]. It's one of the things you had scrounged, and then you put it on your mantelpiece with . . .
AV: . . . the two cats . . .

JR: And the two cats, and then it's like there is a travelling shot, your face is travelling. It is delicious, how did you do that?
AV: You know it's such a simple thing. I'm with my friend, he scrounged that clock and he threw it away. So I put it on my two little Chinese cabinets I have near the window, just put it on and it looks beautiful. So I do the shot of that, and then since the words bring ideas and ideas bring words, I said "well, it's not passing, the time is not passing, but I'm passing, I'm about to go." So I actually did the real physical idea, the clock doesn't move, doesn't pass time, but I pass it behind. So I went to the back, that's my place, the clock is still there, still at the window, I went to the patio of my own place, I took the skateboard of one of my grandsons. So I put myself on the skateboard and there was one of my trainees kneeling, pushing me slowly. This is why the camera was inside shooting itself, so that's the kind of natural idea coming from just words. And I think words mean so much in our mind.

You know how the mind goes on thinking all the time but it's a light thinking, I'm not philosophical, I'm not metaphysical, but my mind goes on and my work flows in my mind, and that's how I think. Time doesn't pass but I pass, it's very simple, makes sense, no?

JR: It does. Agnès Varda, you've had a long and influential career in film but here you are with this.

AV: I did so few films if you think about it, so few. Some people do a film a year you know, I could have done fifty films.

JR: Maybe they wouldn't have been as interesting as these have been. Has the digital video camera been liberation for you?
AV: Oh yes, yes, it has been for this project. I'm not saying that next time I won't take a huge camera but for that subject because of the discretion it gave me, it worked. I mean I had to approach people without frightening them, so I had to be on my own and, you know, I do that because I love to meet people. I try to witness my society. Sometimes I could say that having the camera, it doesn't frighten anybody. But then I will come back with my crew if they accept. "No," I would say, "[only] if you're happy, if you agree to come into that film." I think it makes sense for the people to know who you are and how you behave. Then I said to them, now if you agree then I come with a person who does good sound, a person who does a better camera. And if they accept, we come back and do it. If they don't, we say "well it's okay."

Plus about my own shots, the shots of myself, I was alone and I wouldn't ask a director of photography to do that, I mean I'd feel like I'd become narcissistic or something. And I was speaking to myself, like taking notes, filming myself speaking to the little camera and there was narration I'd improvised when I was filming my hand with one hand. And I felt a little pleasure of being the filmer and the filmed, I mean how could I say that one hand could film the other one. But like explaining our whole life like we want to be part of it, we want to be the subject but we want to be the object, we want everything. And I felt every pleasure. Filming one hand filming the other one, it closes a kind of circle.

Because if I lie to myself the other hand doesn't lie. If I film like a crazy, you know the other hand can't be crazy, something that I like very much. But also it's a nice little tool and it comes out beautifully on the screen. Did you see the shot?

JR: Yes I did.
AV: I shot my cat, I shot the books, it looks beautiful and sharp on the screen, the huge screen.

It's a possibility also to not depend on heavy tech, even though technicians are nice people. But I remember when I did a film called *101 Nights*, there were fifty of us and that's nice also, fifty people at work. But in a way, a little worrying, a little trembling—the personal emotion to be an artist, where is it in the middle of all that? It's difficult.

JR: What's your next project?

AV: Well I've been accompanying this film [*The Gleaners and I*] for quite a while, enjoying people's answers, enjoying the different approach to filming. But I don't know, I don't know exactly if I wish to continue, I could continue in that. I don't want to do *The Gleaners 2* you see—*Return of the Gleaners* . . .

JR: Do you want to go back to the crew of fifty technicians?

AV: No, I don't think so.

JR: And the luxury of a big . . .

AV: I don't want luxury, I don't care about luxury. I love what I did, walking in the fields for hours, being tired in a way, speaking, I love that. But maybe I won't do another documentary right away. I let things happen because I never make a film that people ask me to do or bring me a package with a good book and two actors and all that. I think cinema should be made by coming from nowhere to becoming a film. This I believe in. And that's why I made so few films.

Agnès Varda in Toronto

Gerald Peary / 2008

From the *Boston Phoenix*, March 10, 2009. Reprinted with permission.

The 2008 Toronto International Film Festival last September proved hospitable to Agnès Varda, offering her latest work, the autobiographical *The Beaches of Agnès*, and reaching back for a rare screening of her 1954 first feature, *La Pointe Courte*. The "Mother of the French New Wave" was in an expansive, agreeable mood, and one afternoon she consented to sit down in a hotel room amid quickly gathered journalists and just reminisce. She kicked off her shoes, we took notes, and she spoke fervently of her eighty years on earth, fifty-four of them doing cinema: personal, left-political, feminist, subtly experimental.

"In France," she said, "I started as a photographer and took pictures of Picasso, but I was very shy to ask to go to his studio. I was educated stupidly. I knew nothing of nothing, which also makes you shy. I was scared of men. But I went to Germany to take photos in 1946; I photographed alone in China. I was kind of courageous, thinking I shouldn't do less than my brothers."

In the early 1950s, Varda's ambitions expanded from photography to filmmaking, though all the French directors were male. "I realized you didn't have to be strong like a carpenter. A director doesn't have to do anything but direct actors. Why couldn't I do that? But I didn't want to make a career, make a deal, adapt a beautiful book. Most film followed the path of theater, with rich dialogue, classic form, perfect sense. I wanted to use cinema as a language, like with Joyce and Woolf and Nathalie Sarraute. In 1962, I made *Cléo from 5 to 7*, [which was] shocking to the perceptions of viewers, showing subjective time versus objective time."

"I admire those who now go to film school," she added. "Because at first I was a total autodidact." Fortunately, with *La Pointe Courte*, Varda wandered into the sphere of two great talents of the "Left Bank School,"

Chris Marker and Alain Resnais. "They're so very bright! They taught me many things. Resnais, who edited *La Pointe Courte*, said, 'Your film reminds me of Visconti.' I said, 'Who is Visconti?' They said, 'See lots of films. There's a Cinemathèque here in Paris. See *Vampyr* and *Ordet* by Dreyer, go see Bresson.' When I met Jacquot [Jacques Demy] in 1957, he'd seen Bresson's *Pickpocket* three times. We went to see it four more times." Thus began her romance with the genial filmmaker of *The Umbrellas of Cherbourg*, whom she married.

Demy died of AIDS complications in 1990, and Varda has told of his life twice on film, in *Jacquot de Nantes* (1991) and in *The Beaches of Agnès*, which is more directly about AIDS.

"The life of a couple is very fragile. We had ups and downs, and we recovered from some downs. Losing Jacques, he was fifty-nine, it's not like losing someone [who's] twelve, and then I think of the millions with AIDS in Africa, and female circumcision everywhere. Still, filming *Les Plages*, I had to go back to the pain of feeling his death, to a time when AIDS was always a death sentence. And in the editing, I had to go back again to that. But I decided it should be peacefully told. The world is in very bad shape, but cinema in a way is a peaceful life.

"I don't try to make my place in the history of cinema, but others place me, because of a daring film in 1954, or because of *Cléo from 5 to 7*: my little research in black-and-white about a woman pulled by the hair from death. I've done fifteen long features, fifteen long documentaries, not very much.

"Some people shoot every day. But being called 'Mother of the French New Wave'? I don't care! I love that!"

The Beaches of Agnès: An Interview

David Warwick / 2009

From *Electric Sheep*, www.electricsheepmagazine.co.uk, October 2, 2009. Reprinted by permission.

Renowned veteran director of the *nouvelle vague* Agnès Varda returns to UK screens this month with *The Beaches of Agnès* (*Les Plages d'Agnès*). Part autobiography, part documentary, part cinematic essay, Varda's latest film is a lyrical, free-flowing recollection of her life in and around the cinema.

Varda studied art history and photography in Paris before making her first feature, *La Pointe Courte*, in 1954. Thanks to her friendship with Jean-Luc Godard, Varda went on to make the dazzling *Cléo de 5 à 7*, which won the Palme d'Or at Cannes in 1962. Between 1962 and 1990, Varda was married to fellow director and master of "the film in song" Jacques Demy. Side by side, they made films in both France and Hollywood over the years. More recently, Varda has returned to her visual art roots, and created installation exhibitions for such institutions as the Cartier Foundation and Venice Biennale.

Slightly unsure of what to expect from a "short, plump old lady" with such a glittering past, I meet Agnès in a small office in Holborn, London, to discuss her latest film. She speaks with English clearly learnt in America, and wears a curious mixture of tasteful, floaty clothes and a two-tone "punk" haircut. I find her to be at once amiable and venerable.

David Warwick: Where did the inspiration for *The Beaches of Agnès* come from?

Agnès Varda: I wanted to make a point because I was turning eighty. I thought I should do something. You always remember passing by a zero, and when I was younger I could never imagine being eighty.

DW: You didn't like the idea?

AV: Not at all! I can remember thinking that people who were forty were very old, and people who were fifty—they were out! I remember vividly being disinterested in these people and thinking, "I hope I don't live beyond forty-five." I thought it was poetic to die young.

DW: In the film you say that imagining yourself as ancient is funny.

AV: Haha, yes. Do you know that my grandchildren call me "Mamita Punk"? It's like the name of a stripper! I love it. I'm glad I'm still in the mood for enjoying jokes and punk behavior . . . Most of the papers like to quote the first sentence of the film, "I'm a short, plump, old lady," but the second part of the sentence is more important—that it's the others that I like, the others that interest me, that intrigue me passionately. That's the statement of the film. It appears at the end of the film when they give me all those brooms for my birthday, and I sit here and I think, what are all these brooms. And I say, "it happened yesterday; it's already gone, it's already in the film," and then, "je me rappelle pourquoi je vis"—"I remember why I'm living." Making this film is a way of living on, living and remembering.

DW: How did you go about making *The Beaches*? How much was scripted, and how much emerged from your talents as a gleaner?

AV: A lot was scripted and planned. When we build a set, when I decide I want to show my courtyard as it was, we have to be organized. When we have the boat on the river Seine, and the whale on the beach, we have to be organized. It's set up and constructed. But I remember to let myself be disturbed, like when I go to my childhood house: I visit the garden, and I remember my sister, and then I meet the man who lives there and his wife. They are collectors of little trains, and since I have the soul of a documentarist I can't stop myself. I question them, I make them speak about how they found them, how much they cost, the value of the collection—and I'm gone! So I stage a lot of things, it's organized, but open to things happening.

DW: What about the narration?

AV: I wrote most of the narration before shooting, so that I knew where I was going. But sometimes during the shooting, I have an idea and I say it to the camera. A lot of the narration was finished later or changed—because it has to fit, and also be sometimes contradictory. I like to play off words, which becomes a play of images.

DW: I imagine it was a difficult film to edit?
AV: Yes, the editing was long—nine months—but I had to figure out how to make it free . . . I think it is free, and that's what makes me feel good. Like the scene with the naked couple in the courtyard. It is interesting that you have this in the middle of the film, and then you go to something else . . . By the way, I heard that because of this scene the film is banned—because the man has a hard-on. Earlier in the film, we use a fake hard-on, but this is a real one, and because of that it's banned . . . I should have used a real one both times, but at the time I didn't think of it, and then it was too late.

DW: You praise new digital techniques in *The Beaches*.
AV: I praise it? . . . I use it.

DW: You seem impressed by it though. Grateful for it.
AV: Yes. I could have shot it in 35mm and had a second camera, but I knew that I wanted lots of little editing tricks; and if I had done it in 35mm it would have been hard. When you do any kind of tricks in 35mm, you have to go backwards and forwards between film and digital. Also, sometimes, when something was missing from the film, I'd take my camera, I'd go in the street or in my courtyard, I'd film something, bring it back in, and five minutes later I'd put it in the film. So for a film so complicated, that relies so much on collage, I think we had a good tool.

DW: The form of *The Beaches* is very interesting. You mix lots of different material and styles.
AV: Yes. The technique is collage, and many artists have done that—painters like Rauschenberg for example. It's a way of disturbing the paper. Collage can just be a puzzle in which you have to figure out the real figure or the real landscape, but you can also make a collage that doesn't end as a recognizable figure. You can make a collage that is just a collage.

DW: And you'd define *The Beaches* as a collage that is just a collage?
AV: No. It's hard to define. I see it as an Unidentified Flying Object, because it doesn't belong to documentary really, even though I speak about real people, and it's not a fiction film because it's my life. And it's not action, it's not totally fantastical, it's not a thriller. It's a film that comes out of me. As a cinematic object, that's the way I see it.

DW: It's quite a history lesson too, full of radical people and radical ideals.

AV: It's mostly about showing many people. Alexander Calder on the beach, dancing like a bear, images I have of Fidel Castro, pictures I took in China. It's about part of my life but mixed with a big period of history, the second half of the twentieth century. Even though I never belonged to a political party, never signed anything, I have been with it, and I try to understand it.

DW: You explain in the film how you were an angry feminist in the seventies. Is the fight for feminism still important to you now?

AV: Yes, it's still important. I mean, read the paper. The fight is just beginning in many parts of the world. In France, in England, in some educated countries, it has changed, not totally, but at least the thing about birth control is coming to be understood and used. But in many countries it is not . . . The freedom of women though, it's exciting. And more and more women make films. We have some very good directors. Claire Denis for example: her work deals with something fantastic coming out of life, and it's so strong, so powerful. Have you seen the one with all the blood?

DW: *Trouble Everyday*?

AV: Yes. It's incredible; very powerful. She's very powerful.

DW: What about her latest film, *35 Rhums*?

AV: Yes. That one's strange; difficult to understand, but interesting. She's always interested in people, black people.

DW: In *The Beaches* you recall how, when you were just starting out, you thought that you could make a film by just putting words and images together.

AV: Yes, I was ridiculous at that time. It's obviously not just that at all. It is movement, it is editing, it is music. It is creating a world, a mixed world, like in *The Beaches*, in the first sequence on the beach with the mirrors. The big thing in this scene is the wind. My scarf goes like this, and it pushes me like that. The wind makes the scene feel much more alive.

DW: *The Beaches* reminded me a little bit of Godard's *Histoires du cinéma*, in as far as both films use this technique of collage, and both pursue this old question of "what is cinema."

AV: Yes, I think it deals with this question, "what is cinema?" through how I found specific cinematic ways of telling what I was telling. I could have told you the same things that are in the film by just talking to you for six hours. But instead I found shapes. Like in the scene when I wanted to show the five men their fathers, whom they'd never met. I made a sort of exhibition with a 16mm projector and a screen, and they have to push the images of their fathers into the night. I could have just shown them a picture, but I found something that people will share and feel. It's a ritual and a burial. I found things like this in many places in the film. I made a fool of myself, and I made a fake car in which I tried to park. It's interesting to do that at eighty, and I enjoy doing it and showing it to people and to my grandchildren.

DW: Will you ever stop making films?

AV: Manoel de Oliveira, the Portuguese director, is one hundred and he's still making films. I hope I don't get very old though. Very old age is terrible, apart from in a few cases. I will continue to do installations until the end, and they include films. You have the space, you have to build, you have to invent. But fiction films, I don't think I'll do any more of those. *The Beaches of Agnès* is already a hybrid.

Gleaning the Passion of Agnès Varda

Andrea Meyer / 2009

From Indiewire, www.indiewire.com, December 5, 2009. Reprinted by permission.

The films of Agnès Varda are always infused with Agnès Varda—her reality, her thoughts, her voice, and her passions. Her fiction films—*La Pointe Courte* (1954), *Cléo from 5 to 7* (1961), *Le Bonheur* (1964), *Vagabond* (1985)—are great feminist works that experiment with subject and form like the best of the French New Wave. She was considered a precursor to the revered cinematic movement of Truffaut and Godard, and was clearly influential in tone and style. Varda is perhaps best known, however, for her talent as a documentarian, which enhanced both her fictional and non-fiction films. Even dramatic works like *One Sings, the Other Doesn't* (1976) serve as documents of their times—in this particular case, the feminist struggles of the sixties and seventies. Varda's brilliance is most evident, however, in works like *Jacquot*, a portrait of her late husband, filmmaker Jacques Demy (*Umbrellas of Cherbourg*), *Vagabond*, and stunning shorts like *L'Opéra Mouffe* and *Salut les Cubains*, that utilize the skills she honed during her early years as a photojournalist.

For her latest documentary, *The Gleaners and I*, Varda turned her mini DV-camera on an old practice—foraging for wheat left after the harvest—to create a portrait of modern day "gleaners," those hungry people who live on the leftovers the rest of us have discarded, and those, like herself, who create art of the images and materials they collect. Andrea Meyer speaks with the legendary director about connecting with her audience, intuition, editing, and cine-writing.

Andrea Meyer: Gleaning is such an unusual subject. I wonder what drew you to it as the topic for a documentary.

Agnès Varda: Gleaning itself is not known—is forgotten. The word is passé. So I was intrigued, by these people in the street picking up food. And then I thought, what's happening to the fields of wheat? Nothing is left in the fields of wheat. So I went to the potatoes, and I found these heart-shaped potatoes, and it made me feel good. Made me feel that I was on the right track.

AM: You put so much of yourself and your emotions into your films, it makes the audience put themselves into it.

AV: Exactly. You know, that's what I really want—to involve people. Each person. An audience is not a bunch. You know, it's not "Audience." For me it's one hundred, three hundred, five hundred people. It's a way to meet her, meet him. It's exaggerated, but, really, I give enough of myself, so they have to come to me. And they have to come to the people that I make them meet [in the film]. And I don't think that we forget them. Because the people [I interview] are so unique, so generous—they know so much about society. They are not bitter, mean. They are generous. They are gray, anonymous—you know, humiliated people, in a way. In a way, they make us feel we have to be ashamed, not them. And, obviously, I put a lot of energy to make them look good, express clearly things, including the pain, the hassle, the difficulty to live, to eat. You know, we overeat all the time. Everybody does. And half of the world is starving.

AM: You seem to relish the experience of making the film?

AV: Sometimes I'm touched to tears, you know. That one in the caravan [trailer] was painful. He lost a job, he lost a wife, he lost the kids. Then you feel like you should be silent, listening, and trying to be very small in the caravan. With a small camera, I try not to disturb the flow of his words. And then the editing, you see what you'll do with it. And in the open markets, I was so moved. So painful to see old women, you know, having difficulties to bend—and coming out with one piece of food. And bending again to get another thing. You know, there is an old woman there? She goes into these eggs. Most of them are broken. She finds a box and ends up finding some not-broken eggs. When you know the price of an egg, you understand that she needs the money. She wouldn't be doing this for half an hour to get six eggs. And so my heart was really hurt by that misery.

AM: How much of what you shot was planned?

AV: Very little is planned. What is planned is to meet this one or this one. After looking for them, which took a lot of time. I didn't have a list of gleaners handy. I had to find them.

AM: Gleaning becomes a metaphor for so many things, even filmmaking.
AV: Yeah. It is true that filming, especially a documentary, is gleaning. Because you pick what you find; you bend; you go around; you are curious; you try to find out where are things. But, you cannot push the analogy further, because we don't just film the leftovers. Even though there is some analogy about people that society pushes aside. But it's too heavy an analogy.

AM: One of the other things that makes the film so appealing, like your other work, is that it's as much about you as the people whose lives you document. You film yourself—your hands, your face, even the moldy spot on your ceiling.
AV: I have two hands. One has a camera—the other one is acting, in a way. I love the idea that with these handheld cameras—these new numeric things—very light, but, on the other hand, very "macrophoto." You know what is macro? You can approach things very near. I can, with one hand, film the other one. I like the idea that one hand would be always gleaning, the other one always filming. I like very much the idea of the hands. The hands are the tool of the gleaners, you know. Hands are the tool of the painter, the artist.

AM: I noticed that you have almost the same exact shots in *Jacquot*, only it is Jacques' hair and hands. Those shots are so beautiful, so loaded with emotion.
AV: When I did my own film, I thought I was just doing my self-portrait, in a way. Now, many viewers—and I'm glad you brought it up, because nobody did here—came to me and said, "It was so touching that, over the years, you reached the same shots that you did for Jacques: his hair, his eye, and then his arm. And his hand, with the little ring there."

And they say, "In a way, it was like touching his hand of the film, over the years." And when the man told me that, I cried. I had not realized it. You know, thank God I try to be very clever in the editing room. But when I film, I try to be very instinctive. Following my intuition—is that a word? Following my connection, my association of ideas and images. And how one thing goes to another. But then, when I do the editing, I'm strict, and trying to be structural, you know. And when he told me that, I never thought of it. But he said, "You did the same shots."

I was so impressed, I cried. And he said, "I didn't want to hurt you." I said, "You don't hurt me—you make me feel good." I was crying, but he made me feel, oh, that I was joining [Jacques], you know, in some way. And I thought: Well, I'm glad I work by intuition. Because if I'd organized it, I wouldn't like it so much. I understood that this is to be an artist, you know—because you work by intuition. You go to the right thing, to the right place, to the right image, with your own feelings.

AM: Following your intuition is also responsible for all your wonderful digressions in *Gleaners*.

AV: It's like a jazz concert. They take a theme, a famous theme. They play it all together as a chorus. And then the trumpet starts with a theme and does a number. And then, at the end of his solo, the theme comes back, and they go back to the chorus. And then the piano takes the theme again. The other one goes crazy, you know, then comes back to the theme and back to the chorus. I had the feeling my digressions were like this—a little fantasy; a little freedom of playing the music of things I feel, things I love. And come back to the theme: People live off of our leftovers. People feed themselves with what we throw [away]. And I say "we" because it's you, it's me—it's everybody.

AM: What does this retrospective of your work mean to you?

AV: Well, I'll tell you. I had a retrospective at the MoMA; I had one at the American Cinematheque; I have one at the Walker Art Center of Minneapolis; in France I had one at The Cinematheque. Well, I'm getting older, and people start to put my films together.

AM: What do you think your films offer to people today?

AV: Well, you have to tell me.

AM: That would be cheating. What do you think?

AV: I would say energy. I would say love for filming, intuition. I mean, a woman working with her intuition and trying to be intelligent. It's like a stream of feelings, intuition, and joy of discovering things. Finding beauty where it's maybe not. Seeing. And, on the other hand, trying to be structural, organized; trying to be clever. And doing what I believe is *cinécriture*, what I always call cine-writing. Which is not a screenplay. Which is not only the narration words. It's choosing the subject, choosing the place, the season, the crew, choosing the shots, the place, the lens, the light. Choosing your attitude towards people, towards actors. Then choosing the editing, the music. Choosing contemporary musicians. Choosing the tune of the mixing. Choosing the publicity material, the press book, the poster. You know, it's a handmade work of filmmaking—that I really believe. And I call that cine-writing.

I think, if a film is well-done, it's well-written for me. Cine-written.

So I fight for that. And even though I know that some screenplays can be beautifully made together with another director, and then another editor. I've seen films beautifully made that way. But the way I film is, I love to be responsible for the whole thing. I never work on other people's projects, on other people's screenplays. It's modest, but I did my own work, trying to make it believable, touching. Try to be clever, bringing the audience to be intelligent. And I tell you—they do behave like an intelligent audience with me. They raise beautiful questions; they speak to me after the screenings; they tell me personal things—they want to be involved.

They tell me they are touched. This is a good feeling. It has nothing to do with the box office. I hope it does well, but it's totally different. I'm happy when it works. You've seen *101 Nights*—it was a total flop. But when people speak about it and like it—fine. It doesn't break my energy; it doesn't make me feel like I'm a loser or anything. I had flops, I had success.

AM: This one is so beautiful, everyone's going to love it.

AV: I'm just on the road again. Going to be on the road—yeah. Free—trying to be free. Of what other people do; of success. You know, trying to be free of minor things. I feel very much on the road. Even though I live in a city, and I have a roof.

AM: A beautiful roof, I might add.

AV: A rotten roof, I may add—but I fix it. Don't you think it's funny the way I say [the ceiling] could be a painting—that we could admire it in a museum? Yeah, anything could be art. Anything could be beauty. And let's not be, "This is the ceiling rotted. And this is the museum." The ceiling is rotten—it disturbs me, the leak. There is water coming—tack-tack-tack. But look, why should I go in a museum and say: "Tapies is beautiful when I have this on [the ceiling]?" [In the film], I say, "my ceiling is a piece of art." And that's turning life into—you know, finding not only beauty—amusement, joy, fun. Finding fun where sometimes it's just a bore; finding fun when it's a burden. You can always make something look different. Which is a way of saying that I'm, in a way, protected from being unhappy. There is a big unhappiness in my life and big pain. And I'm protected, in a way. You know, I feel that even the dead people around me protect me. So I'm not too much entitled to complain.

Additional Resources

Anthony, E. M. "From Fauna to Flora in Agnès Varda's *Cléo de 5 à 7.*" *Literature Film Quarterly* 26.2 (1998): 88–96.

Aquin, Stéphane, et al. *Global Village: The 1960s.* Montreal: Montreal Museum of Fine Arts, in Association with Snoeck Publishers, 2003.

Austin, Guy, *Contemporary French Cinema: An Introduction.* Manchester and NY: Manchester University Press, 1996.

Backe, Lone. *Agnès Varda's Den Ene Synger: Og Begrebet Kvindefilm.* S.L.S.N., 1978.

Barnet, M.-C., and S. Jordan. "Interviews with Agnès Varda and Valérie Mréjen." *Esprit Créateur* 51.1 (2011): 184–200.

Barnet, M.-C. "'Elles-Ils Islands': Cartography of Lives and Deaths by Agnès Varda." *Esprit Créateur* 51.1 (2011): 97–111.

Bastide, Bernard, and Agnès Varda. *Les Cent et Une Nuits: Les cent et une nuits d'Agnès Varda: Chronique d'Un Tournage.* Paris: P. Bordas, 1995.

Betancourt, Jeanne. *Women in Focus.* Dayton: Pflaum Publishing, 1974.

Biro, Yvette, and Catherine Portuges. "Caryatids of Time: Temporality in the Cinema of Agnès Varda." *Performing Arts Journal* 19.3 (1997): 1–10.

Boisleve, Jacques. *Agnès Varda.* Nantes: Trois Cent Trois, 2006.

Bonner, Virginia. "The Gleaners and 'Us': The Radical Modesty of Agnès Varda's *Les Glaneurs et la Glaneuse.*" *There She Goes: Feminist Filmmaking and Beyond.* Eds. Corinn Columpar and Sophie Mayer. Detroit, Michigan: Wayne State University Press, 2009. 119–31.

Bozak, Nadia. "Digital Neutrality: Agnès Varda, Kristan Horton and the Ecology of the Cinematic Imagination." *Quarterly Review of Film and Video* 28.3 (2011): 218–29.

Breillat, Catherine, et al. "French Cinema Now—Unbelievable but Real: The Legacy of '68." *Sight and Sound* 18.5 (2008): 28.

Bunney, Andrew. "The Gleaners and I," *DB Magazine,* no. 286 (August 28, 2002), 32.

Butler, Cornelia H., and Alexandra Schwartz. *Modern Women: Women Artists at the Museum of Modern Art.* New York: Museum of Modern Art, 2010.

Calatayud, A. "*Les Glaneurs et la Glaneuse*: Agnès Varda's Self-Portrait." *Dalhousie French Studies* 61 (2002): 113–23.

Callenbach, Ernest. "Review of *The Gleaners and I* (*Les Glaneurs et la glaneuse*)." *Film Quarterly* 56.2 (2003): 46–49.

Caughie, John. *Theories of Authorship: A Reader.* London; Boston: Routledge & Kegan Paul in association with the British Film Institute, 1981.

Chapman, Jane. *Issues in Contemporary Documentary.* Cambridge: Polity, 2009.

Cheu, Hoi F. *Cinematic Howling: Women's Films, Women's Film Theories.* Vancouver, Toronto: UBC Press, 2007.

Chrostowska, S. D. "Vis-à-Vis the Glaneuse." *Angelaki* 12.2 (2007): 119–33.

Clouzot, Claire. *Le cinéma français depuis La Nouvelle vague.* Paris: F. Nathan, 1972.

Cooper, Sarah. *Selfless Cinema?: Ethics and the French Documentary.* London: Legenda, 2006.

Crain, Mary Beth. "Agnès Varda: The Mother of the New Wave." *L.A. Weekly*, August 1–7, 1986, 33.

Crittenden, Roger. *Fine Cuts: The Art of European Film Editing.* Amsterdam; Boston: Focal Press, 2006.

Cruickshank, Ruth. "The Work of Art in the Age of Global Consumption: Agnès Varda's *Les Glaneurs et la glaneuse*." *Esprit Créateur* 47.3 (2007): 119–32.

Darke, Chris. "Refuseniks (Agnès Varda's DV Documentary, the 'Gleaners and I')." *Sight and Sound* 11.1 (2001): 30–33.

Darke, Chris. "Agnès Varda: A Narrative Filmmaker Moonlighting as a Short-Film Essayist, Or Vice Versa?" *Film Comment* 44.1 (2008): 22–23.

de Béchade, Chantal. "Entretien avec Agnès Varda." *Image et son: revue du cinéma*, February 1982.

Dechery, Laurent. "Autour de Mona dans *Sans Toit Ni Loi* d'Agnès Varda." *French Review* 79.1 (2005): 138.

Decock, Jean, and Agnès Varda. "Entretien avec Agnès Varda sur *Jacquot de Nantes*." *French Review* 66.6 (1993): 947–58.

DeRoo, Rebecca. "Confronting Contradictions: Genre Subversion and Feminist Politics in Agnès Varda's *L'Une chante, l'autre pas*." *Modern and Contemporary France* 17.3 (2009): 249–65.

Devaux, Claudine. *Agnès Varda.* Bruxelles: Association des Professeurs pour la Promotion de l'Éducation cinémathographique, 1987.

Dieuzaide, Jean. *Agnès Varda: Catalogue d'exposition, Galerie municipale du Château d'eau, Toulouse, Novembre 1987.* Toulouse: Galerie municipale du Château d'eau, 1987.

Domenach, Elise, and Philippe Rouyer. "Entretien avec Agnès Varda—Passer sous le Pont des Arts à la voile." *Positif*, no. 574 (2008): 17.

Durgnat, Raymond. *Nouvelle Vague: The First Decade.* Loughton, Essex: Motion Publications, 1963.

Erens, Patricia, ed. *Sexual Stratagems: The World of Women in Film.* New York: Horizon Press, 1979.

Estève, Michel, and Bernard Bastide. *Agnès Varda*. Paris: Lettres modernes: Minard, 1991.

Falcinella, Nicola. *Agnès Varda: Cinema Senza Tetto Né Legge*. Recco: Le Mani, 2010.

Fiant, Antony, Roxane Hamery, and Éric Thouvenel. *Agnès Varda: Le Cinéma et audelà*. Rennes, France: Presses Universitaires de Rennes, 2009.

Flitterman-Lewis, Sandy. *To Desire Differently: Feminism and the French Cinema*. Urbana: University of Illinois Press, 1990.

Flitterman-Lewis, Sandy. "Magic and Wisdom in two portraits by Agnès Varda: *Kung Fu Master* and *Jane B. by Agnès V.*" *Screen* 34.4 (1993): 302–20.

Forbes, Jill. "Agnès Varda: The Gaze of the Medusa." *Sight and Sound*, Spring 1989, 22–24.

Forbes, Jill. *The Cinema in France after the New Wave*. Macmillan, 1992.

Ford, Charles. *Femmes Cinéastes*. Paris: Denoël, 1972.

Gorbman, Claudia. "*Cléo from Five to Seven*: Music as Mirror." *Wide Angle* 4.4 (1981): 38–49.

Grant, Barry Keith. *Auteurs and Authorship: A Film Reader*. Malden, MA: Blackwell, 2008.

Grant, Barry Keith, and Jim Hillier. *100 Documentary Films*. London: British Film Institute, 2009.

Grob, Norbert, et al. *Nouvelle Vague*. Mainz: Bender, 2006.

Guest, Haden. "Emotion Picture: Agnès Varda's Self-Reflexive *The Beaches of Agnès* and the Cinema of Generosity." *Film Comment* 45.4 (2009): 44.

Handyside, Fiona. "The Feminist Beachscape: Catherine Breillat, Diane Kurys and Agnès Varda." *Esprit Créateur* 51.1 (2011): 83–96.

Harkness, John. "Agnès Varda: Improvised Inspiration." *Now*, June 19–25, 1986.

Harvey, Stephen. "Agnès Varda in Her Own Good Time." *The Village Voice*, May 20, 1986, 64.

Hayward, Susan. "Beyond the gaze and into femme-filmcriture: Agnès Varda's *Sans toit ni loi* (1985)." *French Film: texts and contexts*. New York: Routledge, 1990.

Hayward, Susan. *French National Cinema*. New York: Routledge, 1993.

Heck-Rabi, Louise. *Women Filmmakers: A Critical Reception*. Metuchen, NJ: Scarecrow Press, 1984.

Hillier, Jim. *Cahiers Du Cinéma: Volume II: 1960–1968. New Wave, New Cinema, Re-Evaluating Hollywood*. 6th ed. London: Routledge, 2001.

Holiday, Billie. *Femmes et Arts: Sarah Bernhardt, Edith Piaf, Simone Signoret, Agnès Varda; Suivi De Lady Sings the Blues*. Romorantin, France: Martinsart, 1980.

Hottell, Ruth, "Including Ourselves: the role of female spectators in Agnès Varda's *Le Bonheur* and *L'Une chante, l'autre pas*." *Cinema Journal* 38.2 (1999): 52–72.

Hurd, Mary G. *Women Directors and Their Films*. Westport, CT: Praeger, 2007.

Insdorf, Annette. "Filmmaker Agnès Varda: Stimulating Discomfort." *International Herald Tribune*, June 11, 1986.

Jackson, Emma. "The Eyes of Agnès Varda: Portraiture, cinécriture and the Filmic Ethnographic Eye." *Feminist Review* 96.1 (2010): 122–26.

Johnston, Claire. "Women's Cinema as Counter-Cinema." *Movies and Methods: An Anthology*. Ed. Bill Nichols. 1 Vol. Berkeley: University of California Press, 1976, 208–17.

Jordan, Shirley. "Spatial and Emotional Limits in Installation Art: Agnès Varda's *L'Ile et Elle*." *Contemporary French and Francophone Studies* 13.5 (2009): 581–88.

Kausch, F. "Agnès Varda—*Les Plages d'Agnès*—La mer, éternellement recommencée." *Positif*, no. 574 (2008): 15.

Kozloff, Max. "Review of *Le Bonheur*." *Film Quarterly* 20.2 (1967): 35–37.

Kuhlken, Pam Fox. "Clarissa and Cléo (En)durée: Suicidal Time in Virginia Woolf's *Mrs. Dalloway* and Agnès Varda's *Cléo de 5 à 7*." *Comparative Literature Studies* 45.3 (2008): 341–69.

Lanzoni, Rémi Fournier. *French Cinema: From Its Beginnings to the Present*. New York: Continuum International, 2002.

Lee, Nam. *Rethinking Feminist Cinema: Agnès Varda and Filmmaking in the Feminine*. Ann Arbor: UMI, 2008.

Lubelski, Tadeusz. *Agnès Varda: Kinopisarka*. Kraków: Wydawnictwo Rabid, 2006.

Lucas, Tim. "Tim Lucas Celebrates Agnès Varda." *Sight and Sound* 18.4 (2008): 88.

McKim, Kristi Irene. *The Astounded Soul: Cinematic Time and Photogenic Love (Wim Wenders, Agnès Varda, Hirokazu Kore-Eda)*. Ann Arbor: UMI, 2005.

McNeill, Isabelle. "Agnès Varda's Moving Museums." *Modern French Identities* 83 (2009): 283–94.

Miller, Nancy K. "Review of *L'Une chante, l'autre pas*." *French Review* 52.3 (1979): 499–500.

Monaco, James. *The New Wave: Truffaut, Godard, Chabrol, Rohmer and Rivette*. New York: Oxford University Press, 1976.

Mouton, Janice. "From Feminine Masquerade to Flaneuse: Agnès Varda's Cléo in the City." *Cinema Journal* 40.2 (2001): 3–16.

Neroni, Hilary. "Documenting the Gaze: Psychoanalysis and Judith Helfand's *Blue Vinyl* and Agnès Varda's *The Gleaners and I*." *Quarterly Review of Film and Video* 27.3 (2010): 178–92.

Neupert, Richard John. *A History of the French New Wave Cinema*. 2nd ed. Madison, WI: University of Wisconsin Press, 2007.

Nicodemus, Katja. "Mitarbeiter Der Woche—Die Filmemacherin Agnès Varda." *Die Zeit* 64.37 (2009): 60.

Ofner, Astrid, et al. Jacques Demy / Agneès Varda: Eine Retrospektive Der Viennale Und Des Österreichischen Filmmuseums 2. Bis 31.Oktober 2006.
Wien: Viennale, 2006.

Orpen, Valerie. *Cléo de 5 à 7: (Agnès Varda, 1961)*. Urbana: University of Illinois
Press, 2007.

Pallister, Janis L. *French-Speaking Women Film Directors: A Guide*. Cranbury, NJ: Associated University Press, 1997.

Patterson, Katherine J. "Deflecting Desire: Destabilizing Narrative Univocality
and the Regime of Looking in Agnès Varda's French Film *Vagabond*." *Film
Studies: Women in Contemporary World Cinema*. Ed. Alexandra Heidi Kar-
riker. New York: P. Lang, 2002.

Piguet, P. "Paris: Agnès Varda: Les Plages artistiques de la Réalisatrice de cinema."
L'Oeil: Revue d'art mensuelle 610 (2009): 78–83.

Portuges, Catherine. "Review of *The Gleaners and I* (*Les Glaneurs et la glaneuse*)."
American Historical Review 106.1 (2001): 305.

Powrie, Phil. "Heterotopic Spaces and Nomadic Gazes in Varda: From *Cléo de 5 à 7*
to *Les Glaneurs et la glaneuse*." *L'Esprit Créateur* 51.1 (2011): 68–82.

Prédal, René. *Sans toit ni loi d'Agnès Varda*. Neuilly-sur-Seine (Hauts-de-Seine):
Atlande, 2003.

Ramanathan, Geetha. *Feminist Auteurs: Reading Women's Film*. London: Wall-
flower, 2006.

Rich, B. Ruby. "Gleaners Over Gladiators." *The Nation* 272.14 (2001): 33.

Romney, Jonathan. "Film: The Scavengers—Agnès Varda's Documentary *The
Gleaners and I*." *New Statesman*, 2001, 47.

Rosello, Mireille. "Agnès Varda's *Les Glaneurs et la glaneuse*: Portrait of the Artist
as an Old Lady." *Studies in French Cinema* 1.1 (2000).

Rouyer, Philippe. "Exposition—Actualité d'Agnès Varda." *Positif*, no. 548 (2006):
72.

Shivas, Mark. "*Cléo de 5 à 7* and Agnès Varda." *Movie*, October 3, 1962: 33–35.

Signorelli, A. "*Les Plages d' Agnès* di Agnès Varda: Nel ventre della balena." *Cinefo-
rum* 50.10 (2010): 75–77.

Singerman, Alan J. *French Cinema: The Student's Book*. Newburyport, MA: Focus
Pub./R. Pullins Co., 2006.

St James Women Filmmakers Encyclopaedia. Visible Ink Press USA, 1999.

Smith, Alison. *Agnès Varda*. Manchester University Press, 1998.

Smith, Alison, and Susan Gasster-Carrierre. "Reviews—Film—Agnès Varda."
French Review 73.2 (1999): 363.

Sabine, Jennifer. "Agnès Varda" (interview). *Cinema Papers*, no. 42 (March 1983).

Udris, Raynalle. "Countryscape/Cityscape and Homelessness in Agnès Varda's

Sans toit ni loi and Leos Carax's *Les Amants Du Pont-Neuf.*" *Spaces in European Cinema.* Ed. Myrto Konstantarakos. Portland, OR: Intellect Books, 2000, 42–51.

Ungar, Steven,. *Cléo De 5 à 7.* Basingstoke; New York: British Film Institute, 2008.

Valence, G. "Agnès Varda, l'Hommage juste." *Positif,* no. 553 (2007): 66.

Varda, Agnès. *Varda par Agnès.* Tamaris/Cahiers du Cinéma, 1994.

Vincendeau, Ginette. "How Agnès Varda 'Invented' the New Wave." *Four by Agnès Varda.* Criterion, 2008.

Wagstaff, Peter. "Traces of Places: Agnès Varda's Mobile Space in *The Gleaners and I.*" *New Studies in European Cinema 2: Revisiting Space: Space and Place in European Cinema* (2005): 273–90.

Wallimann, Susanne. Aufzeichnungen Einer Schwangeren Frau: Gedreht Von Agnès Varda (Carnet De Notes d'Une Femme Enceinte: Tourné Par Agnès Varda). Luzern: Hochschule für Gestaltung und Kunst, 1998.

Wise, Naomi. "Surface Tensions: Agnès Varda." *Berkeley Monthly,* June 1986, 16–17.

Index

CPSIA information can be obtained at www.ICGtesting.com
Printed in the USA
BVOW07s0421190115

383626BV00003B/5/P